The Temple of Mut in Asher: An Account of the Excavation of the Temple and of the Religious Representations and Objects Found Therein, As Illustrating the History of Egypt and the Main Religious Ideas of the Egyptians

Margaret Benson, Janet A. Gourlay

Photograph by A. Beato, Luxor.

TEMPLE OF MUT.

THE TEMPLE OF
MUT IN ASHER

AN ACCOUNT OF THE EXCAVATION OF THE TEMPLE
AND OF THE RELIGIOUS REPRESENTATIONS AND
OBJECTS FOUND THEREIN, AS ILLUSTRATING THE
HISTORY OF EGYPT AND THE MAIN RELIGIOUS
IDEAS OF THE EGYPTIANS

BY MARGARET BENSON AND JANET GOURLAY

THE INSCRIPTIONS AND TRANSLATIONS BY
PERCY E. NEWBERRY

WITH PLANS AND ILLUSTRATIONS

LONDON
JOHN MURRAY, ALBEMARLE STREET
1899

LONDON:
PRINTED BY WILLIAM CLOWES AND SONS, Limited,
STAMFORD STREET AND CHARING CROSS.

PREFACE.

—◦◦—

It has been said that a book, like a joke, confesses failure in offering an explanation of itself, yet the account of an excavation undertaken by amateurs would seem to demand some sort of apology.

Our first intention was not ambitious. We were desirous of clearing a picturesque site. We were frankly warned that we should make no discoveries ; indeed if any had been anticipated it was unlikely that the clearance would have been entrusted to inexperienced direction. Thus we began without any idea of publishing an account of our work. If we had had any such intention we should have kept completer records, and might have ordered many things differently.

We began our second season in the same mind, but unexpected discoveries demanded publication, and the third year added more material. Our idea then was not so much to publish our undertaking as to preserve the names and histories that Egypt had committed to our charge.

We intended therefore at first to put forth these results simply for the use of the expert. Treasure-trove, whether of great or of little value, is the property of the nation, and we desired faithfully to render to those who could better use them the little treasures of history unexpectedly committed to us.

It is easy to remit to the authorities of state a golden torque or a pot of coins by the simple methods of civilisation and the parcel post, but to register results so that they may be of use is more difficult, and the only way in which this could be done without undue risk seemed to be by a book which should combine the necessary facts in an available form for the expert, with an account of our undertaking and its results, for those who, without technical know-ledge, feel the fascination and interest of Egypt.

For the latter class of readers we have given a short sketch of the history of Egypt during the lifetime of our temple. The new and wonderful discoveries of 1897–8, which have made the " mythical " ancient kingdom a reality and have even thrown light on prehistoric Egypt, do not therefore concern us, for the epoch to which our earliest discoveries belong begins with the 12th dynasty. In order to have any

comprehension of the purposes of the temple and of
the statues it is necessary also to have some idea
of the religious theories of the Egyptians; we have
therefore added in briefest outline an account of
some parts of that religion.

Our chief authority for the historical part has
been, to the end of the 18th dynasty, Professor
W. M. F. Petrie's 'History of Egypt'; in addition
to which, for the reign of Hatshepsut, we have used
M. Naville's publications on Deir el Bahari; and
from the 19th dynasty onward Professor Wiedemann's 'Aegyptische Geschichte.' In the study of
the religion we have mainly used Professor Petrie's
'Religion and Conscience in Ancient Egypt,' and
Wiedemann's 'Religion of the Ancient Egyptians.'
Other authorities are also referred to, and we have
been allowed to make use of an article in the
Edinburgh Review.

It is difficult to think that, in any other undertaking, mere tyros should have met with such
generous and kindly help from experts in the
subject, whose time and thoughts moreover were
already sufficiently occupied with important work.
Among many who have helped us our thanks are
first due to M. Naville, but for whose help and
encouragement the work would never have been
begun, and whose advice was always open to us in

all difficulties; to Professor Flinders Petrie, who
has not only looked over the chapters on the religion and history but has given us important and
most helpful suggestions; and to Mr. F. Ll. Griffith,
for the use of a yet unpublished translation. We
have to thank M. de Morgan's liberality for the first
permission to excavate given to women in Egypt.
Some of the most important photographs were taken
by Brugsch Bey, who in all the dealings we have
had with him has been most considerate. Dr.
Borchardt kindly and promptly supplied whatever
information we asked for, and M. Daressy's
courtesy made the difficulties of the first year much
lighter than they would otherwise have been. In
the work of superintendence we have to acknow-
ledge much help, notably from Colonel Esdaile in
the second and third years, and from Miss Katharine
Gent (Mrs. Lea) in the first, and we are indebted to
Mr. Hogarth for advice in the direction of the work.
Mr. Henry Gourlay helped us largely with our
funds; Mrs. Benson with money and personal
supervision; Mr. Mackirdy, who visited Luxor in
our third year, gave us a subscription; Mr. E. F.
Benson, besides helping us with a subscription and
constant and experienced superintendence, drew the
map, and gave us notes and measurements from
which the plan of the temple has been produced.

The photographs for the most part have been done by friends whose names are given, and the vulture (Mut) on the cover has been traced from Mr. Howard Carter's drawing of a scene in the shrine of Anubis at Deir el Bahari.

Mr. Newberry's translations of the inscriptions—the most essential part of the publication—speak for themselves, but we desire here to thank him most warmly for the generosity which has placed his scholarship at our service, for advice, suggestions, and correction, and for the unwearied kindness which he has shown us throughout.

But even thanks would be ungrateful if we did not first emphatically say that no responsibility for mistakes and omissions in work, for error in fact, or unfounded theory, can be laid at the door of those who have helped us. All such failures must be set down to ourselves, to our inexperience, and to certain special difficulties of circumstance. Work was more than once interrupted by illness, which made it impossible, above all in the plan of the temple, to register details as fully as we could have wished. Thus the positions of the pillars in the outer court are taken from James Burton's plan, as our own measurements were not complete. We should have wished also if we had had more time to show the places of the statues wherever they seemed to be *in situ*.

Above all, we should have wished to finish completely the excavation, to clear away the banks of earth which may yet hide treasures of the past, to dredge the lake, or dig, when it was especially low, for statues and monuments which may have been thrown into it.

The limits of time and the interruption of work rendered it impossible to verify our results on the spot after completion of the report. We have however attempted to carry out the work in such a way that though much we hope may be added in the future we trust that little need be altered.

Thus although for the moment we have not finished the excavation, we have thought it better to put forth the book, incomplete as it is, rather than let what has been reclaimed from a buried past fall again into oblivion.

MARGARET BENSON.
JANET GOURLAY.

CONTENTS.

PART I.

INTRODUCTION.

CHAPTER I.

CHAPTER II.

PART II.

HISTORY OF THE EXCAVATION.

CHAPTER III.

CHAPTER IV.

PART III.

THE RELIGION OF EGYPT.

PART IV.

HISTORY.

CHAPTER XI.

CHAPTER XII.

CHAPTER XIII.

CHAPTER XIV.

CHAPTER XV.

CHAPTER XVI.

CHAPTER XVII.

PART V.

INSCRIPTIONS.

CONTENTS.

LIST OF PLATES.

THE TEMPLE OF MUT.

PART I.
INTRODUCTION.

CHAPTER I.

THE Arab village of Luxor stands on the site of
that part of ancient Thebes which was built on the
east bank of the Nile. The cultivated land on
each side of the river, which is in some parts of
Egypt very narrow, here spreads out into a broad
oasis; on the Luxor side this is as much as four
or five miles broad, on the west bank from a mile
and a half to two miles. As one comes up the
river from the north the chain of hills on the left
hand is almost continuous. Near Cairo this is
called the Mokattam range; the hills form a bank
low, perpendicular, cut out like a raised map, or
like a bank of sand through which a stream of
water has eaten its way. As one travels south the
ridges at times approach the water so closely
indeed as to rise a sheer wall from its edge; with
their regular horizontal stratifications, worn and
weathered into small roughnesses, they seem to be

B

graven with vast hieroglyphic inscriptions; and as
seen from the boat, these look scarcely more irregular than the square-hewn doorways of the tombs
hollowed out in the face of the cliff.   Here and
there the rocky walls open out to show, if one has
luck to note it, some ruined city of Roman times
with Titanic walls and great empty gateways: a
city built out of the rock it stands on, and so rough-
hewn and huge that one questions whether this
too is not a freak of nature.   Sometimes the hills
retire again from the river, leaving a broad space
of cultivated land and a belt of desert; and the
clefts that run up these hills end in a top so flat
that one cannot but imagine the summits levelled by
a gigantic plane.

In the north there are no hills on the west side of
the river; but a great raised bank of sand on which
pyramids stand—the only breaks in the long soft
curves of the horizon; but below Thebes the
Libyan hills begin to form themselves, and as
one approaches Luxor there is a chain on the
right hand and on the left; these open out broadly
on each side and nearly close again some way above
the village.   The flat-topped hills on the east break
at Thebes into the points and ridges of the Gebel
el Geir; the square-shouldered Libyan chain of the
west descends with slopes and precipices sharply
outlined against more distant mountains.   The
fainter tints of the north have given place to the
gold of the limestone hills, showing in ethereal

colours of rose and blue in the morning, glowing with a richer rose and more vivid blue shadows in the sunset. The fields between the river and the hills stand deep in corn and luxuriant crops of vetch and bean; there are groves of palm mingled with the thicker foliage of the sycamore-fig and tamarisk. All the plain on either hand is inter-sected with canals large and small, fed from the great sweep of shining river by means of the *shadoof*, whose workers chant their interminable narratives; and by the *sâkiyeh*, whose creaking wood groans out a strange Gregorian melody to the treading of the oxen. Behind the fields a strip of sandy desert stretches up to the barren hills.

This then was the site of that provincial capital, which under the kings of the 11th dynasty, about three thousand years before Christ, became the capital of Egypt.

One must not think indeed that the place was uninhabited before. Egypt was perhaps fuller of life than it is now. All the graveyards since the Arab conquest form but little patches on the country; while the mountains are pierced and the ground under one's feet hollowed from end to end of Egypt for the graves of the old inhabitants of the land. One has only to journey a few days up the Nile to understand the satire of the Israelite's taunt, "Are there no graves in the land of Egypt?"

Thus we find in Thebes traces of habitation

B 2

dating even before the time when the Antefs and the Mentuhoteps made it into their capital—traces not indeed of the houses of the people or the palaces of the kings, for such habitations they esteemed in truth mere "inns" for their life, and built them to endure for a season.   But what remain to us, after four thousand years, are the dwellings of the gods and the "Eternal Habitations" of the dead.

Having once become the capital, Thebes retained the supremacy through the glories of Egyptian history, through party strife of native kings and through sack and destruction of the foreign invader. Builder succeeded to builder and restorer to restorer. The city never wholly declined from its pre-eminence until Alexander established his rival capital in the north.

Even after this the Ptolemaic kings built at Thebes, decorated its earlier temples, and added to their dignity by gateways and precinct walls ; until the name of the hundred-gated Thebes can have been no hyperbole.

In Roman times the current of progress set in a new direction.   The conquering race, whose civilisation was in some ways so much ruder, had yet a force which drew the tide of progress northwards.

"It is Roman" a fellah, who receives two piastres a day for his digging, will say with supreme contempt, turning from the object he has disinterred ; or the Arab guardian of a temple will scream out his fury at the ruthless Roman destruction; "Bad, stupid Romans, not understand hieroglyphics," I heard one cry.

But arts which had been at their finest some three thousand years before, learning such as the priests taught Moses, declined before the sterner qualities of the conqueror, and civilisation, which had dwelt so long in Egypt, followed the Roman to Europe.

While yet Hellenic influences, mixing with the old world of thought, were forming centres of philosophic speculation in northern Egypt, Christianity made its unnoticed entrance into the land.

Though in the north indeed, where it clashed with base mythologies and impious Emperor-worship, there streamed from the combat the blood of martyrs, witnessing in the spectacles to angels and men the truths of an opponent creed; yet through the rest of the land it spread with an extraordinary speed, converting rather than combating the ancient belief. Thus the Ankh, the sign of life, became to the Copts the *tau* cross; and when the Temple of Hatshepsut became Deir el Bahari, "the Convent of the North," the bodies in their mummied wrappings displayed the chalice and ears of corn on the breast, while Anubis, the god of the dead, was painted below.

In quite another wise came the next movement of religious fervour when Mohammed's half-tamed hordes swept over Africa; and above the temples of Egypt there grew up Arab villages whose inhabitants retained in strange stories of Afrîts or in uncomprehended ritual some of the tradition and religious ceremonies of an alien past.

But while a little was thus retained much was lost. Tombs were plundered ; papyri were destroyed, for their lore was judged by the all-sufficient standard of the Koran either impious or super-fluous.

Yet after all the destruction of old foes, ruthless conquerors, and semi-civilised invaders, the wealth of monuments that Thebes has still to show gives some slight indication of the glories of the past.

Three days are judged by the majority of tourists a sufficient time in which to see the monuments of a capital whose rise and fall occupied a longer time than the whole history of Europe from the Roman supremacy to the present day. This time must be parcelled out so that each day shall give a passing glimpse of two or three temples, whose history occupies some centuries, and of tombs of royal, official or private people.

No one during this period, with such a pro-gramme to carry out, can be expected to go round by a small temple which lies between Luxor and Karnak ; and the Temple of Mut can hardly hope to claim even half an hour's study except from the comparatively leisured.

Yet a temple which has been built and added to through a period of two thousand years or more ; on which most of the illustrious Pharaohs during that time have left their record ; which has yielded between thirty and forty statues of themselves and their subjects, some high and important officials, some private persons ; which is unique in its statues of the goddess to whom it is dedicated ; and which moreover occupies one of the most charming temple sites in Egypt, is surely worthy of a little study.

The temple of Luxor is little more than a mile from the great temple of Amen at Karnak, and from the front of the temple at Luxor an avenue of ram-headed sphinxes extended to the southern-most gate of the temple precincts at Karnak. The mouldered bases of these sphinxes can still be seen as the high road leaves the village of Luxor. This high road, an uneven dusty track, raised above the level of the fields so that it may be unaffected by the inundation, continues its way about a quarter of a mile from the river bank until it enters the palm grove which surrounds Karnak.

Just before reaching this grove the road parts into two ; the left-hand track, traversing the grove and striking again the avenue of sphinxes, leads up to the Ptolemaic gateway in front of the temple of Khonsu, where one first catches sight of the whole length of the Great Temple of Karnak. It is a beautiful road, for the palms cast interlacing shadows on the path, and the sphinxes, here in better preservation, hold between their paws little figures of the king who erected them. Before this road reaches the pylon another avenue of sphinxes, some buried, some showing above the dust heads of rams or men, parts from it and runs with an irregular curve to the east, and presently passes before the front of the Temple of Mut.

The road which one left to the right before entering the palm grove, is a broad track. It passes the end of a small ruined temple, roofless and with walls broken down, skirts the outer curve of the Sacred Lake at Mut, and, rising slightly, disappears between sandheaps, forming a gap through which one sees the distant rosy hills of the Gebel el Geir.

Thus the Sphinx Avenue under the palm trees on the west, with its branch which leads to the northern gate of the Temple of Mut, and the broad track to the south, form three sides of a rough parallelogram enclosing the temple with its precinct ; the fourth side of the parallelogram is formed by high mounds of tumbled sandheaps.

The area so enclosed is an arid sandy tract—the sand not so loose that it is blown by winds, but dry and infertile, bound into a hardish soil by the dead roots of thin straggling grass.

At the south-west corner of this area is the ruined temple before mentioned, in front of which two colossal standing statues are pitched forward on their shoulders. At the north-east corner is another ruined temple, and in front of this also a great statue of a king rests on the earth in such wise that one cannot see if the head is buried or destroyed.

Approximately in the middle of the space thus left is a lake, the Lake of Asher, shaped like a horseshoe, and on the promontory of earth which this encloses stands the Temple of Mut.

Towards the end of a stay in Egypt in 1894, I first went to see this temple, having heard no more of it than that there were granite statues with cats' heads to be seen there; the donkey boys knew it, but it was not a usual excursion. Yet it was a place to seize upon the imagination.

The gateway into the first court was filled with earth nearly up to the top. A few yards to the north of this lay yet another gateway, and between the two a triple line of sphinxes. The creature next to the northernmost gate has a man's face, which looks serenely out of the choking earth. From this gate a grove of feathery tamarisks stretches northwards again to Karnak; and beneath the tamarisks runs yet another avenue of mouldered sphinxes.

The temple itself was so much destroyed, and the broken walls so far buried, that one could not trace the plan of more than the outer court and a few small chambers.

The walls of this outer court were banked up slopingly with earth, and out of the earth-bank came here and there at short intervals a lion head in black granite or the headless shoulders of a

woman's figure. The figures were scattered ir-
regularly—at one place a group, at another a single
mutilated head, and again two figures close together
leaned towards one another as if they were secretly
lamenting the downfall of the great gods. On the
east side of the court a doorway opened, and
where the mounded earth grew level a flagged
pathway led to a little shrine high on the sand
heaps.

At the far end of the temple a lion-headed figure
quaintly whitened by saltpetre from the soil stood
out against the background of the lake.

To the south one looked towards Luxor, where
out of the group of Arab houses rose the pylons and
obelisk of the temple ; the great obelisk of Karnak,
and its pylons and halls golden in Egyptian sunlight, showed to the north above palm and tamarisk.
Through breaks in the palm grove to the west one
could see the Libyan hills, with precipices sharply
outlined, azure against rose ; from the higher sand-
mounds were visible, still more distant and faint,
the peaks of the eastern range.

Round the promontory on which the temple
stood lay the lake thick and green ; shoals of tiny
silver fish glanced and darted in the water; here
and there a pied kingfisher hovered over the lake,
dropped like lead into the water, and emerging with
a fish curving from his bill, flew to some jutting
stone, carved or squared in old Egyptian days, to
swallow down the prey ; great fishing hawks wheeled

PLATE II.

To face p. 10.

FIRST GATEWAY.

Photograph by Dr. Page May.

above, and sometimes an Egyptian vulture showed white and black against the bright air.

In the temple courts, browsing on sparse blades of grass, roamed a flock of goats, watched over by an Arab girl with solemn eyes and swathed form, and the little kids skipped and leaped on fallen stones.

As the sun sloped towards its setting, veiled women came down leading a buffalo or two, a young bull or a mild-eyed heifer to water them at the lake ; Arab men came to wash arms and feet, laying a tattered garment by the waterside on which they might step with undefiled feet to offer the evening prayer.   On the road to the south passed now and then the cattle coming to drink, or an Arab in white wrappings on his camel went through the gap down to the fertile fields below.

It is true there was none of the imaginary charm of "Afric's golden sands," crystal fountains and deep green oases ; it was a dusty infertile tract, but the place was full of the mysterious fascination of Egypt, and in the dry exhilarating air one seemed to breathe the very atmosphere of the past.   All the double charm of Egypt was there ; in the present "the East was calling" by the attraction of the sun, the bright intoxicating air laden with strange eastern sweetness, the sight of the palm grove against the distant hills, and the simple but mysterious race that moved about all these.   And mingled with this was the still living past of a race in most ways more modern than that which pastured its flocks in the temple courts—a race at once so near us and so far away, a race of a religion and a history so grand that the people of God could not wholly cast off its effect, yet whose objects of worship were typified, if not embodied, in the rude lion heads around.

Thus, half hidden as the temple was, there was something about the place so beautiful, even so romantic, that a suggestion casually made about digging in Egypt came to mind, and I began to wonder vaguely if it would be possible to get permission to clear the site.

My desire would hardly have got beyond this point of vagueness but that my mention of the half-formed plan came to the ears of M. Naville, who was then excavating at Deir el Bahari, and he encouraged me to think that it was possible to realise it, giving full directions about application to the Government; and thus the plan took shape.

CHAPTER II.

ON returning to Egypt in 1895, I made application to the Government department for permission to clear the site, but met with a refusal. On this M. Naville very kindly wrote himself to M. de Morgan explaining the case ; and M. de Morgan, with the liberality which characterised all his dealings in this respect, immediately gave permission.

The contract which was granted reserved by right (as was most necessary with inexperienced and untried workers) all discoveries for the Museum ; but the authorities were very kind in letting us retain many of those objects which were not of importance for exhibition in the Museum.

Considering the amount of work done in the way of clearance, and even the monetary value of the things discovered, the undertaking was singularly inexpensive. I need hardly say how vastly it was repaid by the interest of the work, by the historical, even personal, interest of the remains, and finally by the acquaintance which it gave one with the character of another race, from the relations we were brought

into with the workpeople. I cannot say the knowledge of their character, for the Arab must remain
an enigma to most Europeans.

We paid the men the regular rate of wages in the
district for work of this nature. Work with the
shadoof is perhaps higher-paid, but it is arduous,
unpleasant and compulsory. Insignificant as the
wages sound for ten hours' work in the sun, they
imply a not inconsiderable value when they are
translated into the purchasing power of the necessaries of life.

The men's wages of 2 piastres or 5*d.* a day, mean
subsistence for a family for three days; the boys'
wages of 1½ piastres make them fairly independent
of their parents. This can be better credited by
those who know that a native can purchase from
80 to 100 eggs for 1*s.*, and can single-handed build
and roof his house with durra stalks in two or three
days. Considering then such daily wages in proportion to their power of providing necessaries of life,
which are very few, it must be remembered, in that
country and climate, they cannot be held as less than
an agricultural wage of 2*s.* 6*d.* a day.

The work indeed lasts for a few weeks only,
and comes therefore only as an addition, and a very
welcome one, to the family income; for the fellahin
so employed have their own fields, well or cattle.

Looking at the question from the employer's
point of view, one can well credit the economic
assertion that the cost of labour is much the same

all the world over. The men—with their comparatively poor physique, their loss of time from childish want of method and from carelessness, with their vigorous discussions and their chants when anything has to be hauled or lifted, with their hoes and baskets instead of spades and wheelbarrows—get through the work in very amateur fashion compared to the men of an industrial nation.

Over and above the regular wages there is the chance of backsheesh for discoveries. There can be no regular rate of backsheesh, and it is not even given on any universally acknowledged principle. The officials of the Government excavation at Karnak during these same years considered it a more satisfactory plan to increase supervision and give practically no backsheesh. Professor Petrie at the Ramesseum inclined to pay backsheesh to the full amount of the object found, if this was small and could have been stolen ; and the excavators for the Egypt Exploration Fund gave as the maximum backsheesh a day's wages. Thus three distinct principles were then reigning in excavations close together.

The principle of backsheesh must be determined by considerations of expediency. The object is to create an inducement to activity and a counter-inducement to the price offered (if the object can be stolen) by tourists and antiquity dealers.

Men working in ground that is not theirs, to discover monuments of a race alien to their own, and working at the excavator's entire cost, can have no right to be rewarded for finds to which as a rule neither natural instinct nor trained observation has led them. At the same time there is an elementary if illogical instinct of justice which leads one to reward the man who unearthed that which one wanted, or who has given up that which he could —dishonestly indeed—have kept and sold.

We roughly proportioned the backsheesh to the value of the find and the opportunities of theft, taking into account the current rate of wages. For certain large finds we gave backsheesh to all the men. The boys had their best chance of backsheesh in sifting the earth which they carried away. In spite of the offered reward it was difficult to enforce such sifting.

As our excavating party, at the best and in strongest numbers, possessed but a few words and phrases of Arabic, orders were given and arrangements made mainly through a donkey-boy who acted as interpreter. This arrangement—the best we could make—was not a good one, as it tended to place the boy in the position of middle-man. Being an Arab he was sure to get his own profit out of one party to any bargain, if not out of both. It also made the attainment of justice difficult, and may possibly have led to increased facilities for stealing.

In most ways we had little trouble with the men. They were remarkably careful in disinterring statues or inscribed stones; in all that we found hardly more than one or two chips were broken by the diggers; they worked fully as well as the average men employed in such work—wonderfully well, considering that supervision could not be constant. They were singularly amenable from the first, and, except under the rule of an incompetent reis, orderly in their work. The first reis we employed demanded higher wages than the average (10*d*. instead of 7½*d*.) to compensate him, as we understood, for the indignity of working under a woman; there was to the end agitated discussion every pay-day among the boys if a piastre or half-piastre was slightly rubbed or, as they called it, "blind"; but the greater number soon learnt that we had no intention of cheating them, and they could wait with patience until we were ready to change any money they distrusted.

We were careful, according to the advice given us, to pay the men and boys ourselves. If this is not done one can never be sure what proportion of the sum reaches the right person and how much is retained by an Arab paymaster. This of course gave some little trouble at the time, but was also a gain to us, giving an opportunity of knowing the people individually and by name.

The more efficient overseers arranged the boys in ranks in front of us when they were to be paid; the men stood behind and the water-girl sat demurely apart, her veil held between her teeth.

Then they were called by name and came up in orderly wise to receive payment. Without a competent reis such order was difficult if not impossible to maintain.

The engagement of the workers was by no means orderly. On arrival at the temple on the appointed day we found waiting twice as many workers as were wanted, each with pick or basket. The men could keep some decent show of order, but no sooner did one begin to call out the names of the boys than they burst all ranks, and surrounded us, each shouting his own name and waving his basket in the air. We were humiliated by the disorder until we received the comforting assurance from one excavator that he himself had broken two sticks in the process.

The immense eagerness to get work at the wages offered proves that the people are not ground down to the economic minimum.

One point we had somewhat at heart. The compassionate tourist in Egypt, realising perhaps for the first time the extreme severity of the fast, is inclined to prohibit the keeping of Ramadan.

Ramadan lasts for a month, and the pious Moslem fasts from three in the morning till after the sun has set—fasts not from food only, but from water and tobacco. The want of food does not try the abstemious people severely; but the want of water is excessively painful to those who are working in the heat; and the crowding of the meals

PLATE ·III.

Photograph by Dr. Page May.

FIRST COURT (LOOKING WEST).

To face p. 18.

between 6 p.m. and 3 a.m., with the broken sleep which this implies, is perhaps as unhealthy as the starvation of the day.

Rich people can lessen the pain of abstinence by turning day into night; the devout poor cannot so avoid it.

Compassion no doubt prompts one to prohibit the fast when the men are working. To stop work during the fast would for us have been impossible, as it fell one year in our only possible season for excavating, and in other years entrenched upon it; though some excavators who began earlier could stop soon after Ramadan began. Work suffers too during this time as the men get more physically unfit, and when one has seen men who have been working four or five hours, and will do as much more, sit drearily down in the sun while the boys eat and drink, it is impossible to urge greater energy.

But even after all these obvious considerations we felt it was still worse to induce them from motives of self-interest alone to discontinue such religious observances. We therefore encouraged them to keep the fast, and purposely asked about it. The first day half of the men kept it, later all did so. In our last season also we consulted them about the most important services in the mosque, and in accordance with what they told us allowed a two hours' break on Friday at mid-day without loss of wages; and to mitigate the severity of the strain let them, at their own request, cease work an hour earlier. This they told us was permitted at the Karnak excavations.

The one difficulty we had, and it is a universal experience, was to prevent stealing.

There is little doubt they stole during the first two years; though we suspected it, we did not discover it until the third year, when a head which had been seen by those of us who were at the temple disappeared during the excitement of a new discovery.

We were very ignorant about the right way to deal with this, took perhaps too many precautions, and bruited our loss too widely. We had not at that stage been able to dispense with the British spirit of justice, and considered it right only to punish one man for any given offence.

Our difficulties in pursuing this head, which we never managed to obtain—our futile beds of justice—the accusations and counter-accusations, some of which must have been absolutely false, all of which were probably partly false—convinced us in the end that the more wholesale methods practised by more experienced people would have been broadly the fairest and certainly the most successful.

We should have treated the men as if they all had more or less connived in the theft, which was probably true; as if all knew about it, which was certainly the case. The head might have reappeared, justice would have been roughly done, and discipline maintained.

One fact that our enquiries as to methods of justice led us to realise was that the old barbarous manner of obtaining evidence is still occasionally practised in Egypt (not indeed by excavators), namely, that of beating out the truth.

What we did as a matter of fact was to try to extort evidence by promises of promotion; to dismiss one boy who was universally accused, but might, we feared afterwards, have been accused from motives of jealousy; and finally to dismiss the reis, who was really responsible and at any rate incompetent.

Finally after much worry we realised that the Arabs were like naughty children; that to press further a vain attempt would be but to convince them of our own incapacity for dealing with them; and that the only thing to do was to wash the slate clean and to begin again with an overseer who was possibly a thief and certainly a liar—in these respects no different to anyone else we could have got—but who certainly knew his business and probably where his best advantage lay.

Beyond this we could only console ourselves with the idea that the head was not an important one and did not belong to any of our best statues; and by trusting that we had made the consequences of theft so unpleasant that it would not be easily repeated.

We were cheered a little after this by the reis bringing to us a boy who had just refused a tourist's offer to buy the hand of a statue, a worthless piece indeed, which he had disinterred. The boy's plea in refusing was that " Miss Benson will beat me."

On this score one may perhaps be allowed a word about the gross temptations that tourists put —ignorantly, no doubt—in the Arabs' way.

To refuse to buy antiquities hawked about Egypt which probably were stolen in the first instance would be absurd. In many cases these have not been stolen lately nor by the vendor, who may have honestly bought them. No excavator wishes tourists to refrain from buying in this way, although an ultimate market for stolen goods is no doubt an indirect temptation to stealing. All excavators lose, and lose largely, in this way, and no one can know how much his own excavation loses. We flattered ourselves that we were to some extent protected by the character of our finds, statuettes being less easy to steal than the yields of tomb-digging. But though this sort of loss is great, it is impossible to help, and the responsibility rests on the excavator, not on the tourist.

It is quite another thing when tourists visit, really by favour, an excavation which is proceeding, and calmly offer, as in the case related, a direct inducement to the workmen to steal from the employer.

It is worse still when the nature of the demand leads to defacement of the monuments. In 1897, for instance, a German collector let it be widely known that he would buy heads.

In the first case, the loss is mainly to the Government and the excavator ; but the further loss to art and history can hardly be estimated when monuments are deliberately defaced to please a head-hunter. It was probably to pleasure this scientific collector that the head was stolen from us ; and one can only breathe a wish that if he has got it, it may be to him as the *Fallen Idol.*

For the rest the relations with the men were singularly pleasant. An Arab has at least the merit of stealing and lying with geniality.

The boys, as they walked to and from the courts with the empty baskets in their hands or the laden baskets on their heads, received us singing. The ordinary song is a mere song of welcome, one line chanted by a single voice, others joining in the chorus. But it is their habit to improvise according to the occasion. When my brother first came to the temple they sang that the Khedive was coming ; when payment took longer one day than was expected they sang sadly: " The sun has set and she has not paid us." The song started the first moment we were seen; truth to tell, if one came suddenly upon them by an unexpected road there was an astonishing increase of energy also.

If we lunched at the temple we distributed the

remains of our meal, chiefly among the boys, but the reis brought us curds in an earthenware bowl. Our most incompetent reis, a gaunt grey-bearded man clad in a rough brown tunic with loose sleeves, had the dignity of a patriarch as he stepped towards us, an earthenware bowl held in both hands at arm's length, the stem of a palm leaf resting like a wand of office on his arm.

Apart from the picturesqueness of it these attentions were a little embarrassing, and the curds excessively sour.

The good humour of the men was immense. If a rope broke while they were pulling it, so that a line of men fell on their backs, they were overcome with laughter. The most elementary joke was well received, and they were quick too to catch a humourous intent. They had singularly little method in their work. We employed a native once to mend a statue, but had to pull his work to pieces and get it redone by a European workman, for he had no definite idea of a straight line. A comparatively experienced fellah will move the stones from the ground on which he is working to that piece which he has next to attack ; and this without any desire to nurse a job.

Their implements are no more professional than their methods. The palm-leaf baskets are of the same make as those belonging to 5th-dynasty times which Professor Petrie exhibited last year. But at least the ancient Egyptians could hardly have used the same palm-fibre ropes to haul their stones, for these snap with any strain. When we had made trial of Luxor crowbars, had used one which promptly doubled up, another so short that it gave no purchase, and had broken a wooden ox yoke in levering a stone, we decided to get our crowbar, as our rope, at Cairo. The men admired our implements, but probably preferred the amusement of their own.

But though these Arabs are irresponsible and merry as children, there is a certain quaint dignity even among the boys, and we had gravely to adjudge a quarrel between two boys one of whom had kicked another in the eye as they swam together in the lake.

They were enthusiastically keen about discoveries. If a find had been made while we were absent from the temple a shout of "Antica" reached us as we approached. They cheered a good discovery, and so great was the excitement when a piece of sculptured stone began to appear that one had difficulty in preventing the digger from trying too soon to prise out his find at the risk of breaking it. The very donkey-boys shared the excitement; shouted out our finds to the passers-by as we went home; and my own boy ran back with a little statue in his arms one afternoon when I was not at the temple, in his haste to exhibit it to me, assuring the friends he passed: " This go to England."

M. Naville kindly lent us a Syrian tent the first

PLAN OF THE TEMPLE OF MUT (FROM MARIETTE'S 'KARNAK').

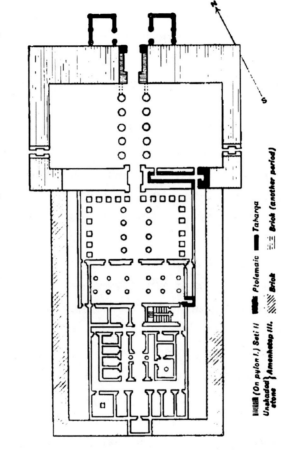

||||||| (On pylon I.) Seti II   ▨▨▨ Ptolemaic   ▬▬ Taharqa

Unshaded }
stone   } Amenhetep III.   ▨▨ Brick   ≡≡ Brick (another period)

To face p. 27.

PART II.

HISTORY OF THE EXCAVATION.

———

CHAPTER III.

EXCAVATION IN 1895.

On January 1st, 1895, we began the excavation.

M. Naville had been with us a day or two previously to interview our overseer. and show us how to determine the course of work.

The outer court, in which we were beginning to dig, had been partially cleared, probably by Mariette. From the mounds which banked it on the north the earth sloped down towards the stone wall between the outer and the second court, and here it had been dug out even below the level of the pavement. This original level was determined by a few paving stones left in place, and by the lower courses of the stone wall, which, being below the level of the pavement, had been left rough.

Mariette's aim had been to make clear the plan of the temple, and he had disinterred in the course of this some few lion-headed statues for the Museum.

He had roughly cleared the outer court and exposed the main walls; noting the small chamber inscribed in the time of Taharqa, which had been at some period completely cleared. But owing no doubt to want of time the plan of the temple had not in truth been sufficiently exposed for accurate reproduction.

We began working according to Mariette's map, which indeed is in the main accurate with regard to the northern courts; but were obliged in the southern portion entirely to relinquish its guidance. The discrepancies may be seen by comparison of the two maps, but we shall have occasion to note some more particularly.

The outer court, as is usual in Egyptian temples, was unroofed. Mariette's plan showed a stone wall only on the southern side, this wall being the dividing wall between the outer and second courts. Round this court, ranged against the wall, he marks lion-headed statues of the goddess Sekhet.

These statues are female figures with lion's heads, the head being joined to the figure in such wise that the lion's fringe of hair is prolonged into a wig. The figures are seated; they bore on the head originally a sun's disk with the uraeus,* but most of these are broken; many have carved on

---

* The uraeus or " asp," as it is sometimes called, is the cobra's head, worn just above the head of the statue. This signifies divinity, and is worn by gods and goddesses, and by royal ·persons as being the descendants of the gods.

them necklaces, anklets, armlets, and rosetted straps across the breast.

These decorations often retain some colour, indeed the whole figure was probably coloured, and we found more than one of which the eyes had been tinged with red. The greater number, including the base, are between 5 feet 10 inches and 6 feet 10 inches in height. Some are uninscribed; others have the name and titles of the king on the front of the throne, at each side of the figure; and some have further a dedication to the goddess.

The greater part of these were dedicated by Amenhetep III., and Mariette therefore ascribed to him the foundation of the whole temple; but as some of these statues were already visible with a dedication by Sheshanq, it is likely that Mariette regarded these as usurped. On the gateway Mariette found the original cartouches of Seti II., and these were still above ground when we began excavating. Mariette also marked a Ptolemaic addition to the gateway, projecting externally. On this part were formerly four representations in relief of the god Bes, incorrectly called Typhon; and two of these are still fairly complete.

Thus the only Pharaohs whom Mariette's enquiry showed to be connected with the temple were Amenhetep III. as founder, Seti II., perhaps Sheshanq, Taharqa, and the Ptolemies.

There was also visible in the outer court a statue

dedicated by Pi-netem, a Pharaoh of the 21st dynasty. The statue is headless but of different workmanship to the rest, the inscription being on the back. The cartouche of Set-nekht on a gateway of the second court was likewise apparent.

We began our work in the gateway and found the pavement about ten or twelve feet below the surface of the ground. In the course of working through the gateway we found some fallen roofing blocks, and as we got to the end came upon another lion-headed statue lying across the way and a small sandstone hippopotamus head of the goddess Ta-urt or Apët (pl. VIII., fig. 2).

We found that the original gateway was of the usual Egyptian shape with sloping sides, and this part bore, as well as Seti's name, the later cartouches of Rameses IV. and Rameses VI. The pylon had been turned into a square-sided gateway by Ptolemaic additions both within and without the court.

We then came on the bases of round pillars standing within the court. There had been four pairs of these (not five, as in Mariette's plan) from the northern gateway to that between the first and second court. The more easterly of the northern and southern pair of these had been joined to the wall nearest to them by a short badly built wall. This again it will be seen Mariette does not give correctly; many of his inaccuracies in fact both here and elsewhere appear to come from the unfounded assumption of a symmetry between that

PLATE IV.

To face p. 30.

PYLON OF SETI II.

Photograph by Dr. Page May.

part which he uncovered and that which he was unable to excavate.

We then worked round the westerly part of the court, uncovering eight lion-headed statues, of which five were fairly complete, two had lost their heads, and one was a particularly large one, of which only the upper half was complete.

Some of these bore the cartouche of Amenhetep III., some that of Sheshanq I. But we found here and elsewhere that it was impossible to find on the latter any trace of an earlier cartouche chiselled out. When this is done it is often very roughly performed. At Deir el Bahari for instance even feminine pronouns are left where Hatshepsut's cartouche is usurped by a king's name, and the erased cartouche shows as a distinctly depressed oval. Here on the contrary, unless all the front was chiselled, which is a refinement the Egyptians were not prone to affect, no erasure has been made. Sheshanq's cartouche is not so well or deeply chiselled as Amenhetep's.

As we turned the corner of the north wall towards the west, we came upon the one good find of the year, and it was a great surprise to all of us (plan no. 1).

We were riding out to the temple when we were met by a boy running towards Luxor. He shouted out " Antica," and told my donkey-boy that he was going for a rope, for there was a fine discovery. " Very good—little man so high," my boy said, holding his hand about two feet from the ground

When we arrived at the temple they were washing the statue (pl. XIV., fig. 1, pp. 189, 325). It was in black granite and was almost perfect, the nose and the feet only being rather rubbed. The figure was in the usual squatting position; knees up, hands crossed, the elbows resting on the knees, the whole figure except the head being roughly outlined in stone without clear definition of the limbs. The figure rendered in this way affords a good surface for inscription, and this statue is inscribed all round. The face was very young and pleasing, the right hand held a lotus, and on the right shoulder were two partly erased cartouches.

We had barely had time to determine this when a great disappointment descended on us. An overseer had been appointed on behalf of the Government, who this first year spent his whole time cross-legged on a wall watching the progress of the work.

As soon as this discovery was made, the first of real importance, he went, as he was bound, to the native Sub-inspector of Antiquities of the district, who now appeared upon the scene, took possession of the statue, bore it away to the small temple of Ap, which was used as a storehouse of antiquities, and turned the key upon it.

The man no doubt was merely doing his duty, but fate seemed hard upon us.

M. Daressy was then Inspector of Antiquities in that district. On our appeal to him, with his unfailing kindness he at once came over, rode with us to the temple, examined the statue, and, congratulating us upon our find, gave us permission to remove it to the hotel and ourselves undertake its safe-guarding.

The statue proved to be that of a royal scribe, and the cartouches on it those of Amenhetep II., whose reign does not abound in monuments. As the statue was apparently *in situ*—being on pavement level, and ranged close to the other standing statues—this threw back the date of the foundation of the temple.

In the same half of the court we uncovered other lion-headed statues, all much broken ; but nothing worthy of special remark beyond the base of another very large one with a cartouche so much broken as to be nearly illegible. As far as we could make out it was that of Rameses II. (plan no. 3).

In crossing the colonnade again we found two small cynocephali in sandstone, much broken and quite defaced, on the back of which were cartouches of Rameses III.

The statues seated against the southern half of the eastern wall were for the most part destroyed above the waist. But as we turned the corner of the wall and came out upon the eastern side we found a very large and fine statue, broken in half indeed, but in such a way that it could be easily mended. It had no cartouche nor inscription, but had a trace of colouring still left on necklace and anklets.

D

Against the east wall were a large number of the statues, some of which had not been more than half buried.   In one group ten or eleven statues were ranged in two lines, and a part of a figure, advanced beyond these, indicated that they might have been three deep.

On this side also we found a block of fine white crystalline limestone (pl. XI., fig. 3), with two or three lines of inscription but no date.   We exposed a piece of the brick wall on this east side, and found it very regularly built in the curving layers which give strength.

Turning again to the north, we uncovered about eight more figures, and some mouldered bases.   Here again it appeared that there must have been more than a single line of statues, for one, erect and square with the line, sat in front of the rest.

In clearing this part of the court we found also the upper part of a woman's figure in a scaly garment, one fold drawn over the arm and the scourge in her hand; there was no name nor indication of date.

Here we ended the first year's excavation, having worked altogether for five weeks.   Very few small things were found, and those not of value; they included some few coins, mostly Ptolemaic, a rough terra-cotta of an Egyptian princess lying on her bed, attired in her wig and crown, beads, a few Roman pots and broken bits of bronze; one of these, a tiny arm, was probably Greek.

Those lion-headed statues which were evidently out of place we ranged with the others round the walls, and mended seven or eight of them. As no guardian was appointed for the summer the Arab children accomplished some breakages ; but we were pleased with the excellent taste of these iconoclasts, for they had wreaked the chief of their vengeance on a fancy arm, which the Italian plasterer told us, with tears in his eyes, he had three times renewed.

The statue of the scribe was sent down to Gizeh by the Museum boat, and the inscribed limestone consigned to the Luxor store-house.

The Museum authorities kindly gave us a cast of the statue.

CHAPTER IV.

EXCAVATION IN 1896.

THE second year the same contract was granted to us at once on our application. This year we had a larger staff of workers, varying from eight men and twenty-four boys, with reis, guardians, and water-carrier, to twelve men with a more than proportionately large number of boys, as our "throw" got longer; for in the southern part of the temple we were further from the place where we must put our earth.

We were able this year also to give more constant supervision, and indeed from the character of the digging it will be seen that close supervision was often needed.

In consequence of the increase of our staff we were able from time to time to work simultaneously in two parts of the temple. We have however in the narrative grouped our results for clearness' sake, so as to give as consecutively as possible the account of the clearance at each place.

We began on the 30th of January, at the gateway between the first and second courts.

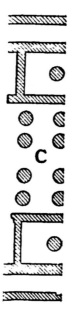

C

WALL NO

AN OF

In working through this it appeared from the straight joint in the dividing wall that this wall or pylon, which Mariette attributes to Amenhetep III., is a composite structure. Further work inside the court confirmed the conjecture, showing that the part of the building which forms the wall of the second court is of later date.

The western part of this dividing wall was completely destroyed, and we found here the remains of more than one row of hollow pots, which may have been used as air-bricks in some late rebuilding. But it is probable that the western side of the pylon was on the same plan as the eastern side at present, with the exception of the narrow passage through the pylon from north to south and the chambers in the thickness of the wall. We cleared the eastern chamber (*k*) during the 1896 excavation, finding nothing in it, and later part of the western chamber (*j*), but the ground was very hard and unrewarding; and as there were other more pressing things to be done we never finished this nor verified Mariette's map with regard to its length.

Pursuing our work through the central gateway we came, just within the court, upon a magnificent lion head in black granite like those we had already found, but of very superior workmanship. The granite of the finely moulded head and disk is still polished. The uraeus was in place when we found it, though there was a crack through the snake head. Unfortunately a boy carelessly throwing stones broke it off, and though we twice had it mended it was finally broken and carried away during the summer. The photograph, which was taken at the temple soon after the head was found, shows the uraeus (pl. X., plan no. 4).

The fragment measures 3 feet 11 inches from the top of the disk to the bottom of the chin. If therefore the figure were proportioned like others of this kind, the whole sitting statue would be by a rough estimate between 14 and 16 feet high.

Going further we found more pieces of this statue—so large that they could belong to nothing else—a piece of shoulder, two feet, the middle part of the body with a huge hand holding a lotus. We could not ourselves put the statue together; parts were missing, and the work of hoisting was far too great for our resources. M. de Morgan however, visiting the temple the succeeding year, was much struck by the head, and ordered that all the pieces of the statue should be sent down to Gizeh, intending if possible to have them put together there.

We had hardly passed the gateway when we struck on what appeared to be part of a large sphere of granite, and while we were still wondering what this could be we found an edge and two rounded projections and suddenly perceived it to be the back of the rounded wig kings wear, with the king's shoulders beneath it.

It tries the patience of an excavator to work

slowly at a statue which is lying flat on its face, so
that the most important point cannot be determined
until the whole thing is free. We must in such a
case too work carefully and slowly, and it seemed
long before all was uncovered and we turned over
the upper part of a king's figure. The arms were
broken off above the elbow; the face was scarred,
but not too much to exhibit a physiognomy of the
most pleasing character.

We then searched further to the east—the direction from which the figure had fallen—and found
the lower part of the statue. Very little was
actually missing, so that we were able subsequently to mend and set it up in the temple. The
statue, with its pedestal, is about 8 feet high
(plan no. 15, pl. XV.).

The one fact which proved disappointing was
that there was no certain evidence of date. A friend
called our attention to the fact that an oval mark on
the shoulder showed that a cartouche had been
chiselled out, and a broad band of roughened
granite up the back of the seat witnessed to the
erasure of an inscription.

While digging out these statues we came on the
bases of the first of five pairs of round pillars, probably campaniform, forming the colonnade across
the second court from north to south.

So far, we had been working close about the
gateway. Now we turned to the west to work out
the western half of the court.

A thinly-built wall stood out in this west half
about four feet from the main wall on the north,
and the part between the two walls was on a higher
level than the rest of the court. This higher level
we found was continued round the court on the west
side behind a row of square Hathor-headed pillars.
We found subsequently that the same was the case
on the north side of the court, and probably on its
east side also.

Here again we note a discrepancy with Mariette's map, which marks square pillars round the
north, east and west sides of the court, leaving out
the unsymmetrical bit of wall in the west half. This
wall he could not have seen ; and it may indeed
have replaced earlier square pillars, for it was not
as well built as the main walls of the court. But
in any case, as will be seen from the map, there
could not be as many of these square pillars as
Mariette marks on the north.

The whole determination of levels in this court
was very difficult, probably from the fact that heavy
statues had fallen, breaking the pavement. The
pavement once broken, the weight of the statues
would cause them to sink still further, and the infiltration of water through the soil would aid this
process. In some such way only can one account
for the fact that for several statues we actually
had to dig down into the earth two or three
feet or more below the level where others stood
in situ.

In clearing the short piece of wall before mentioned we came on another large statue of the
leontocephalous order, smaller indeed than the
great one just mentioned, but very much more
complete. It was broken at the waist and in two
or three places below the waist, but nearly all the
statue could be found. We managed to put it
together by the aid of appliances lent to us by
M. Legrain, who was then District Inspector of
Antiquities, and under the direction of an experienced reis who was working for him at Karnak,
and whose services he kindly put at our disposal
towards the end of the season when we were
mending and putting up our statues.

This statue was dedicated by Sheshanq, and shows
some different work from the rest, for the figure
wears a complete crown of uraei, which was originally surmounted by the disk. The inscription in
this instance is well and clearly carved. The statue,
which still remains in the temple, presents a very
imposing appearance, for although a part of the
pedestal is slightly sunk in the ground it stands
nearly 10 feet high (plan no. 5, pl. XIX.).

Between the short piece of wall and the main
wall of the court we found some more statues of the
ordinary type. We may anticipate by saying that
we found later on that in this court most, if not
all, of those statues which appeared to be *in situ*
were either between the square pillars or ranged
behind them close against the main wall of the

court; thus the greater part stood on the higher level. There were however a few against the east part of the south wall, and pieces evidently out of place in other parts.

The clearing of the court was difficult, owing to the fact before-mentioned that the pavement was almost entirely destroyed. There was also a great deal of stone in the court, which made the work slow.

Turning the north-east corner we worked south again and came across a small black-granite head belonging to a sphinx, partly broken, as well as the shoulder and defaced head of a similar sphinx. The face of the first was evidently a portrait, and the cartouche on the shoulder of the second piece was that of Rameses III. (plan no. 6, pl. XVII., fig. 1).

About the middle of the court we came on a rose-granite pedestal, much injured by the salt of the soil and crumbling. It still preserved however the very rare cartouche of Tutankhamen (plan no. 7).

A little further on a similar block of alabaster was found bearing the partly erased cartouches of Rameses VI. (plan no. 8).

Here too we came upon another fragment which might, with the statue of the first year, have given us a clue to future finds. It was a piece of fine white limestone, on the front of which were the middle parts of two figures; on the back was a delicately cut inscription. The fragment was part of a double statue of a priest and his wife,

and was found to belong to the 18th dynasty
(plan no. 9, p. 335).

Near the southernmost of the round pillars on the
west side of the colonnade, we found a rose-granite
figure, fallen on its side in such wise that a profile,
pleasing except for the fact that the nose was as
usual a little broken, was seen against the soil. The
figure was seated and nearly life-size; it seemed
whole but for a crack through the middle into
which roots of plants had forced an entrance. We
used the greatest care in raising it; but the first
movement broke the upper part of the figure from
the lower, and as we raised the former a part of the
left shoulder, that on which it had been lying, was
seen to be corroded by the salt, and fell off. The
chair on which the figure was seated was so much
destroyed that as we raised it bits of granite
showered down like gravel. What we finally
rescued in fairly good condition was the upper part
of the figure, of which the face had suffered hardly
at all; two other pieces which made up the lower
part of the figure to below the knees; a bit of
shoulder which might be mended; and the two
corners of the chair, on which, happily uninjured,
. were the cartouches of Rameses II. The face is
conventional; the figure wears the crown of Upper
Egypt with the uraeus in front, has the royal
necklace on and carries in hands crossed on the
breast two sceptres, the scourge and the shepherd's
crook (plan no. 11, pl. XVI.).

This statue affords a good instance of the force of the chief agent of destruction in Egypt—if we exclude the tourist and the Arab—an agent whose force must be counteracted if we hope to preserve the temples near the Nile.

On each side of the Nile for about a mile inland runs a subsoil river. When the Nile rises this rises, and in filtrating through the soil waters land beyond the reach of the Nile flood, carrying up with it at the same time the salts of which the soil is full.

These salts enrich the soil, and this infiltration, which is on one side the agent of destruction, is therefore on the other an agent of fertilisation.

The lake of Mut is fed in this indirect way by the Nile, and at the time of inundation rises and floods the temple. A donkey-boy graphically described this: "When Nile rises . . ."—English failed him, and he waved his arms round the banks; "when Nile sit down he sit down by him."

The salts act with greater or less power on different kinds of stone. Sandstone is much affected; granite less. It appears, as Professor Petrie told us, that that which is altogether buried, and thus is never able to dry, suffers much less than that which is wetted and dries year by year; for it is the crystallising of the salt in the interstices of the stone which corrodes it. It is difficult to test this altogether by individual experience, as so many circumstances, even the quality of the particular block, go to make up the result. But it is certain that some of the granite statues, whose unburied tops were so far corroded that their polished surface was quite gone, were whole and uncorroded where they had been covered by damp soil.

If this be so, the work of excavation must lead in the end to the destruction of the statues, unless some way can be found of neutralising the action of the salt ; and the quaint effect now presented in the early part of the year, of black statues with white-stockinged feet, will give way to the sadder spectacle of statues with no feet.

The only device at present, and that is practicable merely in the case of individual and comparatively small objects, is to wash out the salt by soaking in fresh water. M. de Morgan conceived the ingenious scheme of washing out all Karnak by turning the water, which he was sure came into the Sacred Lake by a direct inlet from the Nile, into the temple itself. Although, however, he ascertained that some direct inlet indeed existed, the practical difficulties in the way of the scheme were so great that it was never carried out.

The action of the salt in drying may be easily seen in the case of pottery. We found a small earthenware Coptic lamp of which the surface was complete ; and as we did not then understand the matter it was put away without being soaked. Next year it had grown a crop of salt like mildew ; and this being wiped off another appeared, until the surface began to crumble.

With regard to the Rameses statue it is probable that the position in which it was lying had shielded part of the figure from the action of the salts.

After clearing the west half of the second court, we began at the north end of the east half. A short way from the gateway we found a black-granite head wearing the head-dress of a god (plan no. 14, pl. VIII., fig. 1). The face was well worked, but of the conventional Egyptian type, and both it and the head-dress were broken. With this we found a bit of the vulture head-dress, well worked in black granite. The vulture head-dress is that of the goddess to whom the temple was dedicated, and it was also worn by the queen-mother; and it is odd that we found no other thing of the kind. We worked through this court, finding half a sandstone Osiride figure wearing an elaborate wig which still retained some colour (plan no. 13), but nothing else of interest until we came to the southernmost pillar on the eastern side, and here we unearthed three well preserved sculptured blocks of sandstone. On one side of these were various ugly figures in relief, and on the other roughly incised pictures of galleys, and inscriptions (plan no. 12, pl. XX.–XXII., p. 370). At the moment we hardly realised their importance, but they were found to belong to the 25th dynasty, and to be of considerable interest. We searched for more both then and in the following year, but could only find two more pieces; and more are still needed to complete the scene.

By this time the second court was clear, showing on the south side three gateways, the central greater gateway opening into what was evidently a hypostyle hall as Mariette marks it.   Here we began working, but great masses of stone had fallen in and the work was therefore both dull and slow. As we had now a fairly large staff we decided to employ some of them in digging for foundation deposits.

Foundation deposits, first discovered by Professor Petrie, usually include small models of tools and small specimens in neat brick-like shape of the material used in the temple, together with scarabs, plaques and rings.   Most if not all of these objects bear the founder's name, thus dating the building.   They correspond in fact to the coins etc. that we ourselves put under foundation stones.

We were advised to dig for these deposits in the centres of principal gateways or under the corners or centres of principal walls.   But there are many principal gateways, corners and centres; and though there is generally more than one deposit there is not by any means one at each of these places. Moreover the deposit may be as far as ten yards on either side of the place to which it appears to have reference.   Thus it will be seen that unless one is prepared to give up a good deal of time to such digging, or is skilled in the matter, it is only by favourable chance that one is likely to find.   For

such a search we were not really well equipped; to
carry it out regularly one would have to underpin
walls; and as the stones of a principal wall or
corner are of considerable size we had neither the
means nor the science to do this.

Moreover, since foundation deposits, being of
small valuable objects, are peculiarly liable to be
stolen, the search needs constant supervision. We
could only work one place at a time, and that when
the rest of the digging was not too absorbing; and
it was not therefore surprising that our digging for
foundation deposits proved fruitless as regards that
for which we were seeking. As a matter of fact in
searching for foundation deposits we came accidentally on a find which was one of the chief interests
of the temple.

We dug first in the middle of the gateway between
the first and second court. Here and elsewhere if
our search could not be completed in the day we
assured ourselves by careful measurements and
observations, verified again in the morning, that the
place had not been touched. Our men were evidently quite unaware of our object in this digging,
and we never found a trace of the place having been
touched over-night.

We found nothing in this first place, though we
dug until we came to virgin earth.

While we were prosecuting the search for foundation deposits and that more fruitful search to which
this ultimately led, we were carrying on simul-

taneously both in 1896 and 1897 the clearance of the rest of the temple.

In 1896 this was done hastily for the sake of the plan, as it then seemed probable that we should not be able to return to Egypt. In 1897 we both finished the tracing of the walls and made the clearance complete. Most of this work was slow and unremunerative in the way of small objects of interest, as walls and roof had fallen in and the chambers were full of stones.

As this clearance then went on during two seasons it will be simpler to summarise the result in connection with the 1897 excavation, mentioning here only one or two particular points of interest.

The first of these was the discovery of a small crypt under the chamber (d) on the axis of the temple, at the back of which runs the passage which surrounds the smaller chambers.

The comparison of Mariette's map with all this part of the temple becomes impossible in detail, for the whole is incorrect, but as far as one can judge of correspondences where nothing accurately corresponds, he located the shrine, not in this part of the temple, but in that small building which further excavation showed to be entirely divided from the temple and to have its entrance on the south, from the lake end.

In an Egyptian temple the shrine is placed on the axis and towards the back of the building; it has frequently passages or chambers behind it, but

E

is entered by one door from the main part of the building.* Mariette draws it more or less in this manner, but he mistook the nature of the buildings with which he was dealing, not perceiving that that which he indicates as a shrine is a separate three-chambered building, having its only gateway on the side away from the temple.

Mariette's location of the shrine being then clearly out of the question, the only chamber which corresponds to the conditions is that marked d.

We were digging out this chamber, of which the east wall is so entirely destroyed that a mere indication of its position remains, when the man who was clearing out the earth in front of it perceived that under its pavement was a hole large enough for a little boy to crawl into. We began to work out the hole, and found that it extended inwards from the top of a narrow door, through which, when the earth was removed we descended into a tiny underground chamber, measuring 4 feet 4 inches in breadth by 5 feet 6 inches in length, and too low to allow one to stand upright. The chamber was formed of well fitted masonry, and roofed with three blocks of stone, which extending from side to side formed the pavement of the chamber above. The door or hole at which one got in was broad enough to admit the shoulders of the average person but

* Compare the position of the *Holy of Holies* in the Jewish Tabernacle and Temple. The whole plan of these resembles the plan of the Egyptian temple.

not more than two feet high, and its top being on the same level as the top of the chamber there was thus a drop of about three feet inside. From the top of the door outwards masonry extended for a short way, the blocks of stone being ingeniously placed in such wise that two more stones dropped between them would have filled up the space and completely hidden the little door.

Here then we seemed to have lighted upon a veritable treasure chamber, planned with an ingenuity worthy of an Eastern fairy tale.

Our hopes were still further raised when on having cleared out the earth and rubbish with which the chamber was choked we found that in the paved floor there was a hole extending from the north-east corner to halfway below the door. There was probably but one paving-stone missing, and the hole seemed to have been deliberately made, for it was filled not with earth but with rubbish.

This we worked out, and it was a matter of difficulty. At first a man could work it, but the hole soon grew too deep for a man's arm to reach down, and was then too narrow to admit any one but a little boy, who worked very slowly, but with much enjoyment. One of us had always to be on guard within the chamber, peering into the darkest corner, where the work was carried on by three of the smallest boys in rotation, working with one hand and a trowel.

We could not get through all the work in the

E 2

crypt in a day, so at night we measured what we
had done, pushed a stone to the door of the crypt,
set a seal by writing our initials in sand, and put a
guardian with a gun to keep the place. No one
could possibly enter without obliterating the initials ;
and once we found them rubbed out, but it proved
on enquiry to have been done by a boy who had
let his basket drop as he peered in out of curiosity,
and had gone to fetch it. He was amazed at being
found out, being ignorant of our seal, but confessed,
and we satisfied ourselves that the hole had not been
tampered with.

But if it had been, as is very probable, a treasure-
chamber, the secret of it must have been discovered
long since. We worked at the hole in the floor
through rubbish, finding nothing but some scraps of
pottery, half a Hathor head in earthenware, a
broken bit of blue glaze, until we came to the sand.
Even then we did not despair of finding a deposit
in the sand, and worked through it until we came to
layers of earth that were wet with the infiltration
from the lake, and we knew that no hope of treasure
remained.

We determined then to make a fresh search for
foundation deposit under one of the principal corners
of the temple, and chose for this purpose the south-
east corner.

It will be seen from comparison with Mariette's
map that there is no point which really corresponds
to this corner. His thick engirdling wall is of

brick, and we found it to be of later construction than the rest.

The stone wall next within this Mariette draws to meet the brick wall on the south, which it does not do.   He makes it moreover only of the same thickness as the rest of the inside walls, whereas it is in fact a principal wall of double thickness, which, starting from the stone pylon between the first and second courts, surrounds all the rest of the temple, cutting it off from the small later structure (x, y, z) before mentioned.

It was then at the south-east corner of this wall, the principal stone wall of the temple, that we began to dig for the deposits.

The actual corner stone had to be uncovered, and the wall had been so far destroyed that the top stone left was only in the first course above the foundation layers.   Having dug round this stone then we began to dig round the foundation courses of stone, those originally below the ground, and in doing so came upon the base of an uninscribed statuette.   We dug on and came upon another; this was inscribed.   Excitement began to grow. We put into the hole another man, and for the next two hours there was no moment in which some statuette was not being dug out.

By the end of the morning we had pieces of eight figures, one being the bottom of a double statue—a man and his wife seated side by side.   All but two were inscribed, but we had only found one head, which appeared to belong to the double statue, being a man's head of about the right size and the same yellow sandstone (Trench A, pl. XIII., p. 323).

At this juncture M. Legrain appeared and was very urgent with us to let the statues be taken to his storehouse at Karnak. Although he was so kind as to say that we might have access to this at all times, its distance from Luxor and our constant occupation at the temple would have made the statues practically inaccessible to us for purposes of study.

M. Legrain however yielded to our representations so far as to allow us to take the statues back for the present to the hotel, pending M. de Morgan's decision on the subject, and attached to this permission the condition that we should for the future accurately report all finds, which from ignorance of what was required we had previously omitted to do.

M. de Morgan most kindly wrote back to us and to M. Legrain confirming this permission to keep the finds by us so long as we were in Luxor, under the condition that M. Legrain had imposed.

By evening we had found three more statuettes. All of these belonged to the 18th dynasty.

The destruction and throwing out of the figures were evidently deliberate; a hole must have been dug to bury them, and the fractures were such as must have been made with intent to deface and destroy.

For a day or two we dug still further, but found

nothing more at this time, and came to the conclusion that they had been thrown out merely
at this place, and that the heads had either been
completely broken or buried elsewhere. Some
little bits of heads that we came upon seemed to
confirm the first conjecture.

About four feet from this principal wall we came
to the top of a narrower stone wall; but this latter
was entirely below the level given by the former,
and as nothing showed it to be earlier its purpose
remained something of a mystery.

When the statues came to an end we finished
our search for foundation deposit at the corner, but
though we worked through four feet of the foundation sand, on which the foundation courses of stone
are always laid and in which the deposit is placed,
we found nothing.

We then relinquished this part of the work, filling
up the holes we had made, which in spite of large
notices to the unwary had rendered our temple a
little dangerous.

We now turned our attention to the building at
the end of the temple with a gateway towards the
lake.

On digging round the gateway, we found one of
the lion-headed statues lying across it. It was
partly defaced, but had the disk complete, and we
set it up in its former position on the west side of
the gate, looking towards the lake (plan no. 19).

At the feet of this statue we found a squatting

sandstone figure (plan no. 18, pl. XIV., fig. 2) about three feet high.   It had been thrown out of the temple, like so many others, and was standing on its head in the earth of the bank which sloped up from the edge of the water to the outer wall of the temple.   It has an ugly forcible face and there is a well cut Hathor head carved on the plain surface in front; otherwise the workmanship is rough in the extreme, and there is only a broken line of inscription below the feet, the signs of which are indecipherable.

On either side of the gateway we came upon the wall of burnt brick before mentioned, and built into the small portion exposed by the clearing of the gateway we found the base of a black-granite squatting statue about two feet high.   It had been used simply as building material, and was so firmly embedded in excellent mortar and well made brick that these had to be smashed with an iron crowbar before the statue could be got out (plan no. 22, p. 340).

The excavation was now drawing to a close, and we had dismissed most of our boys.   Mending was going on, and for this purpose we wanted sometimes a large number of men for a few hours, when heavy hauling had to be done, and in the intervals not more than three or four.

Our results, including as they did the Piankhý blocks, the royal statues and the broken statuettes, had been already far better than anything we had anticipated ; but the best was yet to come.

We all intended to go down the river in the first week in March, and the last week in February we were going to close.

On the Thursday of that week four men were working in the temple, and one, a clever boy who had been dismissed, was wandering round the temple by himself.

Presently he came up to us and explained, as far as we could understand his Arabic, that he had found a stone with "a man's foot" underneath it. He brought us to the sloping southern bank of the temple, and showed us what we must have seen but left unnoticed many times before, a piece of inscribed stone sticking out of the ground. The boy showed us where he had grubbed away the earth beneath; putting in a hand one could feel the foot of a statue. Though the piece only looked like a broken stone it was evidently worth while to dig it up. The discoverer—for Osman Amar was the real discoverer of the statue—borrowed a pick and began.

He did not as we expected soon get to the end of the piece. It was Ramadan, and the sun was beginning to decline, and being anxious to finish before sunset we called another man. Still they worked on, and still the statue had not come to an end. We could see now that it was a kneeling statue, in sandstone, flung over as if it had been taken by the heel and dropped. We called yet more men, and though they had to work gingerly they worked quickly, for they too were excited and the sun was near setting. By this time we were filled with fear that the head might be broken; with hope that since the statue was so large it might have escaped.

There was a sudden rumour that the head was appearing, but it proved to be merely the Hathor face on the altar the figure was holding, so we worked on, and certainly the statue did not end at the shoulders.

About this time the pick of the man working below had exposed the side of a white limestone statue, also a large one, lying under that which we were engaged on. This we had to cover for the time being with a thick layer of earth, for fear it should be hurt.

Finally we shouted to all the men who were near to lend a hand; and as the sun set we turned over a statue more than five feet high, in hard polished sandstone, excellently worked, inscribed all over and almost perfect (plan no. 16, pl. XII., p. 299).

The men, full of genuine sympathetic excitement, increased no doubt by the prospect of backsheesh, cheered the statue as it stood. With the backsheesh this time at any rate they were not dissatisfied. Three other men claimed to have seen the piece also and to have told the reis, who had omitted to inform us. They voted very fairly that half the backsheesh should go to the boy who had told us, the other half be divided among the three men.

Then we left two men with guns to guard the statue, and went home for the night. Though we did not yet know whose statue we had discovered, there was no doubt it must be some one of much importance.

By the time we reached the temple next morning Mr. Newberry was already there, and had discovered that the statue was of one Sen-mut, a high official under Hatshepsut and her daughters. Sen-mut was perhaps the man of all others of whom we should wish to have found some record. We hoped that the statue was executed in Hatshepsut's reign, and even as we looked at it we saw her cartouche on the back.

The other statue, which had been lying beneath this, was now disinterred. It proved to be a squatting statue in white limestone of Bak-en-Khonsu, high priest of Amen under Rameses III.; this too was nearly complete (pl. XVIII., p. 343).

Then we had to haul the statues up the bank. M. Legrain's reis lent his aid; Mr. Dixon, who was then on the Land Taxing Commission at Luxor, kindly volunteered to help him with more engineering science; rollers were placed and covered with palm leaves, which, when bruised by the statue's weight, oiled the wood; and the band of Arabs, shouting, singing and pulling, brought Sen-mut to the top, and there he stood, guarded diligently by night, until fetched away to Gizeh.

In the earth displaced by the hauling up of the

statue one man picked up a small chip of granite. This proved to be strangely interesting, for the few words it bore included a 12th-dynasty name (plan no. 17). We had to make a carriage drive round the temple for the truck which carried Sen-mut to the river to meet the Museum boat. His fragments were carefully collected and sent with him. Bak-en-Khonsu we put upright in the place where he was found, until he too was taken to Cairo.

Although we had intended to bring the work for 1896 to an end with the clearance of the gateway giving on the lake, the discovery of these two statues made it impossible to stop without further search in the bank of earth above the lake. We determined therefore to cut away the slope along the face of the brick wall. Beginning on the west side of the gateway we worked towards the south-west corner where Sen-mut was found, and cleared about half this length. No more statues were forthcoming, but a badly built pier of re-worked stones was exposed, jutting out from below the brick wall; the remains of another such pier were evident at the corner where Sen-mut had been thrown out. As only two or three days now remained we began cutting down the corresponding bank on the east side of the gate-way, beginning at the south-east corner, in the hope that this might prove as fruitful as the western side.

A corresponding pier of roughly built stones was soon apparent, and in the brick wall above it we found pieces of two more black-granite statues.

PLATE V.

Photograph by H. B. Gourlay. *To face p. 60.*

CUTTING DOWN THE SOUTHERN SLOPE.

They had been used in the building of the wall, and again had to be broken out with a crowbar. One of these was the middle part of a large squatting statue, fully inscribed (plan no. 24, pl. XXIII., p. 350). This we found afterwards to be of considerable importance. The second proved to be a piece of a similar figure of much smaller size and with an inscription too much mutilated for translation (plan no. 23).

The work had perforce to be brought to a close when about a third of the eastern half of the bank had been cut down. But though much remained to be done we left Luxor satisfied with the unexpectedly large results of a few weeks' excavation.

The Museum authorities very kindly gave us the statue of Rameses II. and the heads of Rameses III. and the unnamed god.

CHAPTER V.

EXCAVATION IN 1897.

WE began our 1897 excavation under circumstances in every way more favourable.

Our funds were large enough to enable us to begin with a fair staff; we engaged at once eight diggers and their boys; owing to a kind and un-expected subscription from a fellow traveller we were able to increase this number at the end of the first week, and we still further augmented it in the weeks that followed. We had also a much larger party to give help in supervision; and we began moreover for the first time with some knowledge of our ground and therefore some definite plan of digging. The plan proved on the whole successful.

We set before ourselves three distinct objects: the clearance of the rest of the temple; the discovery of further statuettes; and a search after the elusive foundation deposits, which must surely exist.

Our indirect object was likewise threefold: to trace the accurate plan of the temple; to determine the history of the building; and withal not to leave the site disfigured with unseemly rubbish heaps, but to give back to it so much of its charm as two thousand years of ruin had left to it and in some ways helped to bestow upon it.

The clearing of the temple was now for the most part straightforward work, though slow, but there was one hope we dimly cherished which might involve a more radical search than anything we had yet been engaged in. One or two indications had been noted that there might have existed on this spot an earlier temple than that we were now working at. These indications were the low wall at the south-east corner bordering on trench A, and the bit of granite bearing a 12th-dynasty name; the first week of our 1897 excavation was to give us another bit of evidence to the same effect.

With regard to the second point—the discovery of any other statuettes that might exist—the study of results already obtained had made it possible to form a hypothesis as to where such statues, if they existed at all, would be found.

It was evident from the position of those already discovered that they had been deliberately thrown out of the temple—the smaller ones first broken and then buried, the larger simply cast right outside the temple area, or used, if they were worth it, as material for a later wall.

We intended therefore to finish the clearance of that trench in which we first found the statuettes; to dig a corresponding trench on the west side of the temple; to search the banks of earth which covered the outer brick wall, especially that above the lake on the south, and finally to examine as far as possible the wall itself, in case statues should in other places have been built in.

All this season we were working in various parts of the ground simultaneously; for clearness' sake, therefore, we will group our results as before.

As regards the search for foundation deposit it is simpler to mention at once that we were again disappointed; although we found this time in the foundation sand, both under the south-west corner and in one of the gateways, the layer of white sand that generally contains the deposit. But of the latter there was not a trace.

We began work on the 10th of January, having hired our men the day before.

We gave them orders to be at the temple ready for work in the morning, intending of course to be there ourselves when they began, which was to be somewhat later than usual. But eagerness to begin, or more probably greed for gain, so worked that they decided to begin by themselves.

At nine o'clock in the morning therefore we got an urgent message summoning us, our new rope and efficient crowbar, to the temple.

The men had begun work where we had ceased in 1896; namely at the brick wall just over the south-east pier. They were gathered here in great excitement, and we did not wonder when, descending the steep path over the edge of the mound, we saw what they had come upon.

Two great masses of black granite had been uncovered, the one the base of a very large squatting
statue, well worked and beautifully inscribed, with a
small Hathor head in front (plan no. 25, pl. XXIII.,
p. 350). This evidently from the finish of the work
was a piece of an important statue; and it was
subsequently found to belong to the piece discovered
in the same wall at the end of the 1896 excavation
—to be part of a statue of the priest and prophet
Mentu-em-hat.

The other was much more extraordinary. The
piece included the head and shoulders of a life-size
statue in black granite. The head was neither
shaved nor bewigged, but showed—a thing quite
unique in Egyptian portraiture—a bald head with a
fringe of hair. The face, of which the nose was
broken slightly, was a beautifully worked and
evidently faithful portrait of a man quite un-
Egyptian in type (pl. XXIV., p. 357).

The forehead, high and commanding, is strangely
flat in front; under the narrow eyes are deeply-
marked wrinkles; the lines above the upper lip
are nearly parallel and strongly marked, the mouth
full, but sharp along the edges of the lip; the
proportions of the face are curious, the length from
eye to lip being very great. Moreover the aspect
of the whole is particularly impressive, not only
from the artistic but from the personal point of
view, being a powerful rendering of a powerful
personality.

F

There is no name on the piece, but from coincidence of titles, similarity of workmanship and lettering, there is no doubt that it is part of another statue of Mentu-em-hat.

Such a find would in itself have been a not meagre reward for the season's excavations, yet though it was by far the best find of the year, perhaps the best yield of the temple, there was much to follow.

Some of our workers were told off for clearing along the wall, and while this work went on and we proceeded with the general clearance of the temple we selected two or three to reopen the trench which had been so fruitful in 1896 (trench A).

It took a short time to clear away accumulated earth and rubbish before we got again to the level of the year before.

Hardly had we begun to dig in the fresh ground however when the trench began to yield statuettes in the same astonishing numbers as before. Again they were all broken, but this time we had better luck with the heads.

The first day's work in the trench gave us fourteen pieces of statues, including one of the most beautiful objects we found, the head apparently of a woman, of the renaissance period of the Saïtes, showing a return to the old 4th- and 5th-dynasty treatment. The face is unbroken, and a crack which runs through the right side of head and face is in most lights hardly perceptible. The hair is

PLATE VI.

Photographs by J. F. Vaughan.   *To face p. 66.*

WOMAN'S HEAD (SAÏTE PERIOD).

parted in the middle and brought down low in front over a crescent-shaped forehead; the head is about three quarters of life-size and possesses the only complete nose that the excavation yielded, a nose straight, fine, and at a seemly angle. Here again we have evidently a portrait of very beautiful artistic workmanship (pl. VI.).

It was in the excitement of these finds that the theft before mentioned was made. The stolen head probably belonged to a squatting statue, as it was broken just underneath the chin; it was not perfect nor as far as was seen in any way remarkable.

With these heads also came out the body of a statue of the Saïte period, of which the head was found next day (pl. XXV., p. 361). This is a pretty figure, finely finished, retaining its polished surface and some trace of colouring. The head and figure fitted perfectly, the break though old was absolutely clean, and they were easily mended.

The double statuette (pl. XXVII., fig. 1, p. 359) is an interesting find from the same place. Unfortunately the name of the king is missing.

An arm in alabaster bearing Sheshanq's cartouche was found in the trench; and a small uninscribed sandstone sphinx in three pieces (pl. VIII., figs. 3, 4, p. 91). This is roughly modelled as to the body, but has a well cut face and wears the uraeus. A cut in the shoulder seems to indicate the erasure of a cartouche.

With the statues from this trench came also that

which gave us another hint of an earlier temple—
namely the base of what is thought to be a statuette
of the first 12th-dynasty king (p. 295).

After finishing this trench we opened a corresponding one on the west side (Trench B), and found
here too a large number of statuettes. One of the
most pleasing of these is the upper part of a figure in
black granite in vizier's dress (pl. XXVI., p. 361) ;
the face, though conventionally Egyptian, is pretty,
youthful, and almost feminine in type. The statue
of Pu-am-ra shows a rare position, for the hands—
which are placed palm upward on the knees—hold
each a small vase, probably for oblation. Both
hands were broken off, but found in the trench
(p. 315).

Altogether we found in the two trenches in 1897
pieces of fifteen inscribed figures, besides the two
heads mentioned, the arm, with some other pieces
belonging to a statue in alabaster, the sphinx, and
a very small conventional Saïte head in sandstone
(pl. XXVII., fig. 2).

When we consider that the 1896 excavation
gave us out of one of these trenches pieces of
eleven other statuettes of which eight were inscribed, it will be seen that this ancient rubbish
heap which we had accidentally lighted upon was
of no small importance.

Since these trenches then had been so rich in
finds we now continued the trench on the east side
(Trench C), turning the south-east corner, between

the main wall of the temple and the later brick wall which surrounds the whole.

We trenched down to the bottom of the foundation layer of the wall, and here too found broken statuettes, though not in such large numbers as before. We were not able to do more than about forty feet of this trenching, but this length yielded a broken black-granite statue of the 18th dynasty (p. 326), the lower part of a statuette in limestone bearing the cartouches of Amenhetep I. and others (pl. XI., fig. 1, p. 297); part of a curious ugly figure of the Saïte period, of which the tunic was merely a smooth cylinder of black granite (pl. XXVII., fig. 5, p. 366), but which held in front of it a tiny broken figure in a sitting position with a book open on the knees; and a fine piece of alabaster which had formed the base of a statuette, though unfortunately the only parts left of the figure which had once knelt on it were two pretty little feet, and all that remained of the inscription was the formal prayer for offerings.

These scanty alabaster remains show how thoroughly the iconoclasts did their work when they had a soft material to deal with.

A few very small objects were also found here, such as a clay mould of the seal of Rameses III. and a similar mould of the Sacred Eye.

In digging this trench we found the lowest course of another wall running parallel to the main wall at a distance of about three feet from it. Nothing of this was left but one course of stone resting on foundation sand, and after a moment's hope that it might be the remains of an earlier temple we were compelled to believe that it was but the stone foundation for the girdling brick wall, though indeed it was a great deal wider than the brick wall, which rested on its outer edge, leaving a stone platform about four feet wide on the inside.

In the mass of earth which covered this platform and concealed the brick wall were many Roman pots large and small. One of the small ones was quite whole, escaping even the pick of the digger who unearthed it. When we had emptied the earth which filled it we found forty-nine *potin* coins of Nero with Greek inscriptions and well modelled heads. One cannot help believing that the pot belonged to some far-off child, for at the bottom of it had been carefully placed a little mat of moss for the coins to rest on (plan no. 26, p. 381).

While this was going on we had continued the clearance of the brick wall above the lake, exposing the whole south front of the temple. A fourth pier of re-worked stones appeared between the Ptolemaic shrine and the pier at the eastern corner, corresponding with one on the other side. The four piers were all badly built, for the weight of the brick wall and the earth which covered it had pushed the blocks out of position. They were made of re-worked stones from the temple, the names of Thothmes III. and Rameses II. being upside down on some of

the blocks.   Another large piece of black granite
had been built into the brick wall itself.   This we
broke out, with great hope that it might prove a
peer to Mentu-em-hat, but to our disappointment
it was nothing more than another lion-headed
statue.

We also finished the clearance of the little Ptolemaic shrine which projected from the wall of the
temple (plan x, y, z) and whose entrance was flush
with the brick wall.   It was very small, consisting
of only two or three tiny chambers about six feet
square, the inmost one being like a daïsed recess of
the second, with no dividing wall.   This shrine also
had been built with re-worked stones, the cartouche
of Thothmes III. being visible on one of the corner
blocks (plan no. 21).

It seemed probable that steps had led from this
shrine to the lake, and on searching for these we
found them, somewhat displaced, and rearranged
them as well as we could.

The lion-headed statue which sat on the east side
of the gate had fallen, like her neighbour, deep in
the earth.   Her we disinterred and set up in her
former position (plan no. 20, pl. XXVIII.).

While digging out this statue we found under
her feet three small Ptolemaic foundation bricks,
two of reddened sotne, one white with traces of
gilding.

A similar shrine to this may have existed on the
west side of the temple, for here we noticed some

jutting stones, and on disinterring them found them to be sculptured and inscribed blocks of Ptolemaic date. There was nothing of importance on those we found, and we could not follow up the digging here as so much clearing had to be done inside the temple that it was impossible to spend much time on the slopes outside it.

On the west side, from the south-west corner to the second court, there seemed to be a passage or corridor between the brick wall and the main wall of the temple. Several pieces of lion-headed statues projected through the earth and seemed to call for clearance. This broad passage being dug out it was found to contain forty-eight of these statues, arranged in a row all down the side next the brick wall and with a pair at each end fronting each other.

Many of these were broken, but a certain number were in fair preservation, and several of the broken ones were readily put together again and set up in their places, so that they seemed to be assembled in dignified and solemn parliament. At one end of the corridor—that near the second court—we found in the earth a store of little bronze Osiris figures. They were however too much destroyed to be of any value.

The blocks of the naval expedition of Piankhẏ, which we had found in 1896 in the second court, were of so much interest as to make it important that others which were wanting to complete the inscription should be found also. But though we searched that part of the court where they might be, digging deep below pavement level, we found no more, and could only conclude that they had been broken in the general destruction of walls and roofing.

In the outer court also we dug a couple of deep diagonal trenches, working till we came to virgin soil, in the hope of coming across some trace of the ardently desired earlier temple. Nothing was forth coming however except two or three more pieces of the ubiquitous lion-headed statues, one of which curiously enough had fallen quite four feet below pavement level, and part of a rough sandstone figure of a man holding a little shrine in front of him. The constant presence of figures of this kind is interesting, as it showed how greatly the temple of Mut was used as a depository for such monuments.

It only remained now to clear the smaller chambers from the *débris* with which they were choked and which quite concealed their number and the walls which divided them. This was very slow work, for the rubbish consisted of broken stones, large and small, which had once been walls and roofing, and which were now more or less buried in sand and gravelly soil. Many of the stones were so large that it required three or four men to deal with them.

From the second or cloistered court a couple of

steps led up to a little hypostyle hall (C); this hall and all the further part of the temple had once been roofed over, so that the heavy masses of the roofing blocks were added to those fallen from the walls. No doubt the temple had long been used as a quarry by any neighbouring Arabs who wanted stone, but there was plenty left to make the work of clearing very laborious.

The hypostyle hall contains four pairs of pillars, and here again we note discrepancies between Mariette's map and the real plan. Mariette makes the hall the whole breadth of the temple and marks six pairs of pillars, whereas in the hall itself there are but four pairs and on each side is a small chamber with a single column in the middle. Even these chambers are not symmetrical, as may be seen by the plan of the temple.

The columns of the hall are not uniform, but in two or three varying styles—one pair being lotiform, another smoothly circular, and so forth. This variety was common in later times. The breadth of the temple from this point onwards is slightly diminished, and on the east side, at the corner of the projection thus formed, is the well-known Taharqa Chamber (a).

A corridor on the axis of the temple, having a gate at either end, leads out of the hypostyle hall to the sanctuary (f). The chambers on either side of this corridor by no means correspond to one another, though Mariette has made his plan almost symmetrical, deducing from the less buried eastern half divisions in the western which exist only on paper and by no means in solid stone.

A glance at the plan will show that the arrangement of these inner divisions differs entirely on the east side from that on the west. Rather more of the wall is preserved on the east side, and even before the chambers were cleared portions of it were visible four to six feet above the ground, whereas on the west side it was all concealed. The only parts which are in reality symmetrical are the chambers on either side of the sanctuary.

It has already been said there was a small crypt under the shrine. The clearing of the rest of the temple revealed other crypts under the pavement in the corridor (f) and one of the chambers. They are merely small stone-lined vaults, too low to stand upright in, and had probably been used for safeguarding treasure. Now they contain nothing but broken stone and *débris*.

In the place marked (g) on the plan, we found four cynocephali of sandstone, about four feet high ; they were evidently not in position, but thrown about anyhow in a small side chamber. They were in the attitude in which they adore the rising sun, and though much defaced (pl. IX.), the palms of their hands, which were painted red, still retain their colour.

All over the temple we found various small and more or less ridiculous objects, hideous little clay figures three or four inches long, apparently dolls, pieces of animals rather better executed, some of them blue glazed ; and there was one really pathetic limestone monkey.

Many of the stones which filled these chambers still showed traces of the sculpture of wall slabs and the bright blue paint of roofing blocks. Here and there among them were fragments of stelae with a line or two of biography still remaining (pp. 367–369).

The objects found in these chambers were naturally of late date, as the last thorough restoration we know of (that of Mentu-em-hat) is in comparatively modern time, about 660 B.C. It was therefore no surprise, in one sense, to find among the rubbish a marble foot of unmistakably Greek modelling, but its realistic treatment gave one a curious sense of modernness and frivolity among the slim severe lines one grows used to in Egypt (plan b).

The only really valuable thing found in this inner part of the temple was a small black-granite head, the portrait of an old man who must have been entirely free from vanity (plan b, pl. VII.). Unfortunately, the neck is broken off so short that no trace of inscription is left. No similar type has been found, so that it is impossible to say to what people this weary old man belongs. Professor Petrie kindly looked through his photographs of known racial types to see if he could be placed,

PLATE VII.

"PHILISTINE."

but nothing nearly resembling him could be found.
What came nearest was the profile of a Philistine
soldier on a wall at Medinet Habu, whose face
might, with old age and worry, have grown to
such an one as this old man's.

The last two or three days of our time we spent
in trying to put the temple in order and to remove
or reduce the disfigurement caused by deep digging
and the accumulation of large masses of broken
stone.   The surface of the courts and chambers was
brought to pavement level by filling up or cutting
down irregularities, and cleared of the rubbish which
concealed their proportions.   This was only necessary in the first two courts, where the pavement had
entirely disappeared.   In almost all the inner part
of the temple the paving blocks are all in place.
With the help of M. Legrain's reis from Karnak,
many of the lion-headed statues were mended, and
restored to their former dignity of appearance and
position.

Nearly one hundred of these—about half that
number being whole—sit round the wide empty
space of the first court.   In the second court there
remain the bases of the columns which formed a
passage up the middle ; on either side is open space,
and round the walls are the square bases of the
cloister columns, supporting here and there the
Hathor-headed capital of the vanished pillars.

Between and behind these sit lion-headed statues
closely ranged, and on either side of the gateway

looks down the solemn majesty of the great lion-
headed Sekhet, with her uraeus crown, and the
pleasant face of the Egyptian king whom envy has
robbed of his name.

Looking further up the temple over many low
lines of broken wall on the west side the figures
of the cynocephali still face the rising sun, with
what is left to them of hands still upraised to
greet him. Beyond sit silent and grave the row
of goddesses in the outer corridor; behind them
lies the glittering lake and above a thick grove
of palms rise the broad shoulders of the Theban
Hills.

In the eastern half of the temple the walls are
rather higher and the spaces larger and more open.
The other arm of the lake gleams behind them.
Beyond the tumbled sand-heaps on the further side
the eye rests with pleasure on the deep blue-green
of the corn-land and, in the furthest distance, on the
trinity of peaks, dreamlike and faintly-flushed, of the
Gebel-el-Geir.

Over all the temple, from where the goddess
guardians sit above the steps down which priests
once carried the sacred bark, and where kings
burnt frankincense before the emblem of the god,
to where the sphinx head still smiles out of the
dust of centuries, lies that air of expectation, still
and assured, which so inspires the remains of that
people, who built not for time but for eternity. All
through the land the spirit of the race prisoned in

stone lives in grave figures which wait through immeasurable years for a hope deferred but sure, looking with level eyes into a distance beyond earthly horizons, as those that watch in the darkness before dawn, for the far-off sunrise which brings in an everlasting day.

PART III.

THE RELIGION OF EGYPT.

———

CHAPTER VI.

THE GODS.

THE study of the Religion of Egypt presents unusual difficulties, from the fact that its immense multitude of deities have neither distinct spheres of action nor invariable characteristics, and that its theories of the soul are parallel and irreconcilable.

To the tourist in Egypt, who is anxious to pigeon-hole and label all his newly acquired knowledge, it is disquieting to find that there appear to be many creators ; that gods whose attributes are sometimes incommensurate and sometimes identical are members of one group or cycle. The ease with which gods and goddesses exchange insignia and attributes makes his brain reel ; he is supplied with manifold interpretations and origins of some god whom, like Osiris, he had thought comparatively comprehensible and familiar ; he finds the demon of one place the deity of the next ; having learnt the names and

studied the appearance of a dozen important divinities he is paralysed to find that the gods are
reckoned by hundreds, and that the temple walls
are crowded with unknown representations; he
reads that one goddess has fifty-one forms, and is
in the habit of going about in the character of
seven identically similar personalities; that new
deities are formed by joining old ones together;
finally, he discovers that the theory of the immortality of the soul, which seemed to make Egypt
so modern and so comprehensible, implies intricate
and dissimilar schemes of the nature of the soul
and the universe; and that these schemes are
placed side by side without annulling and without
adjustment.

In reality the difficulty of comprehension arises
greatly from attempting to explain too much; from
attempting to unify what to the Egyptian himself
was never really unified. The first impression of
the religion of Egypt is in some sense a true one;
it is a collection of theologies rather than a system
of theology—a collection without assimilation; the
rank of its deities varied with time and place, as one
tribe or another carried forward the worship of its
own god, married him to local goddesses, identified
him with the new gods of friendly places, and exalted
him as father or creator over gods of subject tribes.
We are not at fault in finding a want of system in
Egyptian mythology; we err rather in imagining
that this want of unity must have been as un-

satisfactory to the Egyptian mind as it is to our own.

Yet even in our own time people are not scarce who are capable of acting on a variety of inconsistent principles without feeling any urgent need of unification ; but our race and time have so far advanced that in the religious as well as in the intellectual region we have a feeling of disquiet in proportion as we realise our inconsistency. It appears that the Egyptian either did not realise his inconsistencies or supported the situation with complete serenity.

We advance a step towards comprehension when we know that it is the explanation of the Egyptian religion as a phenomenon, not the reconciliation of it as a system, that is chiefly needed. But even on these lines we need expect to have no certain and concurrent explanation.

The main elements of the problem are these : we have animal gods, gods with a human character, gods which represent forces or facts of nature, gods which are hypostases of abstractions. These are grouped, arranged, identified, but on no real system and on no invariable lines. The worship of certain gods spread throughout Egypt; the worship of others was almost entirely local. Most had pre-eminence in some locality, recognition in others.

The question to be solved is : What causes brought together the assemblage ; what was the historical development of the worship of divinities which belong apparently to different grades of civilisation ?

The great difficulty attending this investigation is that the chief part of this development took place in prehistoric times. On the other hand, our most certain clue is found in the fact that there was a great extension of the pantheon, great developments and re-arrangements, during historic times.

With regard to certain instances of identification of gods and development of the inter-relations of deities all are agreed ; as for instance, that the sun god Ra, independent and supreme head of a local cult, was identified with Amen, supreme head of the Theban gods, who then acquired attributes and honours of the sun god ; but the larger question, the connection of human and animal gods with gods of the forces of nature, or gods who express some great idea, is still undetermined and open to manifold conjecture.

That changes were due to the effect of local and successive cults is not a sufficiently far-reaching explanation, for we need first to account for the differences of the latter.

As it is impossible in the present stage of know-ledge to give any universally accepted explanation, it will be well to give in outline two important theories lately put forth, the one by Professor Wiedemann in the 'Religion of the Ancient Egyptians,' and the other by Professor Petrie in ' Religion and Conscience in Ancient Egypt.'

Professor Wiedemann's theory is that the connection of the animal with the human god results from the need felt by the Egyptians (a need shared by many nations in all times) to "morphise," as one might say, the deity in some material way. With a striking power of conceiving abstract and metaphysical ideas the Egyptian combined a strong distaste for dealing with such ideas apart from some concrete material embodiment.[*]

This is strikingly exemplified in the theory of the soul. That the life of the soul could not be dependent on the life of the body the Egyptian saw with a clearness beyond most ancient peoples. Yet the idea of a completely disembodied soul was intensely repugnant, if not absolutely impossible to him.

In the same way, if the god was "to associate with mankind,"[†] as Wiedemann says, "he must of necessity become incarnate, otherwise he could not express himself in human speech, nor act with visible effect." Thus, for example, the god incarnated himself in the king, yet without destroying the personality of the king. But forasmuch as this limited the sphere of the worship of the god, further incarnations were desired. Further human incarnations, indeed, though these were known,[‡] might introduce political

---

[*] Professor Wiedemann speaks of the Egyptian "incapacity for abstract thought" ('Religion of the Ancient Egyptians,' p. 174). It was rather, if we may further define it, an incapacity for *purely* abstract thought.

[†] *Ibid.*, p. 174.

[‡] *Ibid.*, p. 177.

difficulties, and for this reason the nation was led to animal incarnations, the animal chosen being that which illustrated or typified some essential attribute of the given deity. From this again sprang the sanctification and dedication of that whole species to which this animal incarnation of the deity belonged.

In all such speculations as to origin, laws and development of that which lies beyond historic knowledge we have two chief tests of any theory —whether the laws by which we explain the phenomena in question are known to obtain within our sphere of knowledge, and whether their operation is adequate to explain the phenomena.

Here, indeed, the tendency to embodiment is known to have been, as Wiedemann points out, unusually strong, not only in the religion but in the language of ancient Egypt. A word, when spelt, was followed by a picture of the thing intended. All arrangements and ceremonial connected with the deity and with the dead were attempts to provide material embodiment, opportunity and resource for that which the Egyptian yet believed to be essentially immaterial. How strongly the Egyptians felt this, how strongly a nation far above the Egyptian in religious comprehension felt this, we see in the case of Israel, a race with little native disposition towards idolatry : who, though able to worship a timeless Godhead, unembodied, unsymbolised by material form, yet, led only by His radiancy and His obscurity, so yearned in the waste places for the land of Egypt, populous with deities, that the jewels of silver and gold, in which indeed the nation delighted, were freely rendered up to form their calf.

But though the strength of this principle of embodiment is acknowledged, it may be doubted whether it goes far enough in explanation. It does not account for the connection of gods human, cosmic and abstract. Neither does it seem to account sufficiently for the choice of certain animals to represent certain gods; and the theory would seem to imply a crisis of almost deliberate choice rather than a natural history of religion.

Professor Petrie's explanation rests mainly on the extension to prehistoric times of the process which we know to have taken place to a great extent throughout the history of Egypt—the development of mythology through the mixture of races. The combination of local and successive cults would have a subordinate place in this process, for their difference would also be accounted for on the ground of difference of race.

The four chief races which Professor Petrie shows us as combined in Egypt—the Negro, the Libyan, the Mesopotamian, and the dynastic race from the land of Punt *—each bring their contribution to the religion of Egypt.† Earliest and lowest—contribu-

---

* *Cf.* ch. x., p. 161, and note.

† 'Religion and Conscience in Ancient Egypt,' p. 27.

tion of the negro—we have tree and animal worship.

Of all forms of religion, tree worship is perhaps the earliest, the most universal, and the most enduring, lasting from the negro to the Druid, from prehistoric times in Egypt to the maypole and Cornish Furry dance of the present day. This earlier and lower cult we find as a chief element in the popular worship of Egypt, in the domestic worship rather than in the temple worship, though even here we see it in unequal combination with more developed forms; and on this theory the holy animal, reverenced by lower races in itself, became to the higher the accepted sacrifice of the god, the sacred animal of the god, and even his embodiment.

The negro and the Libyan formed a mulatto race in Egypt, who we may roughly say constituted the bulk of the population, as contrasted with the Mesopotamian aristocracy and the dynastic Punite race. But the Libyan, an earlier element than Mesopotamian or Punite, was of a higher type, and therefore had a higher worship, than the negro. He worshipped himself rather than the lower creation, and the gods of the Libyan had a human character.

With the Mesopotamian worship we reach the first stage of analysis, at once an advance and a retrogression on the worship of humanity—for in the cosmic gods we find, on the one. hand, a return to nature; on the other, in the idea of force we find the first step towards an adoration which is not a senseless stupefaction before some amazing object, but an adoration of deity on account of divine attributes. Such analysis is more fully carried out when we reach, presumably in the Punite worship, the deification of abstract ideas, ideas of creation, of formation, of fatherhood.

On such lines Professor Petrie traces the elements which before historic times had already partly mingled in Egypt, exercising indeed a formative influence on each other, so that animal gods are identified with human gods, these again with cosmic forces, or with the abstract deities of the higher race.

Throughout historic times we see the same thing still in process; the gods of the nations, notably of the Syrians, are introduced, take their places with the Egyptian, are joined in family relations with the gods of the land in the triads and in the enneads, or identified with those already existing: but all is done without real assimilation or classification. Finally it is possible that at a comparatively late period of Egyptian history a growing mysticism, seeking for more real unity than exists in these imperfect identifications, found it in a practical monotheism, and thus the soul after death identifies itself with the gods and declares their identity with one another.

Throughout all the chaotic mythology, the disordered theories of immortality, one idea indeed remains impressed on the religion of Egypt. The religion of some nations is a religion for life, not for death.   Strangely enough, at the two poles of morality, the Græco-Latin and the Jewish, religion was a matter for this life, not the next—whence no doubt came the questions that troubled the Preacher.   But the Egyptian did not so regard nor disregard death.   It was neither going down to the dust, nor the blank wall and the blind alley of existence ; it was to him, as to the Christian, the door into a region and a condition which, however strangely limited, was greater and more abiding than this life.

If one can at all regard a religion as realising one pre-eminent idea, we should say that, as to the Jew the beauty of holiness, as to the Christian the paradox of " dying to live," so to the Egyptian the salient idea of religion was the contest and the sequence of life, death, and again life.

Thus if the deities and religious theories have sprung from many different origins, yet they group themselves round this central idea—an idea which embodies itself in the gods of birth, with their hosts of subordinate deities, the gods of vivifying powers of nature, the gods of abstract ideas connected with birth, gods connected with death and destruction, whether in concrete or abstract manner, gods who, whether in sun form or otherwise, rise renewed from conflict and destruction, or reign, dead yet living, over men who have died and yet live.

The triad of Thebes, according to Professor Petrie, originated with the Libyans—Amen, Mut and Khonsu having a human character. The grouping in triads was, it must be remembered, a comparatively late and an artificial arrangement. Indeed this is witnessed from the fact that Mut appeared in other connections—with Ptah and Thoth as her husband and son, and again, even in Thebes, in a triad with Khonsu and Thoth.[*]

Moreover, if we look at their functions and the signification of their names, there is a discrepancy between the three which would seem to indicate, if we can trace independent strains in the religion, a certain difference of origin. Amen, the great god— after whom Thebes itself was known to the Jewish prophets as No-Ammon, city of Amen—appeared as the husband of Mut, whose name signifies "the mother," and as father of Khonsu, who, though acquiring a strange double personality, is essentially like Aah and Thoth, god of the moon.

Although however Mut has been seen combined with other gods than Amen and Khonsu, from a very early time in Thebes this triad was supreme, and their temples chief in Apt. The temple of Khonsu now standing between that of Amen and Mut, though built by Rameses the Third, was in all probability on the site of a still older temple. The great temple of Amen dates back to 12th-dynasty times, and it is probable, as we shall show, that the

* Wiedemann, page 268.

temple of Mut in Asher was founded not later than
that time.

Turning, then, to our own temple, let us briefly
examine the chief religious representations and
emblems, tracing as far as we can in a short sketch
their origin and their signification.

The approach to the temple, as we have said,
is through a triple avenue of stone animals, sometimes with heads of men, sometimes with rams'
heads. These we have been accustomed to call
sphinxes, but it appears that there may be a certain
distinction between the figures.

The sphinx proper is human-headed. Among
the Egyptians, the head is usually, but not universally, a man's head, and is very frequently a
portrait or a representation of the king or queen.
It appears to be sometimes a representation of a
god or goddess, notably of the god Aker, who
guards the sun during his night-time of danger, and
hence acquires the character of guardian of temple
and tomb.

The ram, on the other hand, is the sacred animal
of Amen, and hence the stone creatures, with lions'
bodies and rams' heads, which form the avenues of
Karnak, are more particularly symbolic of the
great god of Thebes.

The Egyptians did not attribute to such composite
creatures a merely fabulous existence, but probably
believed them to inhabit a desert region remote
but real.

The first point which, as we have said, arrests the eye in the temple itself is the number of lion-headed statues dedicated to Sekhet. Sekhet, one of the sun goddesses, represented, like Bast, as lion-headed, is identified with Mut. It is probably from this identification that Mut has, though rarely, a lion head as her emblem.

The statues are dedicated to Sekhet, Lady of Amt; but inscriptions on the votive statues and elsewhere name Mut Lady of the Sacred Lake, and Lady of Asher.

We have other representations of Sekhet in the temple. In the fragment of sandstone stela (no. 6, p. 368), the deceased priest is worshipping Ptah and Sekhet his wife. The Saïte figure (pl. XXVI.) holds an image of Sekhet, and one or two of the votive statuettes bear dedications to Sekhet as well as to Mut.

The temple, however, is definitely dedicated to Mut, and the greater part of nearly all the statuettes are dedicated to Mut, Lady of Asher, as well as to other deities.

The special emblem of Mut is the vulture; indeed, her name, which means "mother," is written in hieroglyphics with the vulture,* and this, enclosed in the sign which stands for a shrine or temple, thus names the temple in the gateway inscription.

* ⟨hieroglyph⟩ = Mut.

It is difficult for the western mind to apprise Oriental symbolism, and it would not strike us at first sight that what Professor Wiedemann calls the " salient characteristics " of the lion and the vulture were motherhood. Thus we learn with a certain surprise also the derivative symbolism of the vulture head-dress, which expressed the idea of maternity and was worn by the queen mother, and of the drooping vulture wings which shielded the cartouche of the king.*

Several of the statues hold before them an altar or a little image of a god.

One of the Saïte figures, as has been said, holds a lion head with the disk, image of Sekhet or Mut. Another still preserves the base of a man's figure with a scroll on the knees. This is probably the figure of Imhetep, " he who comes in peace." " He was generally regarded," Wiedemann says, " as a learned deity," and the attitude seems to be that of reading funerary prayers.† His worship came into fashion during the Saïte period (pl. XXVII., fig. 5).

But far the larger number of the shrines are carved with the Hathor head. The capitals of the square pillars in the cloistered court were also Hathor-headed. Hathor, with her fifty-one forms, " the sum and substance of feminine godhead," as

* ' Egyptian Decorative Art,' by Professor W. M. F. Petrie, page 109. *Cf.* Lepsius' ' Denkmäler,' iii. 122 *a*, where the winged disk without the uraeus surrounds the cartouche.

† Wiedemann, p. 139.

Wiedemann calls her, is far too complicated to deal with in so brief a sketch ; one can but touch a few points of the nature of her worship.

Professor Petrie believes Hathor to have been introduced by the Punite race ; to be essentially the mother goddess, as the Punite Min is the father god. Denderah, the town where Hathor reigns supreme, is opposite Koptos, city of Min. The sacred animal of Hathor is the cow, and in this form she is represented in the Hathor shrine of Deir el Bahari ; more common are such representations of her as these at the Temple of Mut, having a human face with cow's ears or with a human body and cow's head.

Hathor means " house of Horus " ; Horus being the sun-god, the name is equivalent to the heaven. Hathor is thus the mother of Horus.

It will give some idea of the complication of Egyptian mythology if we mention that there is a form of Hathor equivalent to Neith, the tree goddess, which Wiedemann believes to be of distinct origin ; and judges that the seven Hathors, ancestresses of the fairy godmothers who prophesy fates at births, are also independent. On the other hand, Hathor is identified, as Professor Petrie points out, with every goddess throughout Egypt. Hathor appears in one triad as the wife of Mentu, in another as the wife of the crocodile god of Kom Ombos, who was the demon of Hathor's city of Denderah ; and Hathor is in this triad at Kom Ombos the mother of Khonsu ; who at Thebes is son of Amen and Mut.

PLATE VIII.

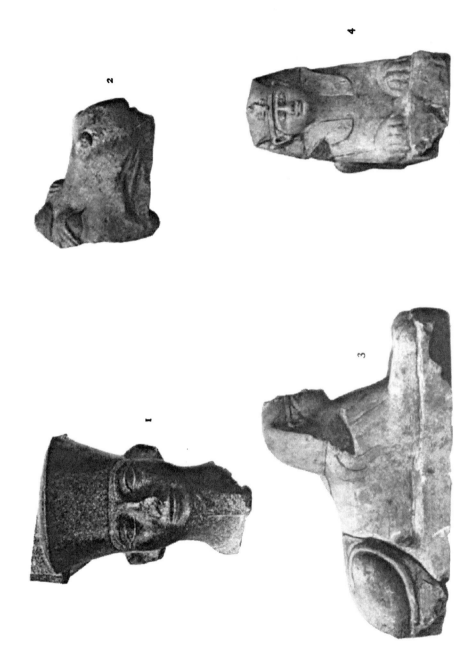

To face p. 94.

Representations of the crocodile god Sebek are very rare at Thebes, or indeed anywhere except in the districts where he was specially worshipped, at Kom Ombos and in the Fayûm. Elsewhere he was regarded as an embodiment of the spirit of evil. It is therefore surprising to find in the Temple (plan no. 10) a sculptured stone representing Thothmes III. making an offering to Sebek.

The black-granite head found in the second court—whose head-dress when complete would have been the cap of Min, surmounted by the feather of Amen—may have been a head of the god Amen-Min—an identification of Amen of Thebes with the Punite Min. There is however too little of the statue left for any certainty on the point (pl. VIII., fig. 1).

In the gateway (Pylon I., pl. VIII.) we found a hippopotamus head of the goddess Ta-urt, or more strictly of Apët, the Theban form of Ta-urt. Ta-urt and Apët are goddesses of birth. This goddess, on Professor Petrie's theory, we must refer to a negro origin. It is generally acknowledged also that to this source we owe the repulsive representation of the dwarf god Bes given in relief on the Ptolemaic entrance. The name Bes is "derived from the word *besa*, which designates one of the great felidæ." * Bes wears the skin of this creature, the head, ears, and mane being drawn over the forehead, the tail hanging down. Bes was thus one

* Wiedemann, p. 160.

of the most ancient gods ; who again rose into a late popularity. Bes, like Ta-urt or Apët, had a connection with birth; he held the child, fed and amused it, danced before it, and hence became a god of laughter. With Ta-urt also he shared the function of being a serpent-destroyer, protecting from serpents the young sun god. It is curious to find this double connection of divinities of birth with serpent foes, and one wonders if any stray influence of such old wide-spread mythologies is seen in the stories of dogs protecting from serpents an infant king.

The Cynocephali, again, must be traced to the same origin. It is believed that the chattering of these dog-faced apes at sunrise led to their specialisation as semi-divinities who adore the rising sun. Representations of the four Cynocephali in this attitude of worship are very common, notably in the 'Book of the Dead.' The two which we found defaced in the outer court may have been members of another group of four.

It will be thus seen that there is no exclusiveness in the dedication of a temple; that a temple dedicated to Mut does not contain representations of her alone, even as the prayers on the Ka statues it contains are not exclusively offered to her; the temple in fact would present much the same aspect as a Romanist church to one who did not understand Christianity—dedicated to one deity, it would contain, as the church would appear to contain, shrines and chapels to other deities.   But the connection of the deity with the temple, and the uses of the temple to the nation, is a large subject, and one which cannot be understood without a consideration of the theories of immortality of gods and men.

CHAPTER VII.

IMMORTAL LIFE.

In considering the significance of the statues in the Temple of Mut we pass from the mythological to the metaphysical part of the religion of Egypt.

In two respects the temple is unique : in the statues of the goddess which, ranked round the courts and corridor, lend a certain impressiveness to its ruined walls ; and in the collection of Ka statues which give peculiar interest to its history.

There are still in the temple, as we have seen, pieces of one hundred and fifty statues of the goddess ; from the way in which these are ranged, from the gaps obviously left by removal, and from the number in other temples and in private and public collections, we may well judge that there must originally have been some hundreds of these statues.

A glance at the list of statuettes will show that there are about thirty of which the inscriptions are not too much mutilated to be intelligible ; there were a few uninscribed, and several inscriptions wholly obliterated or too fragmentary for translation ; there were heads and pieces of heads which belonged to none of the statues we discovered. On a moderate computation, we have evidence for the existence of over fifty statues ; some must have been stolen ; much certainly remains to be disinterred.

In contrast to this we have in other temples occasional statues of a god ; standing or seated figures of the royal builder were frequently placed in front of the pylons, and in Luxor there were besides over a dozen statues of Rameses II. in the court he built ; but the number and diversity of the statues in the Mut Temple are quite unrivalled.

Thus such an explanation as that the statue of the god was placed for adoration ; that the multiplication of statues of the founder (in itself a natural decoration) was due simply to the monumental vanity of Egyptian kings—must evidently fall to the ground.

Neither does the Temple of Mut correspond to our Westminster Abbey, with its statesmen's transept and poets' corner, for many of the statues are of quite undistinguished people.

Again that these are not votive statues in the ordinary sense, that they were not placed in the temple to commemorate some vow or in gratitude for divine help, is also clear. The sailor who has been saved from shipwreck, the sick man who has been healed, burn their vowed candles at a shrine or hang up some suggestive token of deliverance. These statues, whether serenely seated, kneeling with a

H 2

shrine, squatting with swathed limbs, or offering libation, like Pu-am-ra, are not merely commemorative, are not at all tokens of thanksgiving.

The inscriptions are very much alike, and at their fullest may be said roughly to consist of three chief parts : first we have the names and titles of the person represented, with the names of his parents ; secondly the record of his acts and honours ; and thirdly a prayer that "all things good and pure," whether so ethereal as "the smelling of the sweet north wind," or so material as "thousands of bread and beer and oxen and geese," whether so exalted as "glorification, power, justification," so ambiguous as "the gift of a sharp countenance," or so refined as "fine linen, incense, and all flowers," that these should be given by the Lady of the Lake herself or other gods and goddesses "to the Ka" of the person represented and named.

Now while the second part of the inscription may be omitted, as undistinguished people have it not, the first and third parts are necessary, and the peculiar point of the statue is found in the prayer. Clearly then the clue to the meaning of the statues must lie in the meaning of the Ka.

It is now generally agreed that the Egyptian theory of immortality, like the Egyptian mythologies, cannot be harmonised into one scheme ; but that we find a combination of theories belonging to different races, brought together before historic times, but never, throughout history, systematically combined.

Primarily, one must distinguish the Osirian and
the Solar theories.   The main idea of the latter was
that the spirit of the dead fought through the night
with spirits of evil in the form of serpents, even as
Ra himself overcame the Apepi snake of darkness.
The souls followed Ra into the underworld, and in
proportion to their knowledge of magical ritual
kept up with him through the regions he had to
traverse, fighting with him against his enemy and
theirs, receiving gifts of supernatural establishments
in reward.   If the souls were sufficiently well versed
in their ritual to keep up with the sun god through
all the hours of the night, they passed out again with
him into the light and freedom of day.

But the Egyptian doctrine was not a very exalted
one ; those who thus overcame with Ra were "not
necessarily the great ones of the earth," says Wiedemann, "nor yet the very good, but those who
possessed the most minute information as to the
next world and who were best versed in magic." *

Thus, unless the theory is mystical in a much
higher degree than appears, it is not very moral.

It seems not at all impossible that the Solar
doctrine in its complete form—as given, that is to
say, in the paintings in the tombs of the kings—had
already absorbed certain elements of the Osirian
theory of immortality.

Osiris himself appears in some of these regions ;
the unearthly settlements—colonies of the dead—

* Wiedemann, p. 94, 95.

seem to belong to the Osirian theory of immortality.

But the Osirian theory in itself is distinctly a moral doctrine, the most important point being the Judgment in "the Hall of the Double Truth," where the dead appears before Osiris the dead god and the Righteous Judge of the dead; where he pleads that his heart shall not condemn him; where his heart is weighed in the balances against the feather of truth, and he makes his defence, the famous negative confession, before Osiris and the forty-two assessors. Some of the vices which he denies are more or less of ceremonial importance; some, as for instance the plea, "I have not cut off the water," have special reference to the condition of Egypt; but some, again, show a tenderness, a width, a discrimination, not higher perhaps than our standard, but far higher than our commonly recognised code: "I have not been the cause of others' tears," "I have not caught fish by a bait of fishes' bodies," "I have not taken away the cakes of the child," "I have not multiplied words."

The justified dead, those "whose heart condemned them not," dwelt in the Meadows of Rest, played draughts, sailed the canals, tilled the rewarding country of the dead.

What became of the unjustified dead is not clear. In all probability they were "destroyed of the destroyer," who waited in hippopotamus form by the balances.

Though these two theories will admit, it is evident, of further amplification and addition of detail, they appear in themselves to be more or less consistent and complete. Yet there are two parts or aspects of the deceased, singularly prominent in texts and rituals of the dead, which play no part in these theories and seem in no way essential to them —the mummy and the Ka.

In the earlier representations of the *Judgment of Osiris* the deceased appears always in the form of a living man—*the Osiris*, or if we may parallel it in Platonic language, the *idea* of the man. Though in much the mummy is substituted for this figure, and though in the ritual of the dead, that which the Osiris needed, the open mouth, the undefiled feet, is worked out something more than symbolically on the mummy, yet these connections seem comparatively late and artificial, instituted to bring into harmony schemes already accepted on their own merits.

The independence of the Ka is even more obvious than that of the mummy. Though the solar and Osirian theories of immortality do not essentially imply any particular mode of disposing of the body, yet no theory of immortality can disregard the body. The duality of theory is here a duality instituted by nature itself; the dead body being left behind must be somehow disposed of, and nature, theory, or circumstances can only decide the particular mode of disposal. On the other hand, the body cannot by itself form the staple of a theory of immortality.

Another link, possibly an important one, is added in the theory of the "divine Sahu," mentioned, for instance, in the inscription of Senemaah (p. 320).

If *the Osiris* is to be defined as the idea of the man, the Sahu may be called the idea of the mummy—"the husk," an ideal counterpart of the body prepared for burial.

The Ka does not make the same imperative material demand for recognition as the body. Its connection with matter is of a secondary order; though immaterial itself, it needs the material; satisfied in this life, it is only at death that the Ka begins its everlasting claims.

The nature of the Ka is best understood by examining its requirements, its powers, and its manifestations.

Though possessed of a potential immortality, the Ka has not, as some other parts of the man, an essential and independent immortality; it cannot live of itself, without support, and its first requirement is food.

As we have seen, the prayer on the statues at the temple requires among other things material support of the most substantial kind for the Ka, a truly Elizabethan diet of bread and beef and beer and geese, or, more comprehensively, "all that which heaven gives and earth produces, and that which is brought by the river from his cavern," which means no less than the whole produce of the land of Egypt! Nay, so persistent was the Ka in these demands that it would haunt neglectful survivors, and Maspero instances a suit at law brought by a husband against a wife's Ka, which was haunting him thus without due cause of complaint.

But how, it may be asked, was the Ka to receive these? A satisfactory way of administering food to a disembodied spirit would not occur to everyone of us. It appears that the earliest way of satisfying the Ka was by sacrifices and offerings of actual material food. All such sacrifices were offered theoretically to the gods. Thus it is the gods, Amen, Mut, Khonsu, and the whole "cycle of Karnak," who are prayed, as on our statues, to give part "of what appeared upon their altars daily," or "at monthly and half-monthly festivals, and at all the festivals of earth and heaven daily," to the Kas.

At the outset it is probable that men did indeed believe that the actual material food offered was consumed by the gods and the spirits of the dead ; later, it is probable that the spirit of true oriental symbolism—the belief that a symbol does not merely illustrate, but instrumentally effects what it implies—led men to believe that the sacrifice offered in actual material form conveyed an immaterial counterpart into the world of spirits, so that the Ka of the god or man fed on the Ka of the food.

We have a phrase closely corresponding to this idea in "the acceptable *savour*, smell or *smoke* of a sacrifice"; such emanations having, as intangible and invisible, a quasi-spiritual existence.

This then would be the link between the grosser material idea of sacrifice and the spiritual idea of it as of value in the will and devotion of the offerer.

How quickly the more material idea passed we see in the consideration of the second great requirement of the Ka, in the arrangement of his dwelling-house.

The earliest essentials of the tomb were a receptacle for the body and a passage thence to the open air; by means of which the Ka and the Ba or soul (which is in this theory always conjoined with it) might pass out and feed on the funereal offerings, placed on a heap which marked the tomb; in the later development of the tomb chambers were built for the reception of these offerings, which were at first renewed by the pious survivors.

But even the most pious survivors must die, and provision was made for the feeding of the Ka by priests attached for this purpose to the tomb.

Then with the more spiritualised belief in the Ka there came in a way, both safer and less material, of providing for its wants. Priests might neglect their duties; but if the Ka could feed on the idea of the sacrifice rather than on the sacrifice itself, surely this might be more easily and more securely conveyed to it by images of the sacrifice than by material sacrifices which must be perpetually renewed.

Thus the Ka's chambers were sculptured and

painted with the forms of all such things as the Ka needed ; small images of food were modelled in blue porcelain, and we can trace an idea of sacrament in sacrifice, where a material image of a food can convey an immaterial food to an immaterial being.

A further refinement took place.

Prayers were written up so that passers-by by repeating them might supply the Ka with all good things desired ; it is even possible that the sculpturing of the prayer was in itself efficacious. Hence we see that all the statues of our temple are sculptured with the prayer for all things that were needed, for "all things good and pure."

But the Ka's chambers were not only furnished for his feeding, but all that is essential or pleasing to the Ka must be contained in them.

The walls of the tomb were decorated with scenes from the man's life, and show him fishing in the marshes, teaching his servants how to tread the winepress, re-living the scenes of Egyptian country-house life ; or the rough-hewn ceiling is decorated with a creeping vine, and the rock-cut pillars show figures of the deceased sitting in his arbours.

These are decorations and furnishings of Ka life, but there are other necessaries to be provided.

"The essential part of the chapel or tomb," * says Maspero, is the stela, which "perpetuated the name and genealogy of the deceased, and gave him a civil status, without which he could not have pre-

* 'The Dawn of Civilisation,' by Professor Maspero, p. 254.

served his personality in the world beyond; the nameless dead, like a living man without a name, was reckoned as non-existing."*

On this stela are sculptured foods and prayers for foods, scenes and occupations in which the Ka takes pleasure, and which he can enjoy through the efficacious suggestion of his sculptured image. Here too is what is called a "false door," that is, an imaged door which will not open—successor to the little way of escape of the earlier tombs. But the term "false door" is misleading; the false door is not the work of jerry-building masons, as the swathed bundle of sticks is one of the tricks of the embalmer's trade. The false door was never intended to open, never intended to be more than the suggestion of a door, for that is sufficient for the Ka's purpose. Through the very Idea of a door the Ka can pass in and out, feeding on its sacrifices or imaged foods, passing into the outer world to keep its relations up to their duties.

But it is evident that if the Ka needs the suggestion of a door through which to pass, the suggestion of food if it is to be fed, a sculptured name that its identity may not be forgotten, there is still one central all-important requisite, which we have not yet mentioned. The Ka is an immaterial entity with material needs; but material needs are satisfied with the suggestion or figure of material things. To harmonise these requirements and these

* 'The Dawn of Civilisation,' p. 252.

satisfactions, it is plain that the Ka will want a material body, but that the suggestion or figure of a material body will be sufficient for its requirements.

The Ka, separated from its own body, which is inert in the well of the tomb, needs some solid suggestion of a body.

This was at first shown merely in relief, then became, as children say, " more real " as a statue. The tomb in its later developments has a special room for the statues or bodies of the Ka. One body only is necessary, but there is safety in numbers; if one is broken the Ka can still exist on the material basis of another. The temple of Khafra, of the 4th dynasty, contained no less than seven statues.

Ideally, the Ka statue should be as like the original body as possible, so the Ka will be most comfortable. It should resemble the body not in infancy or age, but at the prime of life. But, practically, any statue of a person is an extra body for the Ka, an insurance against extinction.

We may compare this impulse towards providing a material basis of the immaterial existence to the everlasting impulse towards doll-making.

Ideally, the doll should represent a child at the appropriate age—small enough to be cared for ; but if this is unattainable, an old bottle dressed in a rag, or Cosette's little leaden sword, may be hushed to sleep.   The immaterial doll grows, goes through adventures, reverts at will to the most pleasing age, and the real doll may be shut in a cupboard while her adventures are pondered. The material basis may be put out of sight altogether, but its existence adds a solidity to the existence of the immaterial. If no such basis is attainable, the imaginary creature gains reality from a mere pencil scrawl, recognisable only by the eye of affection or the artist.

It is this same impulse, to provide a material basis for an entity known to be immaterial, which is at work in the childhood of the world.

If we consider the statues found in the Temple of Mut, we shall see that whereas some of them, as Ser the priest or Amenemhat the scribe, have mere conventional Egyptian faces, others, as Sen-mut, Tahuti-shera and Bak-en-Khonsu, or the old Philistine (pl. VII.), are evidently portrait statues, and a few, like Mentu-em-hat and the unknown head (pl. VI.), are portraits of a very high degree of artistic value.

With a body or a hoard of bodies in temple or tomb, the Ka became an entity indeed. "The statues," says Maspero, "were not mere images devoid of consciousness. . . . When the double of a man was attached to the effigy of his earthly body a real living person was created and was introduced into the tomb."* Even the Arabs of the present day believe that there lingers about the statues a malicious personality, from which tomb-spoilers

* 'The Dawn of Civilisation,' pp. 256, 257.

can only be safe by destroying the statues. This same belief we may trace, perhaps, in the Egyptian interpretation of the Mohammedan statute against portraiture as idolatrous. To every picture of himself, they say, a man must give a soul at the last day.

The Ka is no more limited by his material embodiment than doll adventures by the capacities of china and wax. The Ka can make itself visible. According to Maspero, the idea of the Luminous meant originally the appearance of the Ka in faint ghostly light. And the Ka can move from place to place; his dwelling-house is no prison, it is merely the local basis of his movements.

Sen-mut's inscription runs: "Grant that he may go forth a living soul to smell the sweet scent of the north wind in every festival of heaven and earth ' ; another prays for "a good time in Thebes, a good life in the temple daily " ; and a third for "joy in this house as the reward of my work."

In the story of Setna,* the Ka of Ahura, who is buried at Koptos, is sitting with her husband, Na-nefer-ka-ptah, in his tomb at Memphis. But there is evidently the same inconvenience about this arrangement that there would be in life. A wife living at Koptos might visit her husband at Memphis, but it would obviously be more convenient if they lived in the same place. So Na-nefer-ka-ptah desires that the bodies of his wife and child

* 'Egyptian Tales,' second series, W. M. F. Petrie.

may be brought to Memphis. Again the Ka can take forms as of life. · In the same story the Ka of Na-nefer-ka-ptah takes the form of a very old man, and goes to show Setna the way to the Koptos tombs.

The fact that the Ka becomes an all-important element after death in no way implies that it is an entity only after death. It becomes only then a separate entity, but is an element of man all through life, and we have not infrequent representations of the Ka during life. In one scene at Deir el Bahari Hatshepsut is followed by a little bearded man, crowned with the same entreating arms. The birth scenes of Hatshepsut at Deir el Bahari, or of Amenhetep at Luxor, show not one child but two, in every respect identical except that the Ka child is sometimes marked by the fact of bearing the Ka arms upon its head—upheld beseeching arms significant if not symbolical of the many requirements of the Ka. In one of Hatshepsut's temple scenes there are twelve such children, and the extreme number of Kas which it is possible to have is, according to M. Naville, fourteen. Only royal persons can have so many; these royal Kas moreover had distinct names enclosed in an oblong which represents the false door, instead of in the cartouche.

This, then, is the biography of the Ka; it is born at birth; remains, so to speak, concealed in the personality during life, to issue at death with all

PLATE IX.

Photograph by J. F. Vaughan.

CYNOCEPHALI.

To face p. 112.

the material needs of the man, which yet it can receive in a symbolic manner. It can appear in the form it wore during life; it can take upon it other forms; but it needs some material embodiment at any rate if it is to be comfortable and satisfied; it is mortal and immortal—mortal in that it is not self-sustained, immortal in that it will go on eternally beseeching. It is closely connected with the body and tomb, though not absolutely limited by them; attention to the after-death wants of the Ka does not supersede the need for "a good burial" for the body.

The physical powers of the Ka, as Professor Petrie points out, are obviously limited in some directions, extensive in others. The Ka, he says, "can talk, . . . it can argue, it can play games with mortals, it can inflict supernatural penalties. But its powers cease where physical force is concerned";* and he instances that in the story of Setna, the Ka of Na-nefer-ka-ptah, who discoursed with Setna, played draughts with him, beat him, and sank him into the earth with a spell, yet could not resist Setna when he snatched the magic roll from his hand.

If this is so it is a very important point; but though the physical powers of the Ka seem limited in this direction, still it must be remembered that the Ka has played and presumably moved his draughts, and that after he has laid a spell upon

* 'Religion and Conscience,' p. 32.

I

Setna he sinks him into the earth *with the draught board*, which undeniably suggests a hard knock on the head. Thus the spell seems of value in bringing Setna within the range of the limited physical powers of the Ka.*

How then can we interpret the Ka? What term best corresponds to these powers, needs and limitations?

Wiedemann suggests that the Ka, as distinct from the soul, the body, and the other essential parts of man, is the "Personality." Maspero calls it the "Double"; Miss Edwards, in 'Pharaohs, Fellahs and Explorers,' suggests that it is the Life. To make the Ka the Personality or the Life would no doubt harmonise well with the metaphysical scheme of man, but would so much the less harmonise with the Egyptian character, which was not systematic. And neither of these would fully explain its needs and its powers, the necessity for material symbols of those things which supply ordinary human needs, its freedoms and its limitations. The Double is not a happily chosen title, for a man cannot have a dozen doubles. Moreover, the Double is, at any rate in English, used of a visible

---

* Such a combination of weak physical powers with the powers of a spell is a frequent element in fairy tales. A spell is so to speak a hand-engine, or may be compared to the fascination of a serpent which acts in arresting the victim or annulling its superior physical powers. If the theory of the Ka is indeed of negritic origin it is more than likely that the power of the serpent suggested this attribute of the Ka.

replica of the original while he is still walking the earth, and is supposed to be a sign of death ; whereas the Ka becomes chiefly active after death, and other important representations of it are at birth.

Though we can have no word which will exactly express an idea which is not native to us, the old English word "ghost," with its large range of meaning, gives certainly some which are very essential to the Ka. The ghost is, so to speak, at the same stage of civilisation as the Ka, has something of the same relation to the body and the tomb, has the same relation to the survivors. The soul which is set free from the body after death does not haunt the survivors nor appear to them. But the Ka can haunt as the ghost does. There is a tendency, it is true, to specialise the word ghost and confine it to appearances after death, but an older usage—preserved in such phrases as "giving up the ghost," or in the equivalence of ghost with "wraith," an appearance before death, or in its application to any intangible appearance of living man—corresponds more generally to the nature of the Ka. In this idea too we have the same freedom and the same limitations, the ghost being able in old English tales to wander at will, but compelled at cock-crow to return to its basis—the grave.

The plaint of the Ka, quoted by Maspero, implies the same theory, strongly akin to our English theory, of the ghost wandering by night but banished from daylight.

"The West is a land of sleep and of heavy shadows; a place wherein its inhabitants, when once installed, slumber on in their mummy forms, never more waking to see their brethren; never more to recognise their fathers or their mothers; with hearts forgetful of their wives and children. . . Since I came into this funereal valley, I know not where nor what I am." *

The ghost exhibits the same limitation of physical powers; powers of speech not being absent, certain abnormal but unmuscular powers in the physical sphere being present; the story of a ghostly branding hand being thus comparable to Na-nefer-ka-ptah's powers with combined draught board and spell, but any exercise of muscular force being similarly debarred. Na-nefer-ka-ptah cannot resist Setna when he would snatch the magic roll, as the perpetually recurring ghost of a man who has mislaid a will can lead people to the place where it is, but can never itself move the will into sight.

The ethereal or astral body of the Theosophists—an intangible replica of the real body which can be projected during life and endures for a time near the real body after death—is to some extent parallel to the Ka theory; the extraordinary length of time during which the body is preserved by embalmment giving to the Ka, in comparison with the others, a quasi-immortal existence.

The consideration of theories more or less parallel indeed may give help in deciding whether the Ka is a theory of immortality of a lower order than those before mentioned, or whether it should be

* 'The Dawn of Civilisation,' p. 113.

called strictly not a theory of immortality at all but a theory of a transitional state. Another consideration of special importance is the connection from the earliest times of the Ka with the Ba, or soul, represented as a human-headed hawk. The Ba, like the Ka, passes out of the tomb through a passage made for it. The Ba receives certain material blessings from the tree spirit, with which both are so intimately connected that in the earlier cemeteries sacred sycamores were planted, so that the tree spirit inhabiting them, as a bird does a favourite fruit tree, might pour out blessings on the dead.

If this be so, we should have three theories of immortality, corresponding to three of the mythologies before mentioned—the Ka and the Ba theory, being associated with the tree spirit, would be that of the lower or Hamitic races ; the Osirian theory would be connected with the Osirian and other human gods of the Libyans, and the solar theory has its connection as is evident with the cosmic gods.

It is thought by Professor Petrie that the mummifying of the dead was brought in by the Punites, and may indicate a fourth system of immortality.

But though the Ka and Ba, as ghost and soul, may belong to a distinct scheme of immortality, the part that the Ka plays is, in a sense, prominent but unessential. The Ka has no essential immortality ; it has all the marks of a transitional condition ; the close connection with the body, the necessity of material support, of material basis of existence, all mark out the Ka, like the ghost, as belonging to an incomplete state of things, as being part of a larger scheme of immortality, as being in itself a mere transitory thing, having a passing existence which will be extinguished when a more perfect immortality supervenes.

Like the wraith, the Double, the ghost, which belong to times of threatened dissolution, or to the imagined condition between dissolution and complete immortality; so the Ka seems to be primarily evoked by conditions of unstable equilibrium, to which the Egyptian would very correctly add birth. It is necessary to the complete man in such a way that its separation from him cannot be a permanent condition, but is only artificially prolonged until re-union.

As the electric spark is born of the interruption of the current, so the Ka, as a distinct entity, exists separately in the dissolution of being.

The Ka theory would then above all point to a final re-union of soul and body, when it should be re-absorbed. Thus we may image the statues round our temple as waiting in hope of a complete immortality.

Among the petitions inscribed on the statues two expressions are given in the words of the original—the "*de hetep seten*" formula, and the "*per-kheru*" offering.

These formulae have been generally considered unintelligible,

but in a paper on the stela of Mentuhetep Mr. Griffith * dis-
cusses the various meanings which have been suggested.

As they stand the words are untranslatable, being abbrevia-
tions of some longer expression.

De hetep seten as nearly as one can translate it would mean
" let the king (*seten*) give (*de*) *hetep*." The gods are also appealed
to for *hetep*.

Hetep may mean simply "an offering," "rest in the tomb," or
" grace." Mr. Griffith inclines to the latter interpretation, and
would render *hetep* a grace or sanction, for which the king is
specially petitioned.

In this case it would appear that the king stands as mediator
between the petitioner and the gods, being himself unable to
grant the supplies which the Ka needs, but being a necessary
link in their granting, inasmuch as without the sanction or favour
of the king the gods will not give their sanction to "enable the
deceased to partake of the joys of the blessed dead."

In the granting of the *per-kheru* the favour of the king is not
asked ; with this it appears he has nothing to do, the *per-kheru*
being solely at the disposition of the gods.

Per-kheru means literally "a coming forth," but the application of the words is open to more than one interpretation.

A study of texts shows "the coming forth" to be connected
with utterance of a voice, and possibly with food. The favour
asked of the gods then is either that the soul should come forth
(emerge from the tomb or realm of the dead) in obedience to
the voice of the gods, as the servant comes forth answering the
call of his master ; or on the other hand that the offerings of
food should "come forth" for the Ka in answer to the voice of
the sacrificer ; thus that the Ka of the deceased should be able
to participate, by the favour of the gods, in the sacrifices made
to the gods.

------

* See on Statue I., p. 295, and reference.

CHAPTER VIII.

THE TEMPLE.

ALTHOUGH the prayers for the Ka include a good life in the temple, and the statues are placed there probably with a view to sharing in the sacrifices "at all the festivals in earth and heaven," the temples are only in certain instances primarily constructed as dwelling-places for human Kas.

On the west bank of the Nile, the side of the City of the Dead, stand the funereal temples of the kings, temples which serve on a great scale exactly the same purpose as the funereal chapels of tombs. Ka statues of the king sit before the gates; he re-lives in the sculptured scenes the glories and triumphs of his early life, and his Ka feeds thus on sacrifice real or imaged. The temple is at once a memorial of earthly greatness and a dwelling-place for the Kas of the dead king and his family.

But on the east bank of the Nile the temples are built by many kings and dedicated primarily to one god or goddess. We have therefore to find the special object for this temple building, as well as of those statues of the goddess with which the temple of Mut is uniquely decorated.

It must be remembered that in Egypt the gods are far from supreme; they are limited by fate, by magic, by each other, and finally by their own nature, and the most important way in which this limit bears upon them is that they, like human beings, are subject to death.

The triads indeed are primarily constructed with a view to the decay and death of the gods, the son being intended, as Wiedemann says, to replace his father as chief god of the triad and husband of the goddess. In this way the god acquires the title of "husband of his mother." The goddess in the same way is potentially mortal, though being of less importance her successor is not provided for.

The gods, being subject to death like mortals, have also the same kind of immortality; as dead gods they are gods of the dead; as dead also they have, like human beings, the dependently immortal Ka, a Ka which is fed on those sacrifices for a part of which their worshippers petition.

But if the gods have Kas like men, they need not only *Ka*-statues like men, but places for the Ka to dwell in.

Wiedemann, indeed, gives a double explanation of the temples : that they were primarily intended both for fortresses and to be the abode of the god or sacred animal. It seems possible therefore that, in vague combination with the latter theory, the temple of the god may, like the funerary temple of the king, be a home for the Ka of the divinity worshipped; that as the funereal chapel is the abode of the Ka, the funereal temple the house of the king's Ka, so the temple dedicated to a god is the dwelling-place of the divine Ka.

Here the divine Ka would receive sacrifices, grant portions to the Kas of the worshippers, as Joseph gave portions from the king's table. Here it would dwell, giving "joys in the temple"; here too we should find its material basis or *Ka*-statues.

The god becomes incarnate in a sense in the king or in the divine animal; but the Ka of the god needs, as the Kas of men need, some material imaged basis of his existence, and we find in the four or five hundred statues ranged round the walls of the temple this material imaged basis for the Ka of the goddess Mut.

Thus the piety of Amenhetep III. and Sheshanq preserved in a sense the immortality of the goddess of whom they were votaries.

We can indeed find no other sufficient reason for these statues. Simple meaningless decoration was alien to the Egyptian, as to all young races. Art begins by being symbolic before it is decorative, and pictures end by becoming patterns.*

Neither can simple adoration account for so large

* This does not imply that all patterns originate from pictures, nor that the process takes place within the history of any given nation, which may have borrowed its decorative art or conventionalised pictures from an earlier race.

PLATE X.

Photograph by Dr. Page May.   *To face p. 122.*

GREAT HEAD OF SEKHET.

a number of similar statues. We could imagine
worshipping a gold and ivory Athene, but not three
or four hundred statues on exactly the same pattern,
and of approximately the same size. The votive
statuettes also seem to connect this place in a
peculiar manner with provision for the Ka.

On the other hand we cannot from the theory of
the mortality of gods conclude that the gods of
Thebes, like the god Osiris, were dead gods and
gods of the dead. The Egyptian is not so systematic. All gods potentially die, but few are celebrated as dead. The son of Mut is potentially in
his turn husband, but the permanent honours of the
great god are paid to Amen.

Thus, though the Ka of Mut should be so provided with hundreds of statues, it does not follow
that Mut is celebrated as a dead goddess. She is
always living; it is only theoretically that she
can die.

As with men, so with gods, the dwelling-place is
not a prison. The god has his headquarters at one
place but visits at others. The images of Karnak
paid an annual visit to Luxor, travelling in procession to the water's edge, and by boat up the Nile.
So, too, the triad which had its headquarters at
Thebes was worshipped as far as Ethiopia, but the
Mut worshipped at Gebel Barkal, under the Ethiopian kings who built a temple to her, as to Amen,
was still *Mut, Lady of Asher*. There she might
be worshipped, there accept sacrifices, and grant

pleasant and pure things; there even she might visit, as Khonsu of Thebes visited the princess of Bekten to heal her; but where her chief temple is, where her *Ka*-statues sit round courts and corridors, the golden house of Mut in Asher, is her home.

As sunlight and shadow will bring into clearness an outline before blurred and hazy to the eye, so a contrast of creed may make more comprehensible the elusive and confused outlines of Egyptian religion. Such a comparison, perhaps the most forcible in all history, is given by the Hebrew creed, is shown by the study of what the Israelites brought away from Egypt, and of what they, most painfully as it proved, must leave behind.

We can touch but a few points of the contrast here.

The Israelite was not a race to take a passive impress; it had a creed of its own before entering Egypt, and its sojourn had turned to bondage. Yet we should take but a crude view both of history and of the dealings of God's Providence if we could imagine so receptive a nation returning after four hundred years with no new leavening of religious ideas from the race most advanced in the world or the time, with a reformation that was purely a protest.

Yet how immeasurably higher was the belief the Israelites took out of Egypt to that which they left behind. So much higher that we wonder little at

the yearning of the rank and file after the easier
worships through which they passed.   For the outside form of Egyptian worship which they took must
seem to be void of meaning to those who, giving up
the strain after the far higher symbolism of the
Israelite shrine, cried out for the golden calf.

It is very probable that Moses was a priest in an
Egyptian temple, and Miriam, like the wife of Ser
(p. 363), a singer and sistrum player.

Thus Moses would be familiar with the inner rites
of the temple, would know the ark shadowed by the
winged goddess of justice,* and in the pattern
shown him on the mount saw this, as in Egypt,
with the staves passed through its rings, borne on
the shoulders of the priests.

"Their idols are silver and gold, the work of
men's hands," priests sang in the Song of Degrees
of the Passover, for it was the silver and gold
images of Amen, of the vulture goddess and her
son, that travelled in the shrine from Apt and
Asher.   Thus the Israelites kept the ark borne
on the shoulders of the consecrated, kept the
shadowing wings of justice, but left the shrine
without image of divinity.

Yet they left it not without symbol of the attributes of divinity.   As the reformation of the 18th
dynasty had kept, alone of all Egyptian deities, the

---

* It is tempting to think that the wings of Maat, goddess of
justice, are borrowed from Mut. Thus the cherubim of the
Mercy Seat would spread wings of protection ; but although the
wings have the proportion of the vulture wings, it would be rash
to say that they are characteristically the wings of Mut.

goddess of justice and her symbols, so it was now. The worshipper of the life-giving energy of the sun had retained the worship of Maat not as a personal deity but as abstract justice.

The symbols of Maat were the ephah, just measure of capacity, the rod, a standard measure of length, and the stone weights. The Ark contained three things: the omer of manna, the rod of Aaron and the stone tables of the law.

Professor Petrie suggested to us that there might be another meaning in these things than that which we are wont to see in them; that the rod, the omer and the tables of stone may have been the standards of length, capacity and of weight for the tribes—standards after the pattern of which all future weights and measures were made.

Justice was then as always symbolised by weights and measures. "Ye shall do no unrighteousness in judgment," the Israelites are commanded, "in meteyard, in weight, or in measure. Just balances, just weights, a just ephah, and a just hin shall ye have." And the Preacher is not weary of declaring that a false balance is an abomination to the Lord, but a just weight is His delight.*

This becomes more full of meaning if we can think that the Ark of the Lord contained the true meteyard, the true measure, and the just weight, His delight.

Thus the contents of the Ark would exhibit a subtler symbolism than the European mind is ready

* Lev. xix. 35, 36; and cf. Deut. xxv. 15, Prov. xi. 1.

to accept. The rod of the priest in the theocracy would be not a royal scourge, but the righteous "meteyard"; the law would be written on just stones of weight; and the bread of God's mercy laid up in the true measure; and the whole was shadowed by images of Justice, with wings stretched over that which is called not the Seat of Judgment but emphatically the Mercy Seat.

The derivation of the symbolism is rendered yet more probable by the fact that it seems to recur in a vision of Zechariah (ch. v.).

The vision begins by the sight of a flying roll; it is explained as a consuming curse, but its description is by dimension, twenty cubits by ten, and its action by division or measurement: thieves are cut off on one side, swearers on the other, the roll being a dreadful Justice, thus dividing the sinner from the "remnant."

The angel of the vision then shows Zechariah an ephah and a talent or circular weight of lead.* A woman said to be Wickedness is cast into the ephah, and the weight of lead is placed on the top. Wickedness in the ephah, kept down by the weight, would seem to represent the unjust measure, the untrue balances.

Then came *two women with wings like storks' wings* to carry Wickedness in the ephah into the land of Shinar. This is the only mention in the Bible of winged women; but, as we have seen, Maat of Egypt is represented in double form as

* The word in Hebrew signifies weight, not exactly value.

two women with long vultures' wings.   The figures
would be familiar to the Israelites through the
cherubim of the Ark, but it would seem that their
original meaning was not yet lost, if the vision
means that the justice of God banishes from
Jerusalem injustice with the false weight and false
measure, carrying her away to the land of Shinar,
the land of the captivity, to establish her in her
own place.

Again, it is possible that, at the time when the
Israelites left Egypt, there was an esoteric monotheism among the priests, but for the populace the
country was thronged with deities.

Like men, these were born and died.   They
dwelt at one place; they passed to others; they
were wedded and bore children; they became incarnate in king and animal.

But to Moses—seeking the name of the god his
people were to follow into the desert, asking as for
the name of one deity among many gods and
goddesses who might endure for a time, claim
supremacy, decline and die—there came the revelation of the Name "I AM."

The dwellings of the deities, or divine kings,
were seen all over Egypt, rising with their banners
above the palaces and the houses of the people;
but the Israelites—following into the desert a timeless formless deity, carrying with them an image-
less shrine—grouped themselves round no abode
of their God but a goatskin tent, where shone
from time to time the radiance of a Deity who

knew no limit of space nor house that could contain Him.

There is a word bandied among those who love to degrade the sublime, that the commandments of the Israelites are but a selection of precepts, and that not the best that could be found, from the Negative Confession. We need not go beyond the first word before we ask what god in Egypt could say, " Thou shalt have none other god but me."

One point has often asked for explanation. How does it come to pass that the Israelites, coming out of the midst of a nation who lived for immortality, yet have for a long time, with a creed so much more sublime, no word on the subject ?

We are far from professing to solve the question ; but there is at least one consideration which should not be overlooked. We have seen to some extent what kind of an immortality it was that the Egyptian believed in, and how in many respects it was material and not distinctively moral. *This*, then, was not the immortality that could be incorporated into so much more spiritual a belief; yet, on the other hand, the ideal of immortality could in itself not be denied; and until the traditions of the house of bondage are left very far behind, the Jewish Scriptures are silent on this point.

Thus, grand as are the general outlines of the Egyptian religion, it has mixed but little in the thought of the world, except through that religion which was at once influenced by it and protestant

K

against it. It is the little tabernacle, not the Egyptian temple, which is the familiar image. If Isis and Horus have suggested imagery for the Mother and Child, as long ago the sacred bark and winged justice suggested the pattern of the Ark of God and overshadowing Cherubim, what is this but to say that in truth the Hebrews have spoiled the Egyptians? While the Israelites' law and sayings are household words, their temple, their tabernacle familiar images, their prophets and teachers ours also, we must dig down, and discover treasures that nature preserves, and not the hearts of men, if we would re-live the Egyptian past and know again those who set up their statues in the house of Mut "to establish their names for ever and ever."

NOTE.—It appears that the first weights used by the Egyptians were of stone and square, for the determinative of weight is a square. From the 18th dynasty, however, if not earlier, electrum was coined in rings: the form of a circle or ring seems to be that which naturally suggests itself for the coining of metal money, which is by origin nothing more than a certain weight of metal. Thus the symbolism of the stone tables, and of the "circular weight of lead," may equally have been drawn from the weights of the Egyptians. The talent was originally an Egyptian weight (Wilkinson, 'The Ancient Egyptians,' ii., p. 259).

The Israelites borrowed also the ephah as a measure of capacity from the Egyptians. Though the homer (10 ephahs) and the omer ($\frac{1}{10}$ ephah) are not known to be Egyptian measures, they are calculated on the basis of the ephah, and on a different system to the other Israelite measures, thus suggesting that they too were borrowed terms.

If it seems that the time of Zechariah is late for the revival of the inner symbolism of Egypt, it must be remembered that a large number of Jews went down to Egypt at the beginning of the captivity and found a refuge at Defeneh (Tahpanhes of Jeremiah xliii.). Thus there must have been a renewal of the knowledge of the images and usages of Egypt among the "remnant of Judah."

PART IV.

HISTORY.

CHAPTER IX.

DYNASTIES XII.–XVII.

THAT period in Egyptian history which includes the
dynasties from the 7th to the 10th is one of confusion and strife. The country was partially conquered
and held during the 10th dynasty by invaders from
Northern Arabia, who ruled in Lower Egypt, while
the native kings were restricted to the upper
country, and to futile efforts to recover their lost
inheritance. This was an opportunity for a strong
man, frequently granted to such men in Egypt, of
establishing his own family as a new dynasty.

The *erpa*-princes of the Theban nome were
quick to seize the moment, and gradually enlarging
their boundaries and building up their power they
established their own as the ruling house, and made
the capital of their province the capital of a kingdom.
The struggles of five hundred years slackened with
the accession of Antef I. to the throne, and slowly

B.C.
c. 3322–
2985.

B.C.
c. 2985–
2778.

K 2

died out during the period of the 11th dynasty. These princes, the Antefs and Mentuhoteps, whose names alternate in the dynasty, could with truth use again the title which had lost its meaning, "lord of the two lands." *

The throne-names which each assumed on his accession show the gradual progress of order and dominion. Antef III. is "beginning justice"; Mentuhotep III., "uniting the two lands," while Sankh-ka-ra, the last king, is "making his two lands to live." † The way was thus prepared for the great kings of the 12th dynasty, who raised Egypt to place and consideration among other nations, and ruled at home with a just and strong hand. The founder of this great dynasty was the prince Sa-Ra-Amen, who took later the name of Amenemhat I.

Part of a small limestone seated figure which we found in the temple of Mut represents the prince Sa-Ra-Amen (Trench B, p. 295). The upper part of the body is broken away; only the lower part remains with the base, upon which two figures are incised. The workmanship is clearly early; the prince sits with his hands upon his knees, and wears a short skirt. What is left of the inscription contains the usual prayer that all things good and pure upon which the gods live may be granted to the "Ka of Sa-Ra-Amen."

As this must be held to be a statue of Amenemhat

---

* *I.e.* the two banks of the Nile.
† 'History of Egypt.' W. M. F. Petrie, vol. i., p. 148.

it seems to point to the probability that he was the founder of the temple of Mut. This is the more possible, that in the time of the 11th dynasty the worship of the god Amen—and of the whole Theban triad—rose into prominence. As the rulers of Thebes grew into kings of the whole land of Egypt their god rose in consideration, until, assimilated with the sun-god Ra of Heliopolis as Amen-Ra, he took his place as king and ruler of all the gods. With him the goddess Mut grew in honour.

Mentuhotep had already laid at Karnak the small beginnings of that temple which was to grow so great, as king after king for two thousand years added his tribute to the god and to his own glory. Amenemhat added to that foundation, and of his work a granite altar still remains. It is not wholly unlikely that Amenemhat should have dedicated a temple to the companion of the god whose son he so clearly claimed to be, nor was he perhaps unwilling to begin a building at Thebes on his own account.

This Amenemhat was one of the strongest and most original men who ever ruled in Egypt. His connection with the 11th dynasty is not clear; his success was not founded on its weakness and decay, for the last kings were also the most powerful, but no record remains of the struggle by which he won his way to the throne.

His throne-name means "renewing births"—that is, he gave a fresh impulse to the social life of the country and reorganised it in every department.

A change in the mode of government had
gradually come about during the 11th dynasty, and
its results were in fullest force during the 12th.
Whereas in the days of the Old Kingdom the
governing power was centralised, and the king
ruled from his capital directly over the whole
country or as much of it as he held, during the
Middle Empire, on the other hand, government was
carried on by a sort of feudal system.   The country
was divided into nomes (or provinces), in each of
which its own prince held power, a power practically
royal and hereditary.   But these princes were answer-
able to the king for their administration, and could
be in the last resort deposed by him.   That this
royal prerogative, though not lightly used, was not in
name only, a long inscription from the temple of
Min at Koptos bears witness.   This is an inscription of Antef V., and is a record of the solemn
deposition of the prince of Koptos for the crime
of high treason, and the confirmation of another
ruler in his stead.

In a tomb at Beni Hasan the owner Khnumhotep tells in a long inscription of the founding of
his family as princes of the Oryx nome.   His grandfather—another Khnumhotep—had been established
in this province by Amenemhat ; and in simple and
telling words he speaks of the unmistakable signs of
the order brought about by the wise king—how he
restored landmarks, settled disputed boundaries,
insisted on just dealing in the all-important matter

of water distribution, and made law efficient throughout Egypt. The inscription goes on :—

"He [the King] arose and placed him [Khnumhotep] great
chief of the Oryx* nome, establishing for him the south land-
mark and making firm the northern one like heaven, and divided
for him the great river down its middle, setting its eastern half to
the nome of the 'Rock of Horus,' reaching to the east desert.

"Whereas his majesty came that he might abolish wrong,
gloriously appearing even as the god Tum† himself, that he
might set right that which he found ruined, and that which one
city had taken from its sister city; that he might cause one city
to know its boundary with another city, establishing their landmarks as heaven, reckoning their waters according to that which
was in the writings, apportioning according to that which was in
antiquity, of the greatness of his love of right. . . . He set up
the landmarks . . . he divided the great river-valley down its
middle, its water, its fields, its wood, its sand, as far as the western
desert." ‡

Could there be a more vivid yet simple picture
of a great king, who with one hand welded Egypt
into a homogeneous kingdom, and with the other
moulded the details essential to the well-being
of his people ?

Amenemhat was not only a statesman but a
builder, and what he wrought in stone has long out-
lasted his wise and equal laws. There are remains
of his work scattered along the whole length of the
river valley, from Tanis in the Delta to Korosko in
Nubia ; it is evident that these have been parts
of great buildings, and the workmanship and finish

---

* The oryx is a species of antelope.
† The sun-god at his setting.
‡ 'History of Egypt,' vol. i., p. 149.

are of a very high order. Many of them were
usurped by later kings, notably a fine statue at
Tanis, on which Merenptah wrote his arrogant
name. In his old age, by the agency of his son
Usertesen, he brought the wild country of Nubia
into subjection, making it part of the kingdom, and
it was never again wholly lost to Egypt. The
inscription which records the conquest is dated in
the twenty-ninth year of Amenemhat—and he only
reigned thirty years. The inscription is as simple as
his others, and the more convincing that it is without
the florid hyperbole in which the small as well as the
great deeds of kings are recorded. On a wall at
Korosko is cut: "In the twenty-ninth year of
Sehetepabra ever-living, they came to overthrow the
Wawat."

During the last ten years of his reign he associated
his son Usertesen with himself as co-regent, thus
bringing in a custom which became habitual with
12th-dynasty kings. Amenemhat seems to have
thought this step necessary on account of a conspiracy against him, which originated in the palace
itself, with the object of making Usertesen king, and
which nearly succeeded in depriving Amenemhat
of life. He answered the plot by making the crown-
prince co-regent; he resigned the active conduct of
affairs into his hands, and contented himself with
playing the part of *deus ex machinâ*. He may have
been worn out by the strain and toil of twenty years
of rule, or so filled with bitter contempt for the

treacherous friends and familiars that he cared no longer to lead them. Usertesen justified his father's splendid confidence in his loyalty, but the "foes of his own household" turned the old king into a cynic. His "Teaching" addressed to his heir shows the scornful bitterness which filled him :

"Let one be armoured against his associates as a whole; it befalleth that mankind turn their hearts to him who inspireth them with fear. Enter not to them singly; fill not thy heart with a brother; know not an honoured friend. . . . Keep to thyself thine own heart, for friends exist not for a man in the day of troubles. I gave to the beggar, and I made the orphan to exist. I caused the man of no position to obtain his purpose even as the man of position.

"It was the eater of my food that made insurrection; he to whom I gave a helping hand produced terror therewith; they who put on my fine linen looked on me as shadows; they who were anointed with my frankincense defiled me while using it.

"My portraits are among the living, my achievements among men, making for me dirges that none heed, a great feat of combat that none see. Behold, one fighteth for a lassoed ox that forgetteth yesterday. . . . I was a maker of barley beloved of Nepra; the Nile begged my mercy in every hollow. None were hungry in my years, none were thirsty therein; the people sat content in what they did, saying, with reference to me: 'Every command is in its right place.'

"Is it the function of women to captain assassins? Is the interior of a house the nursery of insurgents? . . . But thou art my son, Usertesen . . . thou art my own heart, as my eyes see, born in a good hour. Behold what I have done at the beginning thou hast arranged finally. Thou art the haven of what was in my heart." *

_____

* 'Teaching of Amenemhat,' translated by F. Ll. Griffith, and given here by his kind permission from the section 'Egyptian Literature' of a forthcoming publication, by Messrs. Hill & Co., of New York, entitled, 'Library of the World's Best Literature.'

Amenemhat died after a reign of thirty years, during which he had made of Egypt a powerful kingdom among the nations who then formed the world, and given her a state at home just, well ordered and prosperous. Such words in his mouth are not idle boasting, but a simple consciousness of work well done.

His pyramid was called "Ka-nefer"—the beautiful Ka—but the site of it is not known.

At the moment of the old king's death Usertesen was carrying on a campaign against the Libyans; he was returning with many captives and much spoil when a messenger met him with the word "that a hawk had soared with his followers." The prince understood, and hastened at once to Thebes to take full possession of the kingdom.

But no trace of any king of the 12th dynasty has yet been found at the temple of Mut except this little statue of Amenemhat I. The history therefore of the dynasties between the reign of Amenemhat and that of Hatshepsut must be passed over in slightest outline, and merely as a link between the two periods.

But it is well worth while to linger for a moment over the picture of life in the Egypt and Syria of Amenemhat and Usertesen which is given us in the story of Sanehat.* The gulf of four thousand years is bridged over by the simple words, and the Egyptian, of a civilisation then older than our own

* 'Egyptian Tales.' First Series. W. M. F. Petrie.

is now, and the life of the pastoral chiefs of Syria before the time of Abraham, is brought vividly near us.   That it is most probably a fragment of contemporary biography adds to its conviction.

Sanehat, who was possibly a prince of royal blood, thus begins: "In the thirtieth year, the month Paophi, the seventh day, the god entered his horizon, the king Se-hetep-ab-ra flew up to heaven and joined the sun's disc, the follower of the god met his maker."

Sanehat had heard the message given to the Prince Usertesen, and understood it as well as he; for some reason which he does not explain he was seized with panic, and without waiting to see whether the accession of the new king really meant ill-fortune, fled out of Egypt into Syria, where he was kindly received by the Sati.   There in Syria he went through an experience very like that of Moses in Midian so many centuries later.   He was welcomed by an important chief of a "goodly land," married to his daughter, and became a chief on his own account.   His father-in-law, says Sanehat, gave him the "best of that which he had," in a land where "there are figs and grapes; wine is commoner than water; abundant is the honey; many are its olives; and all fruits are upon its trees; there is barley, and wheat, and cattle of all kinds without end."   From the place-names which Sanehat uses, and his descriptions, it is likely that the country he fled to was a part of Edom, and his territory might very well have been in the hill country of Hebron, which is a land of milk and honey and olives.

Sanehat ruled his domain after the fashion of his master Amenemhat in Egypt. "When a messenger came or went to the palace he turned aside from the way to come to me; for I helped every man. I gave water to the thirsty, I set on his way him who went astray, and I rescued the robbed." As superior in the discipline of armies to the Syrians, he acted as general to the soldiers of the prince, and "played the champion" in many border wars. On one occasion he was defied by an opposing champion who challenged him to single combat, which was carried out much in the manner of David and Goliath.

There were other Egyptians besides Sanehat in the tents of this prince, and they, with Sanehat at their head, were treated with distinction, for Egypt was a far more powerful kingdom than Syria, with its multitude of petty chiefs, and the king of Egypt was to be feared and propitiated. Thus Sanehat is eagerly questioned by the prince about the new ruler, and sets forth his character in a judicious mixture of enthusiasm and diplomacy. Usertesen, a strong and energetic man like his father, is well portrayed.

"There is none like him: he is a master of wisdom, prudent in his designs, excellent in his decrees, with goodwill to him who goes or who comes. . . . He is a brave man; he breaks the horns and weakens the hands; those whom he smites cannot raise the buckler . . . he is a lion who strikes with the claw, and has never turned his back.   His heart is closed to pity, and when he sees multitudes he leaves none to live behind him. . . . He is a friend of great sweetness, who knows how to gain love; his land loves him more than itself, and rejoices in him more than in its own god; . . . he enlarges the borders of the south, but does not smite the Sati or crush the Nemau-shau.   If he descends here, let him know thy name by the homage which thou wilt pay to his majesty.   For he refuses not to bless the land which obeys him."

After many years of prosperity in a strange land the passion of the Egyptian for Egypt overcame Sanehat, and the desire to die and be buried at home got the better of his fear.   Therefore he sent a petition to the king to ask forgiveness for his flight, and to entreat leave to return, "that I may see the place where my heart dwells; how great a thing it is that my body should be embalmed in the land where I was born."

Usertesen, secure on his throne, easily granted the prayer, and bade him come leaving all his wealth behind, promising no less in Egypt while he lived, and also that the longed-for funeral rites should be carried out in fulness for him when he died.

So Sanehat came home in peace, casting from him in a moment the ways of all those years of life, and returning with joy to the dear familiar customs of his youth; and best of all the favours heaped on him by the king was the building of the pyramid tomb, whose growth he watched with entire content until the day came when they should "lead him to the city of eternity.'

Usertesen ruled Egypt, like his father, with a strong hand. He crushed the tribes of the " vile Kush," to the south, he kept his northern borders clear of invasion, and he compelled his feudal princes to govern their provinces with equity. At Beni Hasan is the tomb of one of them, Ameni, who sets forth on its walls his successes as a general and his righteousness as a governor.

"There was not a pauper around me; there was not a hungry man in my time. When there came years of famine I arose. I ploughed all the fields of the Oryx nome, to its southern and its northern boundaries. I made its inhabitants live, making provision for them, there was not a hungry man in it, and I gave to the widow as to her that had a husband : nor did I favour the elder above the younger in all that I gave." *

The reign of Amenemhat II., who followed User-tesen, was unimportant. The pyramid and pyramid town of Usertesen II., who succeeded him, have fortunately been preserved. In the years during which a pyramid was being built a town grew up beside it to house the multitude who laboured on it. This town on the completion of the work was commonly deserted.

Professor Petrie† has excavated these remains of Usertesen II. Hundreds of dwellings were cleared and the plan of them exposed, from the palaces of the high officials superintending the work to the tiny two-roomed houses of the workmen.

To this reign too belongs the well known picture

* ' History of Egypt,' vol. i., p. 161.
† ' Illahun ' and ' Kahun.'   W. M. F. Petrie.

in a tomb at Beni Hasan of the reception of a
group of Semites bringing a tribute of kohl or eye-
paint to the prince of the nome. These people, from
the hill country of North Arabia, show signs of a
high civilisation; their arms and musical instruments
are like those of the Egyptians, and their clothing is
fuller. A coat of many colours was evidently the
usual dress; these garments have elaborate tinted
patterns woven in the stuff.

The brick pyramid of Usertesen III. still stands
at Dashûr. In it M. de Morgan found the jewel
casket of a princess of the royal family. Nothing
could be more beautiful or of more delicate workmanship than the inlaid work of her dowry—gold-
smith's work inlaid with precious stones; in colour
and design these pieces are a miracle of skill.

This king Usertesen made a canal through the
rocks and waterways of the first cataract, so that
boats could pass up the rapids into the Nubian Nile.
It was called the "most beautiful way of Usertesen,"
and he carved a record of his work on a rock on the
island of Sehel in the cataract. This island served
as a natural house of archives, for its rocks were
covered for centuries with the inscriptions of many
kings. The canal was reopened in the days of
Thothmes III., a thousand years after; he added the
decree that the fishers of Elephantine should keep
it clear for ever. Wiser they than those who
came after; for twice that time men have been
content to leave their boats below the cataract, and

B.C.
c. 2660–
2622.

after laborious portage through the sand re-embark
above. The end of this century even may not see
the completion of the great new barrage which is to
give water to Upper Egypt, and which will enable
boats to pass straight up the river; boats could
float from Egypt into Nubia in the days of Usertesen, and that not at the expense of the beauty of
the cataract and of Philae.

Usertesen fixed the southern frontier of Egypt
above the second cataract, confirming the conquests
of the first king of his name.

B.C.
. 2622–
2578.
The long reign of Amenemhat III. marked the
flood tide of the material prosperity of the dynasty,
prosperity bringing with it inevitable decay. Victory
abroad and good government at home had brought
wealth and security to the country, and Amenemhat III. reaped where the first Amenemhat had
sowed.

He had time and riches to spend on great works
of peace. The province now called the Fayûm was
then a great lake—(Lake Moeris)—in a hollow
of the desert, fed by the Nile. Amenemhat I.
conceived the idea of reclaiming the soil, yearly
enriched by the mud-bearing river, and he began
the huge work of damming the waters of the lake.
This undertaking was continued on a large scale by
Amenemhat III., who added a province to his country,
and that the most fertile in Egypt, by the building
of enormous dams, and the digging of a canal to
regulate its water supply.

On the shore of the bridled lake were raised two high platforms of stone, on which sat two colossal figures of the king, about forty feet high, carved in glittering stone, looking out over the wide water. At the edge of the newly won province he built his pyramid, its tomb-chamber hollowed out of a single block of quartzite, a miracle of workmanship. Here too his pyramid-temple formed a portion of the enormous maze of buildings called by the Greeks the Labyrinth, raised partly by Amenemhat and partly by Sebekneferu his daughter, who reigned later as queen in her own right.

This long and prosperous reign was followed by the two short reigns of his son and daughter, Amenemhat IV. and Sebekneferu. The power of the dynasty, enervated by long freedom from struggle, quickly waned under a weaker rule, and passed into other hands.

The 12th dynasty ranks with the 4th and 18th in interest, as well from the intimate and detailed knowledge we have of the life of the time as from the character and force of the men who ruled over Egypt, the greatness of the monuments they reared, and the excellence and beauty of the art which produced, not only these astonishing records in cut and sculptured stone, but the minute arrangement and exquisite colour of the Dashûr inlaid work.

One slender link between the Temple of Mut and the 12th dynasty still remains to be mentioned.

L

A small piece of a statue in black basalt was found, bearing on it the name of the " *sem*-priest Amen-emhat-ankh," and having the name Amenemhat enclosed in a royal oval (p. 296).

It is very unusual to find a private name compounded with the royal cartouche, and such instances of it as are known nearly all belong to the 12th dynasty. It is possible therefore that the statue of this priest belonged originally to an early temple founded by Amenemhat I., and kept its place through later restorations.

A state of affairs parallel to that which obtained from the 7th to the 10th dynasties is found in Egypt in the time from the end of the 13th to the end of the 17th.

Few authorities remain for this part of history, and these are discrepant. The invasion and dominion of the Hyksôs (the so-called Shepherd Kings), a people about whom much has been said and little is known, belongs to this period.

It seems clear, however, that these invaders did not enter Egypt during the 13th dynasty.* The kings of this dynasty held Egypt in its entirety; their work is found from Tanis in the Delta to above the third cataract. These remains are chiefly statues; the most notable is that of Sebek-hetep III., which lies on the island of Arqo, above the third cataract. But of far the greater number of these fifty-five kings the monuments supply no record.

* 'History of Egypt,' vol. i., p. 205.

Of the 14th dynasty our knowledge is even more B.C.
c. 2112–
1928. shadowy. Egypt seems to have fallen by degrees into a state of disorganisation and weakness after the strong hands of the 12th dynasty were withdrawn. ·Numerous kings, whose reigns are of the shortest, seem to point to the breaking-up of the country into petty kingdoms with contemporaneous kings.

Into a country thus weakened poured the strong fierce bands of the Shasu, a Semitic people from the highlands of Syria, who, after a hundred years. of fighting, established their chiefs as kings over the whole of Egypt.

Much controversy has centred round the name " Hyksôs," but no better derivation has been found than the orthodox Heq-Shasu, "chief of the Shasu."

It is to be noted that the word Hyksôs occurs only in Manetho. This people is always called Amu by the monuments. The sceptre used by these princes was in the form of a shepherd's crook, and this crook, which has the hieroglyphic value *heq* (prince), was retained by the native kings after their restoration, as a symbol of sovereignty.

The kings of the 15th and 16th dynasties were B.C.
c. 2098–
1738. Hyksôs; the best-known name among them is that of Apepi. Although a nomadic people they were by no means barbarians, but they earned the bitter hatred of the Egyptians by the iron severity of their rule.

The Hyksôs kings of the 16th dynasty held all Egypt, governing from the Delta through the native princes, who acted as local administrators.

The story of the Hebrew slave and governor
Joseph cannot be assigned to any particular time,
but there is no evidence to contradict the tradition
that it was to a Hyksôs Pharaoh he owed his sudden
advancement from prison to the vizier's chariot.
Such a king indeed might have welcomed a servant
who came from a land and people akin to his own,
and whose religion was of a type perhaps more
familiar to his hereditary faith than that of his new
subjects.

The latter part of the Hyksôs dominion was
again filled with struggle and revolt, while success
swayed now to this side and now to that. The
princes of the royal Theban house had been
driven far to the south, and there had mingled
their line with a Berber race. They now gradually worked their way north, even reaching Thebes,
until the prince Seqenen-ra felt himself able to
again assume the title of king. His reign, if we
may call it such, and those of two of his sons,
were occupied by perpetual efforts to shake off
the foreign tyranny. Finally victory rested with
the Egyptians, when his third son Aahmes succeeded to the leadership. This was a man strong
enough to draw all the resisting power of the
country to follow him, and under him the fierce
united effort to break the hated yoke ended in the
expulsion of the foreigner from the land he had
trodden down for five hundred years.

B.C.
1610–
1597.

B.C.
1587.

CHAPTER X.

EIGHTEENTH DYNASTY.

AAHMES TO HATSHEPSUT.

WITH the 18th dynasty we come to one of the most fascinating periods of Egyptian history—one of the most attractive periods as regards the character of its remains and the personality of its rulers.

With the earlier rulers of the dynasty we have little to do. The great work of Aahmes was the deliverance of Egypt from the Hyksôs yoke. Interest attaches also to his wife and half-sister Aahmes Nefertari, as being one of those rulers of Egypt to whom divine honours were paid. Her worship seems to have had an extraordinary popularity. No king reigning in his own right can vie with her as a popular deity, and she even took rank among the great gods of Thebes. It is questioned whether Nefertari was a negress, as the face of her coffin-lid is black. But later rulers assuredly not Ethiopian have been represented in the same way, and death is symbolised, in paintings of the gods, by a darkish hue.

B.C. 1587–1562.

B.C.
1562–
1541.
Of the reign of Amenhetep I.—a reign not of the first importance in the history of Egypt—Thebes has some remains, and here our temple gave us one little record.

We have mentioned the discovery in 1897 of the base of a small statuette in white limestone (Trench C, pl. XI., fig. 1, p. 297). The fragment includes the lower half of a female figure, preserving also the legs and feet of a little child which is sitting on her knee. The inscription on the front is the usual dedication to " Mut, the lady of Asher," and shows the cartouche of Amenhetep I. Professor Petrie conjectures that the statue represents the goddess herself nursing the little king. On the right side of the seat is an incised figure of Aahmes Nefertari, "royal mother, royal wife," no other than the divine Nefertari, Amenhetep's mother. On the other side is an incised figure representing a young girl, one would guess about sixteen years of age, holding, as the other does, her sceptre at arm's length. This side gives also a dedication to Mut, and the name enclosed in a cartouche is Sat-amen (daughter of Amen), to which are added the titles "royal daughter, royal sister, divine wife."

We find mention of two Sat-amens as having lived about this time; one the infant daughter of Aahmes and probably of Nefertari—thus sister or half-sister of Amenhetep I. Of the second the record is more dim. There is a legend of Sat-amen, wife and half-sister of Thothmes I.—daughter therefore

PLATE XI.

AMENHETEP I. (FIG. 1).

STELA OF THOTHMES III. (FIG. 2).

LATE 18TH-DYN. STELA (FIG. 3).

To face p. 190.

of Amenhetep I.—but there is such insufficient proof
of her existence that she may well be mythical.

Thus if the child on the lap of the goddess is
Amenhetep I. the representation must clearly be of
his sister ; and the two apparent difficulties—that
a child who died as an infant is represented as
grown up, and that she is called *divine wife*—are
not inexplicable. An infant might, it appears, be
represented as many years older than the age at
which it died, and an infant heiress who would, if
she had lived, have married the reigning king, could
be entitled, in virtue of essential priesthood, divine
wife though not royal wife.

It is a pity that the statue, like so many others,
has been broken, for the work is very delicate.
The base up to the knees of the goddess is not
more than four inches high, yet the incised portraits
at the side show with exquisitely true lines the
difference between the matronly face of Nefertari
and the girlish profile of Sat-amen.   There are only
two other records of this child—her coffin, containing a mummy which is not hers, and a toilet-
box preserved in the Louvre.

We found one other statue which may possibly
belong to this period—a double statue, much mutilated, of a husband and wife, the wife's name being
Aahmes ; but there is no evidence which would
allow us to place it definitely in the first two
reigns of the dynasty, though it is probably early
(Trench A, p. 297).

With the reign of Thothmes I. the peculiar interest of the 18th dynasty begins.

Thothmes I. was the son of Amenhetep I. and his queen Sensenb. The portraits of Thothmes and his mother are found in the Thothmes chapel at Deir el Bahari.* They are very much alike; each profile shows a slightly receding forehead, that of Sensenb being more upright than her son's. The nose in each case is aquiline and rather long, the mother's being more rounded than the other; the lips are full but not negritic, and the chins short and rounded. Of Queen Aahmes, half-sister and wife of Thothmes I., we have more than one portrait at Deir el Bahari. Aahmes' face again is, as might be expected, of the same cast, but it is more graceful and finished and altogether more pleasing. She has a longer mouth, lips that smile upwards with complaisant lines, and the proportions of her face are more regular. Of Mutnefert, also half-sister and wife of Thothmes, there is a statue at Gizeh, but the nose is broken.

Thothmes I. was the pioneer of Egyptian conquest in the East. He overran the whole of Syria to its extreme northern border, and set up his tablet at the city of Ni (near Aleppo). Later kings, notably Thothmes III., brought Syria into far more complete subjection to Egypt, but no king ever pushed the boundary of the empire beyond the stela of Thothmes I.

* 'Temple of Deir-el-Bahari,' by Ed. Naville. Egypt Exploration Fund, part i., pl. XIII., XIV.

His valour is described in the usual terms by one of his generals : " His majesty became furious at it like a panther, and he shot his first arrow, which stuck in the breast of that wretch, and these (fled ?), fainting before his asp." *

Thothmes I. added two pylons to the temple at Karnak, which had been begun in the 11th dynasty, and added to by his father, Amenhetep I. On the other side of the river, just under the point where the rugged Libyan hills fall with precipices and slopes of rock and tumbled sand-heaps to the plain, he began the very beautiful little temple called now the "Thothmes Temple" at Medinet Habu.

One of his pylons at Karnak bears a long inscription relating to his daughter's position in the kingdom, for a full comprehension of which it is necessary to understand the Egyptian law of inheritance.

Women occupied a peculiar and interesting position in ancient Egypt. In most countries where polygamy is widely practised and recognised, as in Mahomedan countries at present, we find that women occupy a very subordinate position in social life and we are inclined to regard this as a natural consequence of polygamy. But in ancient Egypt it was not so. It appears on the contrary that the wives had separate establishments and could be called in their own right " Mistress of the house." We have several instances of this in inscriptions on

* 'History of Egypt,' vol. ii., p. 62.

the statues of the temple of Mut. On the statue of Minhetep, " Superintendent of the inner chamber" about this time, Minhetep says he was "born of Abu, *the lady of the house*" (p. 319). On a statue of the "Superintendent of the treasury," also of this dynasty, Senemaah states that his father was Uazmes the doctor, and his mother "the *lady of the house*, Aahmes" (p. 320).

In the same anomalous way the Egyptian law of inheritance through the mother, or rather the determination of inheritance by the rank of the mother as well as of the father, a custom which is generally associated with a low standard of social life, we find preserved in Egypt when the country was even highly civilised. So too the marriage with so near a relation as a half-sister, which we are inclined to treat as altogether a mark of barbarism, is absolutely the rule in the royal family.

Thus we have even at this period in Egypt polygamy, inheritance by the female line, and marriage with the half-sister. Yet these points which we are accustomed to associate with a barbarous condition of society, low morals, and a despised and subject condition of women, we find associated in Egypt with a high degree of civilisation and an independent and powerful position of women. It is an interesting point as illustrating in its social condition a principle which we find in the religion of Egypt, and even, as Wiedemann[*] says, in their art of

* ' Religion in Ancient Egypt,' pp. 1, 2.

writing, namely, a curious combination of the pro-
gressive and of the conservative spirit. Wiedemann
characterises the Egyptians as essentially conservative, but they are not conservative as the
Chinese are conservative. Their conservatism is
no "stationary state"; it is new wine in old bottles,
yet the bottles are not burst. The youth of a nation,
the advance of civilisation—in one sense, of the arts
—is conjoined with a strange conservatism of custom.

The two points—of inheritance through women,
and marriage with the sister or half-sister—are, it
will be seen, intimately connected. Women did not
often rule in Egypt, though they conferred the right
of succession; but since succession was thus doubly
determined it happened that the person next in
birth or even superior to the king was frequently
his sister or half-sister.

The king and his sister were thus joint heirs in
a sense to the throne: the latter able without
reigning to confer a right to reign; the former
having a right through birth to become king-
consort and thus actual ruler.

Thus Aahmes the first king married his sister
Aahmes Nefertari in order to secure through her
the right of himself and his heir to the throne.
That heir Amenhetep again had two queens: one
his sister Aahhotep, daughter of his father and his
own mother, by whom among other children he
had two daughters, Aahmes and Mutnefert. The
descent of his other wife Sensenb is unknown, but

though probably not royal she was in any case made a queen wife.* Her son Thothmes I. was Amenhetep's successor.

Thothmes I. then was in an inferior position as regarded his right to the throne to his half-sisters Aahmes and Mutnefert, and in marrying them he established his own right as well as that of his successors to the throne. By Aahmes, probably the principal and at any rate the eldest and first wife, Thothmes had one daughter Hatshepsut, and probably two sons who died early † ; by Mutnefert one son Thothmes II.

Towards the end of his reign then, when Aahmes' two sons had died and his own health was probably failing, Thothmes I. found himself, as Professor Petrie points out, in a difficult position.‡ He had one daughter and one son. The daughter was about seven years older than the son and probably showed already her vastly superior power and character. A marriage with her was necessary to assure the right of his son's children to the throne, if not of the son himself. Thothmes I. found a way out of the difficulty. He associated the daughter with himself as co-regent and subsequently married her to the son.

With the reign of Hatshepsut we come to one of the most brilliant periods of Egyptian history, and

B.C.
1516–1503
with
Thothmes
II.
1503–1481
with
Thothmes
III.

* 'La Succession des Thoutmès, d'après un Mémoire récent,' by Ed. Naville, p. 3.

† *Ibid.*, p. 12.

‡ 'History of Egypt,' vol. ii., p. 66.

the rule of the greatest queen who ever reigned. It was a unique reign, for Hatshepsut was co-regent with her father before his death, was co-regent with her husband and brother, and finally associated her nephew and son-in-law with herself on the throne.

Her reign was what a queen's should be in its foreign relations and in the progress of its arts and the piety of the ruler. It was religious and rich in temple building.

Thus she speaks of the two great obelisks she erected at Karnak, almost the highest in the world, monoliths of rose granite 102 feet in height, quarried at Aswân, carved, transported and set up in the incredibly short space of seven months.

"I have done this," she writes, "from a heart full of love for my divine father Amen. I have entered upon the way in which he conducted me from the beginning; all my acts were according to his mighty spirit. I have not failed in anything which he hath ordained. . . . I was sitting in my palace, I was thinking of my Creator, when my heart urged me to make for him two obelisks of electrum" (red granite tipped with electrum) "whose points reach unto the sky. . . . Oh, ye who see my monument in the course of years, and converse of what I have done, beware of saying 'I know not, I know not, why these things were done.' . . . Verily the two great obelisks that my majesty has wrought with electrum, they are for my father Amen, to the end that my name should remain established in this temple for ever and ever." *

Hatshepsut and Thothmes II. also built the main part of the exquisite little temple at Medinet Habu which Thothmes I. began. The late French excava-

* 'History of Egypt,' vol. ii., p. 86.

tions have shown this up in all its simplicity and completeness. The square window frames, through which one sees a pillar or two of the proto-Doric order, sixteen-sided and without capital; the doorways with steps up to them and the winged uraeus painted above, through which again one catches a glimpse of pillar and windows and square-built doorways beyond—remind one in some inexplicable way of Italian architecture, simple, straight, and fair.

But the greatest work of Hatshepsut's reign, eclipsing the obelisks in grandeur and the Medinet Habu temple in beauty, was the temple at Deir el Bahari—the funerary temple of herself and her family. This is as original, as unique, as it is architecturally beautiful.

The systematic clearing of the temple has been carried on by the Egypt Exploration Fund under M. Naville for four winters. Earlier excavators had explored only parts, and much of their clearing has been reburied. " The temple of Hatshepsut," M. Naville wrote in the report for 1895, " now presents a striking sight to the traveller. . . . The proto-Doric columns give one the impression of a Greek temple, and the white limestone of which they are made, though by no means to be compared to white marble, contributes to that illusion."*

Hatshepsut chose for her temple an incomparable site. It lies in an angle of the Libyan hill, bounded

* 'Egypt Exploration Fund Report,' 1894-95, p. 33.

on two sides by ramparts of almost vertical rock. The slope of ground from west to east has been levelled and squared into three great terraces, rising step by step up the mountain. Up through the middle of these ran a broad staircase, now a rough slope; and in front of each terrace is a colonnade of white limestone. This colonnade turns east on the north side of the second terrace, so that its proto-Doric columns shine out white against the golden limestone of the hill.

Where the staircase rises to the third terrace there stands a gateway of rose granite leading to a large court. From here all lies open to the east, and raised above the level of the Nile one looks down, as they did in old time, on fertile fields cut through by the silver streak of river, and across to the obelisks of Karnak. In the western cliff are hollowed niches and a sanctuary is tunnelled deep into the rock. North and south of the great court lie other courts and chambers, one containing the only altar left in Egypt. This, built of the same white limestone as the temple, is a most imposing sight; it measures about sixteen feet by thirteen, stands five feet from the ground, and has a flight of ten steps leading up to it.* The altar was not used for sacrifice but on it were placed offerings to Ra Har-akhti, the sun god at his rising. In the present ruined state of the temple one is tempted to think that the sun at his rising would shine

* 'Deir-el-Bahari,' part i., pl. VIII., p. 78.

upon the altar or be seen by a priest standing there, but the cornice of the court would originally have rendered this impossible.

At the south side is the Hathor chapel with a vaulted roof (not on the keystone principle, of which the Egyptians were ignorant)—where Hatshepsut as a little boy is suckled by the Hathor cow. There are other representations of Hatshepsut in the temple: held as a baby boy in the arms of her mother or the goddess in the scenes of her divine birth, for Hatshepsut claimed as her father the great god of Thebes, Amen; again she is seen as a man in the dress of a king. Her face is worn, strong, thoughtful and masculine, but with something moving and pathetic in the expression; it is far from beautiful, and the god Amen has certainly not fulfilled his promise that she should be "of an appearance above the gods." But in many places where the figure of the queen should have been it is erased, as in the Thothmes chapel, which opens out of the altar court and still exhibits the portraits of her mother and Thothmes I. with her grand-mother Sensenb. The cause of this we shall see later.

The sculptures on the wall of the middle terrace record the most interesting public event of the reign.

The foreign relations were peaceful. In the beginning of the joint reign of Hatshepsut and her husband, indeed, wars were undertaken in his name

with the " vile Kush " (Ethiopians) " who had gone
into rebellion to injure the people of Egypt and to
raid their cattle." " And his majesty raged at it like
a panther," and " sent a great army to overthrow
the rebellious." * But for Hatshepsut herself, her
" spirits," she says, " inclined towards foreign people."

Thus the subject of these sculptures is no campaign of conquest, but a peaceful expedition to
Punt † (Somaliland), to trade for frankincense, gold
(or electrum, an alloy of some kind), ebony and
ivory, cattle and apes.

The ships, in which the work of the rowers is
helped by one great bellying sail from a mast in the
middle, are seen setting out from Thebes. The
water is light blue, which denotes fresh water, and
the fish are fresh-water fish.‡ These, accurately
drawn, are of night-mare size; one appalling
creature like a lobster takes the same space in the
water as six rowers in the boat above.

Later the expedition passes into green salt water
and new kinds of fish appear, among them a turtle.
Thus it is argued that the expedition must have
gone down the Nile and across by a canal to the Salt
Lakes, which we know the Egyptians made use of

* Petrie, 'History,' vol. ii., p. 73.

† Punt was, according to Professor Petrie, in all probability
the home of the Egyptian race. The Egyptians would be thus
" a kindred race to the Phœnicians, or Pūn race, whose farthest
and latest great colony in the Mediterranean was known as
Punic."—'History of Egypt,' vol. i., p. 14.

‡ 'Pharaohs, Fellahs and Explorers,' by Amelia B. Edwards,
pp. 276 ff.

M

at a later time; and so down the Red Sea to
Somaliland.

Besides the rowers and their superintendents there
was a small force of soldiers and without doubt the
artist of the expedition, for it must certainly have
been an artist who so delicately and accurately has
portrayed for us the men, the creatures and the countries. Reaching "the Holy Land," the expedition
was met by the royal family of the country, who
saluted them with surprise: " Have you descended
hither by the paths of the sky or have you sailed the
sea of To-Neter?"* As regards the appearance of
the royal family all one can say is that the chief is
more attractive than his wife or daughter. These
we trust fulfil some standard of Puntite beauty,
or the artist of the slim Egyptians has been too
unkind. The Puntites themselves were not negroes,
for they are painted red, a colour which Egyptians
used to denote their own men; and the type of
features is not negritic; but there are negroes among
them. The houses, like large beehives, some of
them made of wicker work, were built on piles
and ascended by ladders. The country produced
ebony, cocoanut palms, up which monkeys are
shown climbing and an incense-bearing tree; and
M. Naville's latest excavations have shown that the
Puntites kept dogs. The Easterns traded by
presents then as now; the more civilised gave

* 'Deir-el-Bahari,' Introductory Memoir, by Ed. Naville, Egypt
Exploration Fund, pp. 23 ff.

manufactured trifles, the less civilised rich raw products.

The Egyptian envoys were again royally set on their way and took back with them, when they re-embarked, trees in pots for the gardens at Deir el Bahari. These gardens occupied the lower terrace, and late excavations have found there the stump of a palm tree. Deir el Bahari stands now on arid sand heaps in the hottest corner of the Libyan hills, but its architect brought water for the garden and the ponds and filled the holes in which the trees grew with earth.*

Besides these odoriferous sycomores the Egyptians brought back great heaps of the myrrh they bear; logs of ebony (out of which was made the ebony shrine of Deir el Bahari), tusks of ivory and rings of gold or electrum. And as the navy of Tarshish brought back for Solomon not only gold, silver and ivory, but also apes and peacocks, so for Hatshepsut were brought, with her precious things, her ebony and ivory, myrrh and electrum, strange animals for delight, apes and long-horned cattle, a giraffe and an elephant.

The work of the temple at Deir el Bahari is as fine as any in Egypt; the portraits so true that even a part of a face can be identified; the hieroglyphic signs are drawn with a delicacy and finish that makes one recognise the origin of the sign, as one cannot in ordinary inscriptions. The

* 'Egypt Exploration Fund Report,' 1895–96, p. 1.

M 2

very petals and calyces of the flowers are delicately marked, the bee's wing in the royal titles is veined and his body ringed, the white calf's head has neat black spots on the cheek, and it is possible to see that the sign for *Mes* ⚘ represents three strings of onions, and to identify the *Seten* ⚘ with Scirpus grass *

The temple of Deir el Bahari is the glory of Hatshepsut's reign, but it is the memorial also of another name than hers; the Queen might command, but an artist must execute.

Hatshepsut had the power which all great queens should have, of raising up great men. Chief among such men was Sen-mut, the architect of the beauties of Deir el Bahari. A man of low birth, for " his ancestors were not found in writing," he aspired to some of the greatest offices in the kingdom, and if his work there were but half as great as his work in architecture, they were worthily filled.

We have already spoken of the finding of the statue of Sen-mut at the temple of Mut; we have still to consider the import of his inscription (p. 299).

Much was already known about Sen-mut from his tomb, a rock-cut inscription at Aswân, and the only statue existing, that at the Berlin Museum. This is a squatting statue, and from its inscription

* See the coloured plates, ' Deir-el-Bahari,' I. and II.

PLATE XII.

To face p. 164.

Photograph by Brugsch Bey.

SEN-MUT.

we learn that he was, above all things, chief architect,
"director of the directors of works"; that he was
"chief tutor to the king's daughter . . . Neferu-ra";
that his parentage was not distinguished, as his
"ancestors were not found in writing"; that he was
created a prince, the "companion greatly beloved,"
keeper of the temple of Amen, and keeper of
the granaries of Amen. "Other official charges
were also held by him; and it is not difficult to see
that he was the favoured official of the queen, after
the death of her husband and in the minority of
her other brother" (or nephew), Thothmes III.[*]

Besides this his funeral stela represents him as
sitting between his father Rames and his mother
Hat-nefer. " He appears there to have had special
charge of the sacred cattle, of which many are
figured and named." One of them is called "her
[the queen's] great favourite, the red."

"His stele at Aswân shows him standing before Hatshepsut,
and entitled the royal seal-bearer, the companion, greatly beloved,
keeper of the palace, keeper of the heart of the queen (see
'keeper of the king's conscience,' the Lord Chancellor), making
content the lady of both lands, making all things to come to
pass for the spirits of her majesty. It is stated that he there
carved the two great obelisks for the queen."

In his tomb were found terra cotta cones stamped
with his name, on which he is called "priest of
Aahmes," and he "held offices for the younger
daughter (Meryt-ra) as well as for the elder one

[*] 'History of Egypt,' vol. ii., pp. 88, 90.

Neferu-ra." His tomb at Thebes "was very magnificent, but the painted facing of the walls is almost
entirely destroyed."* There are besides a few
small objects belonging to him, but these give no
new information.

To these points already known the statue found
at the temple of Mut adds much that is interesting
and important, some touches vividly descriptive.

Sen-mut, created a prince (though he is called
"hereditary prince" upon the Mut statue), describes
himself as "the Great one of the Great," "the
Noble of the Nobles." To be the Great one of the
Great was evidently no sinecure, for "the affairs of
the two lands were reported to me and I wielded the
North and the South." He was "the Great one of
the Southern and Northern Tens," "the chief of the
land to its extremity," "the Reporter and mouth of
the King" (Hatshepsut) "of Lower Egypt, and the
glorious friend of the King of Upper Egypt"
(Hatshepsut still). In some ways his position seems
not unlike that of Joseph; he was "Royal Chancellor," probably as Mr. Newberry says (p. 312)
vizier, the "Chief Steward of the Queen," and
"Regulator of the Palace."

The "King's" favour was well earned but it
was worth earning, for the statue was "Presented
by favour of the Sovereign, the Queen of Upper
and Lower Egypt living eternally"; it was presented "in order that he may be before [Mut,

* 'History of Egypt,' vol. ii., p. 90.

Mistress of the] Sacred Lake, and in order that he may receive the offerings presented before the goddess . . . the favours of the Queen, who lengthens the duration of his time to eternity, so that his memory might be good [before the people] in after years as they come."

"I filled the heart of the Queen," writes the "glorious friend," "in very truth, gaining the heart of his mistress daily, . . . I was upright, not giving to one side, and the mistress of the two lands was pleased with that which came forth from her [? his] mouth, the *ari-nekhen* and Priest of Truth, Senmut." "I knew her comings in the Royal House, and was beloved truly of the ruler."

He does not omit, as we shall see, to show his method of earning this affectionate gratitude, which Hatshepsut so rewarded, and decorated with "the order of the gold of favour."

His priestly functions were not few; besides being "priest of Aahmes," he is called on the Mut statue "leader of the guides of the gods," "Superintendent of all the priests of Mentu-em-ant" (Mentu in Erment), "Chief over the secrets in the Great House," or "in the Temple," "Overseer of the Temple of Neith."

Not only so, but besides the various offices we already knew that he performed for the god Amen he was keeper of his fields, his garden (the garden of Deir el Bahari, which was dedicated to Amen), his heifers, his cattle in general; he was chief

steward of Amen, keeper of his house, chief over
his slaves, overseer of his husbandmen, and superintended the filling of his store-houses "every ten
days."

As his princely and priestly functions were carried
on without reproach, so into his architectural work
he put his whole heart, and in very truth his
architecture gives full confirmation of his boasts.
"Chief architect upon all the works of the Queen,"
"guiding all the handicrafts" (clerk of the works as
well as architect), "there was not his equal, strong
of heart, not fainting, upon all the monuments of the
gods;" "chief steward in the *Usertkau*, who is
within the heart of the Queen in Thebes in establishing monuments."

Among his architectural functions we come to
that most important to the history of our temple,
and hitherto unknown—"Architect of all the works
of the Queen in Karnak (the obelisks), in Erment,
Deir el Bahari, and in the *Temple of Mut in
Asher*."

Thus the discovery of the statue does not give
us merely, like the evidence we have for the existence of a 12th-dynasty temple, a probable date; but
we have the certain statement that it was under
Hatshepsut's orders that the temple was built, and
that it was Sen-mut who designed and built it.

So stands Sen-mut, a man of colossal talents.
To an age of specialists, when the quasi-critic
intuitively decides that a man of two thousand

years ago, and of the most talented race in the
world, cannot be at once the visionary mystic of
the Revelation and the meditative mystic of the
fourth Gospel, the idea of such many-sided talent
must be inconceivable. Our great men may be
eminent in a profession and a hobby: " Le peintre
Rubens s'amusât d'être ambassadeur." In the
Middle Ages our priests indeed were our statesmen, and Italy had a man who was at once a
great architect, a great sculptor, a great painter,
and a poet. But this fades into nothing by the
side of a man who was a great prince, the chancellor,
a priest, a superintendent of priests, an architect,
and the clerk of the works; and was, moreover,
tutor to the queen's daughter.

The quaint portrait of this princess, " that brilliant
and beautiful girl," as Professor Petrie calls her, was
preserved until lately at Deir el Bahari, the smiling
face with graceful long neck and hair neatly arranged
under the head-dress and uraeus.

What did this amazing man teach the princess?
The history of their own land, of which they had
already three times the length of record behind
them that we have since the Norman Conquest; such
morality as the maxims of Ptah-hotep—for surely
the smiling princess could not imbibe the cynicism
of Amenemhat; the secrets of the temples over
which he was chief; the rites of the religion in
which he must have been an adept; astronomy,
with the rising and setting of the stars, on which the

religious festivals depended? Certainly he must
have been able to teach her as much of the " wisdom
of the Egyptians " as she could take in.   If we
imagine Michael Angelo and St. Jerome, Beacons-
field and Elizabeth's Burleigh, combined in one man,
who has not so far lost the touch of reality but that
he can oversee the works he has inspired, who is not
ashamed to honour his obscure parents at his side,
such a man would bear some likeness to Sen-mut.

But there is still more to be known about this
building of the temple.   The statue of Sen-mut
gives the date of the building and the name of the
architect.   The same year we found (Trench B,
p. 68) another of the statuettes, of rather later
date, bearing the cartouches of Hatshepsut and her
nephew.   This is of one Pu-am-ra, " The *erpa*- and
ha-prince, the skilled noble, the royal chancellor, the
second priest of Amen " (p. 315).

Pu-am-ra is kneeling, and holds in his hands two
bowls for libation.   The statuette is of black
granite and the pedestal is inscribed with his testi-
mony, giving us the record of the actual material
of the fabric and the shrine :—

" The Royal Chancellor, the second priest of Amen, he says:
' I saw the erection of the great house, the shrine *in ebony worked
in electrum* by the Queen of Upper and Lower Egypt, Ra-ma-ka
[Hatshepsut], to her mother Mut, mistress of Asher.'
" ' I saw the erection of . . . *in good white stone of Anu* [lime-
stone] by the Queen of Upper and Lower Egypt, Ra-ma-ka, to
her mother Mut, mistress of Asher.' "

So the temple of Mut was built in white

limestone, like the temple of Deir el Bahari, and the shrine of Mut was also of the merchandise of Punt.

The only limestone wall which remains is that of the chamber (h). This, then, is probably part of the actual building which Hatshepsut commanded, Sen-mut designed, and Pu-am-ra saw built.

But although this chamber is all that is left, we can, to a great extent, realise what appearance the temple of Mut would present at this time.

We cannot say how far the plan of the temple was ultimately altered by the later builders and restorers. But later restoration was probably more or less on the same lines as Sen-mut's design. The Sekhet statues were certainly not standing, for all these are dedicated by later kings; but the lake was already dug out, and the ground on which the temple was built must have descended more sharply to the water.

Looking at the temple of Mut from the other side of the lake, then, we should have seen standing on the promontory, some twenty to thirty feet above the encompassing lake, the white limestone colonnades and courts. The shrine of ebony and electrum, black and golden, would stand where we lately found the crypt, not seen except from inside the holy place. In the courts or colonnades there would be already some of the votive statues—Sen-mut in red crystalline sandstone, with his ugly complacent face, would have knelt holding his Hathor altar—the statue placed there perhaps on

the completion of his labours; the squarely cut
white limestone statuette of the first Amenemhat
must have been placed there, and the black-granite
figure of Amenemhat-ankh; a tiny squatting
statuette of the Superintendent of the inner chamber,
with the cartouche of the elder princess; the standing
statue in black granite of Hapu-senb, the high priest
of Amen in Hatshepsut's reign (p. 312); of the
second priest Pu-am-ra, kneeling with his oblation.

If the temple was of that fine crystalline limestone
of which an excellently inscribed block has been
preserved (pl. XI., fig. 3), it would shine and sparkle
in the sunlight almost like marble; if of that coarser
limestone of which the stela of Thothmes III. is
made (pl. XI., fig. 2), it would yet shine golden in the
Eastern sunlight, which lies like a liquid—like milk
of gold—over the stones. Above the yellow sand-
heaps at the east side of the little temple the points
of Gebel el Geir would be seen—visionary hills in the
morning, all crimson in the sunset; southward one
would look to the palaces of the queen and the
dwellings of her people; westward across the Nile
to the City of the Dead, the white colonnades and
terraces of Deir el Bahari, and the Libyan hills,
beginning already to be tunnelled with "eternal
habitations."

Looking northwards, towards the site of the
present temple at Karnak, if no "garden of Amen"
with feathery palms and odoriferous myrrh trees
from Punt intervened, we might see the sanctuary of

Usertesen, the pylons of Amenhetep I. and the first two Thothmes, with a row of colossal statues in white limestone and red sandstone in front of them. Above the obelisks of her father would rise the giant monoliths of Hatshepsut, rose-granite with deep carving and dazzling points of electrum, as she saw in her vision while she sat in her palace and "thought of her Creator." And we too must not say "I know not, I know not," why all these things were done, remembering her record which still stands after nearly four thousand years. Verily they were for her "great father Amen," and to establish her name "for ever and ever."

"That my name should remain established for ever and ever," wrote the queen. Did she guess perhaps when she wrote it what need she had of a durable monument ?

For twenty years after her husband's death Hatshepsut had reigned, associating with herself her nephew. To him she married her second daughter, Hatshepsut Meryt-ra, for the beautiful pupil of Sen-mut had died.

Neferu-ra had been destined no doubt, as eldest daughter of Hatshepsut, to be married to her successor, but death happily removed her from this fate. At what time she died is not certainly known ; as late as 1500 B.C. she was living, for it is recorded that the "keeper of her palace" was her tutor Sen-mut.*

* 'History of Egypt,' vol. ii., p. 78.

Our temple yields one little record of her, the statue of Minhetep, "the one known to the king," who held the office of "superintendent of the inner chamber" to the "divine wife Neferu-ra, living" (p. 317).

When Hatshepsut was about sixty years old she followed her daughter to the grave, and Thothmes began his independent reign.

From that time Hatshepsut's fame is swallowed up by a very midnight of hatred.

Thothmes III., then a man thirty years of age, vigorous, daring and able, must have chafed for long under the restraint of a more powerful and peaceful will than his own, and that will the will of a woman.

Whether it were solely by undisputed right of sovereignty or partly by force of her extraordinary personality that Hatshepsut held the power her father had first confided to her hands, death alone could end her sway ; and no sooner was restraint thus removed from her nephew than with intemperate malignity he sought to erase all trace of her name and her fame. Her face alone he destroyed at Deir el Bahari, leaving untouched not only the portrait of her father, who was also his grandfather, but of her mother, who was in no way related to him—thus attributing to his benefactress a sin indeed original. But not at Deir el Bahari only, at Karnak, and indeed in every place where it confronted him, Thothmes attempted to erase her record. Where he spared her portrait it was with the intent of usurping it; he even destroyed her *Ka*-sign, thus imperilling, as M. Naville conjectures, her status, or even her existence, in the world to come.* If it had not been that in its haste his malignity overshot its mark, leaving the feminine pronoun in inscriptions with the masculine name, it may be that Hatshepsut's name and record would never have re-emerged from the obscurity into which he plunged it.

But with the king against her, was there no one who could cherish and preserve the name of Hatshepsut? Not Sen-mut, who held office under Meryt-ra, after Hatshepsut's death? Could not the royal friend, whose name she had "made to live," make to live the name of his mistress; or Pu-am-ra, who still remained governor under Thothmes, have preserved her fame?

The king was an autocrat in Egypt, and the hand that erased the cartouche on the statue of Hapu-senb was a strong one.

Some trace of the queen her subjects undoubtedly have preserved; Sen-mut retains the unerased cartouche; Pu-am-ra holds both that of Hatshepsut and that of Thothmes. But one longs to know how far these also bowed under the yoke of Hatshepsut when she was alive, and how far they, without the malignity of her nephew, raised themselves with relief when she was dead.

But there was one more bound to her than her

* 'Deir-el-Bahari,' part i., p. 9.

subjects, her daughter Meryt-ra, whom she had given to Thothmes as his wife. How was the case here? Did Meryt-ra share the feeling of her husband, or was she without influence on him? It is strange that her name has not been found in her mother's temple.*

It may be thought idle to speculate on the affections of four thousand years ago—a playing with shadows if we ask whether Hatshepsut was capable of inspiring enthusiasm and obedience but not love; and indeed in many cases it would be idle.

But Hatshepsut's power is no myth, and virulence like that of Thothmes no shadow; and the malignity which repudiates all gratitude or even decent recognition of favours received may well make one pause.

* ' Deir-el-Bahari,' Introductory Memoir, p. 27.

CHAPTER XI.

EIGHTEENTH DYNASTY, THOTHMES III. TO AŶ.

THE reign of Thothmes III. was so long and so crowded with activities that he is in many ways the most conspicuous figure in Egyptian history. That fame was justly earned, and forms a sharp contrast to the baseless glories of Rameses II., prince of plagiarists—for the works of Thothmes were genuinely his own.

Mention has already been made of the ungenerous malice with which he strove to destroy the name and memory of the great queen to whom he owed his throne and the prosperity of his inheritance. The qualities which made him one of the great conquering kings of the world cannot atone for the exhibition of so base a spirit. He was a man of indomitable courage and energy, swift, resourceful, careless of personal danger, and impatient of delay, but possessed at the same time of power to carry out successfully undertakings which might seem to have been initiated recklessly. The boyish good-natured thick-featured face of the head in the British Museum is quite unlike the Thothmes who is known by his works ; it must either have been executed

B.C.
1481–
1449.

N

while he was still a youth or be merely a conventionalised portrait. In the keen, rather fierce lines
of the face on the walls at Deir el Bahari, repeated
in the minute but characteristic portrait on the stela
found in the Temple of Mut (pl. XI., fig. 2), we find
a truer likeness of the revengeful king and the
brilliant soldier.

His genius was for war, and within a few weeks
of his accession he led an army into Southern
Syria. Egypt had not forgotten the warlike
tradition of Thothmes I., and now, stored with
the riches and energy of a prosperous and active
though peaceful reign, was ready to follow him
wherever he chose to go. A hint of rebellion
against the somewhat nominal rule of Egypt in
Syria gave him excuse for plunging into a series
of campaigns which filled many years of his reign.
The annals of these years, of the wars and of the
enormous wealth of plunder they brought, are very
full and picturesque.

The story of the passage of Mount Carmel
belongs to this first campaign, and exhibits the
new king's eager courage and impatience, combined with his general's instinct of the moment
when the rash course is also the safe one.

The Egyptian army had marched by Gaza up
the coast of Syria as far as Mount Carmel. The
most formidable of its enemies was the chief of
Kadesh, a strong and important town on the
Orontes, far to the north. He had instigated a

confederacy of chiefs in Northern Syria to throw off
their allegiance to Egypt and defy the untried ruler.
The army of these princes was collected in the plain
between Mount Carmel and the city of Megiddo;
the Egyptian army lay on the further side of the
mountain.   Two roads led into the plain, winding
round either end of the hill, and one pass, difficult
and dangerous, led right across it, so narrow that
soldiers and chariots must move through it in single
file.   The king asked advice from his officers, and
they gave it: "What is it like that we should
march on this road which becomes a narrow pass?
Men have come saying that the enemy are waiting
to attack where there is no passage for a numerous
host.   Does not one chariot-horse have to follow
behind its fellow, and man behind man likewise?
Ought our vanguard to be engaged while our rear-
guard is waiting in Aaruna without fighting?
Now there are two roads: one road behold it will
lead to the [south], and the other behold it leads us
to the north . . . and we should come out on the
north side of Maketa [Megiddo].   Let then our
mighty lord march on one of these two ways,
whichever his heart chooseth, but let us go not on
that difficult road."

But the king, confident and eagerly impatient,
replied: "As I live, as I am the beloved of Ra,
praised by my father Amen, as my nostrils are
refreshed with life and strength, I will go on this
road of Aaruna; let him of you who will go on the

N 2

roads ye name, and let him of you who will follow
my Majesty.   For they [namely, the enemy], abomi-
nated of Ra, consider thus : ' Has his Majesty gone
on another road?   Then he fears us.'   Thus do
they consider."

Then they said to his Majesty : " As lives thy
father Amen-Ra, lord of the thrones of the two lands,
who dwells in Thebes, who has made thee, behold,
we follow thy Majesty wheresoever thy Majesty goes,
even as servants follow their master."   Into the
narrow defile accordingly the army marched, the
king himself leading the single line, as he had sworn,
" Not a man shall go forth before my Majesty."

When the head of the army issued from the
ravine and began to come out into the plain, they
fell in with outposts of the enemy, set as a pre-
caution to watch the hill road.   The insight of
Thothmes was fully justified, for the main body was
watching in two divisions the roads which wound
round the base of the mountain.   These outposts
were soon put to flight, and now the Egyptian rear-
guard, still entangled, sent to beg for the king's
personal help.   " Let our powerful lord listen to us
this time, and let our lord keep for us the rear of his
army, and the people."   So the king turned back and
stood sentinel for his soldiers, struggling with the new
and bewildering difficulties of a rugged mountain
path, through all the time required for the passage.
" When the van had come forth on this road, the
shadow turned, and when his Majesty came to the

south of Maketa on the edge of the water of Qina
it was the seventh hour of the day."

Then the weary soldiers rested and the great tent
of the king was pitched, and the command given,
" ' Prepare ye, make ready, for we move to fight with
the vile enemy to-morrow ' ; . . . and the sentinels
of the army were spread abroad ; they said : ' Firm
of heart, firm of heart, watchful of head, watchful
of head.' "

The next day Thothmes gave battle to the con-
federated chiefs and routed them completely ; they
fled headlong to Megiddo, " as if terrified by spirits,"
and —for the gates were promptly shut —were
dragged up over the walls of the city by having
clothes let down to them.

Spoil, wonderful to the Egyptians, was left on the
field, and many prisoners and mighty men, " who lay
like fishes along the ground."   " Then had but the
troops of his Majesty not given their hearts to
spoiling the things of the enemy, they would have
taken Maketa at that moment."   But the chariots
of gold and silver so excited the Egyptian soldiers
that they gave up the chase, and Thothmes had to
reduce the city by a siege.   He built a rampart and a
thick wall round it, which was named Men-Kheper-
ra-aah-setu (Thothmes III., encloser of the Sati).

After a short endurance the city capitulated, the
chiefs of the land " came to smell the ground, to the
spirits of his Majesty, asking breath for their nostrils
of the greatness of his power."

Thothmes imposed a heavy tribute and took back to Egypt from Syria an extraordinarily rich spoil. Many of the things, especially the wealth of gold and silver work, were new to the Egyptians, and were highly prized.

Fifteen or sixteen times during his reign, a small pretext served the king for marching his armies into Syria. He subdued it from its southern border even to the great river, the river Euphrates; Phœnicia was subject to him; even Cyprus sent him tribute. Near the city of Ni on the frontier of Mesopotamia he set up his boundary stela, beside that of Thothmes I., who first penetrated thus far. But the conquest of Thothmes III. was a more substantial one. Syria became a real part of the Egyptian empire, and all its riches, wrought and natural, flowed into Egypt.

Metals of various sorts, precious stones, valuable woods like cedar, and animals were exacted in abundance.

The handicrafts of Syria produced suits of armour, woven stuffs and every kind of gold and silver work, inlaid chariots, and golden vases, cups and dishes. Plants too which pleased the king were brought to the banks of the Nile, and the well known hall at Karnak called the Garden of Thothmes is sculptured with clumps of pomegranate and graceful groups of waterplants and birds which the king had admired and brought home. Every year a splendid treasure was laid

at the feet of Thothmes, the unwilling tribute of
vassal chiefs or the spoil of a fresh campaign.

From the South as well as the East poured
the full-flowing stream, from Ethiopia—country of
the vile Kush—and from the " Holy Land" of
Punt came incense, ivory, ebony and "all the good
things of the land" for the honour of the gods of
Egypt, freely dedicated to them by the king.

The softer, more luxurious civilisation of Asia
thus entered Egypt to conquer its conqueror; but
most important of all the factors in the great change
was the multitude of slaves brought from all parts
of Syria. Women who were to be the mothers of a
new generation, men skilful in the arts and crafts of
a richer country were brought in to modify the art,
the language, the religion, the domestic life, the very
type of face, whose rough hard lines began to be
smoothed down into pleasant child-like contours.
Compare the face of Khafra or of Usertesen with
the faces sculptured on the sanctuary at Luxor or in
the paintings of the Theban tombs—and a more
subtle conquest is apparent than that of Egypt
over Syria.

Wars, incessant and arduous, in Asia or on his
southern frontier, were not sufficient to employ the
inexhaustible energy of the king. More buildings in
Egypt owe their foundation to him than to any other
Pharaoh ; they are found through the whole length
of the land, from the third cataract to the Mediterranean. Work of every sort was carried on at

fever heat; it is easier to get a good scarab of Thothmes III. than of any other reign. This king was an enthusiastic servant of the gods. Where there was a god to be honoured there a temple was raised, and if no local divinity was worthy then a new shrine was built to Amen. To "his father Amen-Ra" he dedicated lavishly the best of his spoil, till the coffers of the god overflowed with treasure, his houses with slaves, and his wide lands with cattle. In Nubia, in Upper Egypt, in the Delta, at Koptos on the Red Sea route the king built temples great and small. At Heliopolis he added to or restored the great temple of Ra, who, more especially in his form of Tum, was adored there. Of the two obelisks he erected there, one is now in New York and the other stands upon the Thames Embankment.

But it was in his capital city of Thebes, the home of his divine father Amen, that Thothmes raised his most enduring monuments. While blotting out with one hand the name and face of Hatshepsut, with the other he completed and adorned her designs, cutting his own name deeply upon hers wherever it occurred on her finished work.

The tomb of Pu-am-ra, architect to Thothmes, whose statue found in the temple of Mut was spoken of in the last chapter, is the most beautiful in Thebes. It is in the northern Assassif, and the sculptured reliefs contained in it are finer than in any other of those treasure-houses, the

18th-dynasty tombs. Among the sculptures is a picture of Pu-am-ra before the king, with the six overseers who carried out the work upon the obelisks in the temple of Amen at Thebes. The obelisks are also represented.

At Karnak, as is natural, the greatest work of Thothmes is to be found. His wonderful hall of pillars, his carved "garden" of foreign plants, the rose-granite chambers, the lotus and papyrus columns, the famous lists of conquered foreign peoples and of his own predecessors on the throne of Egypt, all these are too well known to be dwelt upon. Here, too, his unbridled hatred of Hatshepsut caused him to conceal, by a casing round the lower part of Sen-mut's obelisks, her name and dedication of them to her father Amen.

Thothmes did not neglect the temple of Mut in his universal service of heaven. Blocks re-used by later builders, but bearing his name, occur in two or three places in the temple, and one slab, in a wall of the second court, formed part of a scene of Thothmes offering to Sebek (plan no. 10). The upper part of the body of the king, with his name and the head of the crocodile god, only remain.

It is unusual and interesting to find at Thebes any record of the worship of this god, and this instance of it may have sprung from Thothmes' feverish desire to honour every possible divinity. The fragment of the small but finely worked stela already mentioned was also found in the temple (Trench B, pl. XI.,

fig. 2, p. 368), and shows Thothmes adoring his
ancestor Amenhetep I.

While the king himself thus added to the temple,
several private persons in his reign placed in it
Ka-statues on behalf of themselves or their parents.
The most interesting is a pair of figures seated side
by side in a chair.   These represent Tahuti-shera
the doctor, and his wife Thent-nub, and were placed
in the temple by the pious care of their son Aahmes,
the *uab*-priest (Trench A, p. 323).

They were not " people of importance "; neither
their tomb nor any other statue of them is known ;
and it is only by the devotion of the son, whose
wish of " making to live " his mother's name has
been fulfilled, that we are aware that they once
lived upon the earth.

His prayer for the Kas of his parents includes
the suggestive wish, which gives a glimpse of the
Egyptians' joy in living, that they may still be
granted the "smelling of the sweet wind of the
North," and in addition to the substantial benefits
of bread and beer, oxen and geese, that they may
drink the clear water of the mid-stream.   That,
literally translated, means " water of the turbulence,"
and to this day good drinking water is only taken
from the swift-flowing midmost current of the river.

The upper part of these statues is destroyed, but
a head corresponding in size, workmanship and
material, which was found near the figures, is
doubtless that of Tahuti-shera the doctor (pl. XIII.,

PLATE XIII.

Photograph by]   I   *[M. Werli.*

MAHOMED MOHASSUB AND TAHUTI-SHERA.

Photograph by]   2   *[M. Werli.*

TAHUTI-SHERA.

To face p. 186.

fig. 2), who must have been at the top of his profession, to judge by his prosperous complacent face.

We were struck by the resemblance in the shape of this head to that of the well known wooden figure of the 4th dynasty—called the Sheik-el-Beled —in the Gizeh Museum, and still more by its remarkable likeness to the head of an Arab village boy. The likeness was so marked that we photographed the lad with the head of the statue in his hand (pl. XIII., fig. 1), to show the curious similarity between the skulls of the Egyptian of more than three thousand years ago and the country Arab of to-day. The type has remained constant in spite of all the mixture of race.

Another figure found in the temple is that of an official named Senemaah (Trench A, p. 319) a superintendent of the treasury, a post which must have brought plenty of work in the days of Thothmes. He also was the son of a doctor, Uazmes, and his mother is called the "lady of the house" Aahmes. No name of the dedicator of the statue is given; it very likely may have been placed there by his son Pïaay, "chief sculptor of the temple of Amen," who executed a tomb near Gurneh for his father Senemaah. The inscription of the statue contains only the conventional prayers.

Another important person whose *Ka*-statue was placed in this temple was Min-nekht, a superintendent of the granaries (Trench A, p. 321). He is

represented seated and wearing a long garment.
He seems to have combined the portfolio of the
Ministry of Agriculture with the office of Chancellor,
for the inscription gives him the Chancellor's title,
"the two eyes of the king in the towns of the
South and his two ears in the provinces of the
North."

His tomb is known, another statuette of him is
at Gizeh, and his name occurs on a lintel, on two
pallets, and in an account papyrus.

Such were some of the men who lived in the
spacious times of Thothmes. In 1449, while the
son who succeeded him was still young, the long
reign of the king came to an end. His tomb has
just been found, not far from Gurneh. His was a
personality which was always in extremes ; whether
he hated or fought or built or showered treasure
upon the gods, he did it all with the same fierce
thoroughness, and if the end in sight was more than
once a crime, the curse of the unlit lamp and the
ungirt loin can never rest upon him.

B.C.
1449-
1423.

The reigns of Amenhetep II. and Thothmes IV.
are overshadowed by the splendours of the kings
who ruled before and after.

Amenhetep II. possessed a prosperous kingdom
and a wide empire, but was content to enjoy what
had been already won and to follow in the track
beaten so broad by his versatile father. He was
quite a youth when he succeeded ; he is shown in a
great tomb at Gurneh seated on his nurse's knee,

and no wife appears beside him till some years later.
He reigned about twenty-six years, and this fact—
which was disputed—was neatly proved by the discovery of wine-jars at Thebes, dated in the twenty-
sixth year of the king,* and inscribed by Panehsi,
the negro vine-dresser, who stored the wine.

Amenhetep followed the example of his predecessors, and marched through Syria even as far as
the boundary tablet on the Euphrates, but rather to
make his name known and to establish his authority
than to attempt fresh conquest.   Such personal
exploits as he recounts are of a quieter sort than
those of his father.   This expedition took place
early in his reign; of the last twenty years there
is no record.

Amenhetep built at many places; his name is
widely scattered, but few remains survive.   In this
too he suffered at the hands of his successors, for
his modest works have been largely usurped and
monuments of his reign are rare.   His name is
found in the temple of Amen at Karnak, but does
not occur on any existing part of the temple of
Mut.   Statues of two officials of his reign were
however found there.

The first of these represents the royal scribe
Amenemhat (plan no. 1, pl. XIV., fig. 1, p. 325).
He appears in a squatting position and holds a
lotus flower in one hand.

* 'Six Temples at Thebes,' Prof. W. M. F. Petrie, p. 5.
Egypt Exploration Fund, 1897.

He has a singularly pleasant child-like face, but nevertheless seems to have been distinguished for his discretion.   He mentions as his special virtue in the service of the king that "he is one who shuts his mouth on that which his eyes have seen," and he was found a faithful servant on the royal journeys.   His father Antef had also been royal scribe, and his mother was "the lady of the house Mut-em-ua-sat."

The statue of another high official is that of Amen-Ḳen (Trench C, p. 326), whose wife was a royal nurse, and who himself was a superintendent of the cattle of Amen and a royal fan-bearer, "attending his lord upon the water, the land, and every desert."   He kneels, holding a shrine, and his prayers for a "sharp countenance and pleasant heart," as well as the usual petitions for sustenance for his Ka, are all addressed to the goddess Mut, Mistress of Heaven and of all the gods.   The prayers of his travelled contemporary Amenemhat on the contrary appeal to the gods of Heliopolis and Memphis as well as those of Thebes.

The tomb of Amen-Ḳen at Gurneh is well known. The paintings are very beautiful and interesting. The boy king Amenhetep II. appears on his nurse's knee, and the great scene called "The New Year's Presents" is also in this tomb.

Here the king sits contemplating the splendid offerings made to him ; among them are a golden tree, a gold and silver chariot, and many weapons

PLATE XIV.

Photograph by M. Benson.

AMENEMHAT (FIG. 1).

Photograph by J. A. Gourlay.   *To face p.* 190.

FIG. 2.

and ornaments made of or decorated with these precious materials. Statues of his mother Meryt-ra, of Thothmes I. and of the king himself with their Kas are among the offerings, and many sphinxes with the young king's face.*

The tomb of Amenhetep at Gurneh, long known to native dealers and plunderers, has this year been opened to Europeans and placed under guardianship. The tomb had been used as safe hiding-place for royal mummies in troubled times, and nine kings besides Amenhetep himself had here found safety from desecration. As in the tomb of Pinetem at Deir el Bahari the great warlike kings of the 18th and 19th dynasties found a refuge, so here the kings of peaceful times, saved from destruction, have rested for three thousand years.

In the great tomb chamber deep in the rock, its blue gold-starred roof borne by square-sided columns, Amenhetep lies in his rose-granite sarcophagus. The pious hands of the priest-kings of the 21st dynasty, to whom this safety from violation is probably due, have placed in a little chamber near the bodies of his successors Thothmes IV. and Amenhetep III., those of Setnekht and Seti II. of the 19th dynasty, and of three of the Ramessides. Other bodies in the outer chambers, not mummified but preserved by the dryness of the air, notably that of a man stretched and bound on the model of a

* Lepsius, 'Denkmäler,' iii 63 a, 64 a; Petrie, 'History of Egypt,' vol. ii., p. 164.

boat, with wounds in head and breast, seem to point to the confirmation of the disputed theory of human sacrifice.

To Amenhetep alone of Egyptian kings, so far as is yet known, has been granted the universal prayer that the tomb might prove an eternal dwelling-place.

The reign of the son of Amenhetep, Thothmes IV., was a short one. He added nothing to the empire, though he followed family tradition by marching into Syria early in his reign, and against Nubia in the latter part. Nor was he a builder. His name is found here and there, but it is commonly inscribed on works already existing. His strongest plea to remembrance is that he cleared, in obedience to a vision, the great " Sphinx of Khepra " at Gizeh, from the centuries of sand in which it was well-nigh buried. A lintel, hastily taken from the forsaken temple of Khafra hard by, was engraven with a record of the vision and set up between the forepaws of the Sphinx.

It tells how Thothmes, then a youth, was hunting with a follower or two in the great deserted cemetery of Gizeh, where the wild beasts haunted the silent monuments of old kings. Resting in the midday heat of the desert, under—

" the shadow of this god, sleep fell upon him, dreaming in slumber in the moment when the sun was overhead. Found he the majesty of this noble god talking to him by his mouth, speaking like the talk of a father to his son, saying : ' Look thou at me ! Behold thou me, my son Tahutmes ; I am thy father,

Hor-em-akht, Khepra, Ra and Tum, giving to thee the kingdom. On thee shall be placed its white crown, and its red crown on the throne of Seb the heir. There is given to thee the land in its length and its breadth, which is lightened by the bright eye of the universal lord. . . . My face is towards thee, my heart is towards thee. . . . The sand of the desert, on which I am, reaches to me, spoiling me; perform thou that which is in my heart, for I know that thou art my son who reverences me : draw near, and behold I am with thee.'" *

When Thothmes came to the throne, in his first year he cleared the envious sand from the image of the "noble god," and set up the recording tablet. The lower part has been destroyed, so that no hint is left of the name of the king believed to be the creator of the Sphinx, and the most wonderful of Egyptian monuments guards for ever the secret of its maker.

Thothmes reigned but nine years, and naturally of so short a reign the private monuments are few. Two statuettes found in the temple of Mut belong to his time.

The first of these is a little limestone figure of the "true royal son, his beloved one, Tahutimes" (Trench A, p. 328). The prince kneels, holding a Hathor-headed shrine, and his prayers for offerings are all addressed to Mut, the Lady of the Sacred Lake. This prince has hitherto only been known by a scarab, but his identity is established by the fact that on this statue is mentioned the name of the "tutor of the royal child, Heq-er-shu," and the

* Petrie, 'History of Egypt,' vol. ii., p. 167.

O

name of this official also appears in the tomb of Heq-er-nehêh, tutor to prince Thothmes' elder brother Amenhetep. We may conjecture that Thothmes died as a boy, as he was still in the hands of his tutor when his Ka had to be provided for.

The second statue of this reign yielded by the temple is that of Mery-ti (Trench B, p. 330), a royal scribe. He is represented in the usual squatting attitude, with his arms crossed on his knees. On his shoulders are incised the names of Thothmes IV. He was an official of high rank, for he bears the titles of *erpa-* and *ha*-prince, was superintendent of the cattle of Anhur, a title which means a good deal when it is remembered what an important form of wealth were flocks and herds; he is also called guide of the festival of Osiris.

Thothmes IV. married a Syrian princess, according to the custom of the time—a princess who was only obtained, as one of the Tell el Amarna letters proudly records, at the seventh time of asking.* This was the well-known queen Mut-em-ua, a princess of Mitani, whose family intermarried with the Egyptian royal house for two or three generations. She was worshipped and greatly honoured in Egypt as the mother of Amenhetep III., with whom she appears in the famous birth-scenes at Luxor and on other monuments.

* Petrie, 'Syria and Egypt,' p. 34.

Under Amenhetep III. Egypt touched the summit of her prosperity, reached now, after three thousand years of effort. From Ethiopia to Babylon her empire was a well-assured and solid reality, and all that the world could then offer of wealth, luxury and beauty was poured into her lap. Kings and people had laboured and this generation entered into their labours.

It is probable that Amenhetep was but a lad at the time of his accession ; his early portraits as king show the side-lock of youth, and the first ten years of his reign were spent in the joy of sport and war. He records his slaying of one hundred and two lions in that time, and the only war of his reign was also undertaken while he was still little more than a boy. He went far to the south, and smote the tribes living beyond the Egyptian border. During his minority it is probable that the queen Mut-em-ua governed as regent. She appears in the well-known sculptures in her son's great temple at Luxor ; these scenes are on the walls of the shrines and innermost chambers of the temple, and cele- brate the great king's birth as the undoubted son of Amen.

But though Amenhetep undertook no new great conquest, his boundaries were seemingly wider than those of Thothmes the builder of the empire. To the south indeed he had pushed further in his early wars, and in the far north—to the limits of Naha- raina and Mitani—the doubtful borders of Egyptian

O 2

dominion became under his rule obedient parts of
a welded whole.   Evidence of this may be read
between the lines of some of the Tell el Amarna
letters, when for instance a king of Mitani, negoti-
ating a marriage, yields at once to Amenhetep's
demand for a princess, sending her with rich
presents, and recalls in a later letter the former
equality of his country, reminding the king of
Egypt of the seven embassies sent in earlier times
to sue for the same honour.*

Amenhetep had two queens ; one of them was
this princess of Mitani whom he married apparently
for reasons of policy and who makes no further
appearance in his life, and the other " the well-
beloved great royal wife " Tyi whose influence made
—or marred—the fate of the dynasty.

To what race Tyi belonged is not clear, but her
type of face can be traced in Northern Syria ; the
curious likeness between herself and her husband—
shown in a portrait of the king in his middle age—is
perhaps an indication that she was one of that same
family of Mitani to which the mother of Amenhetep
belonged, and from which a princess, whose face
also resembled Tyi's, was brought in after years to
be the wife of her son.

Alliance by marriage between Syria and Egypt
was the rule during the second half of the 18th
dynasty, and it is most probable that Tyi's own
mother was of the Egyptian blood royal, and that

* Petrie, 'Syria and Egypt,' p. 30.

therefore marriage with the princess confirmed her husband's right to the throne and transmitted it to their son.

As the devotion of Amenhetep has made her name to live, so the undying charm of her own personality keeps this far-off queen a living woman to-day.

The portrait of Tyi [*] gives the clue to her character and influence in history. The face is peculiarly attractive, though the long prominent chin and slightly receding forehead forbid one to call it beautiful ; but there is something wise and sweet about the mouth, something at the same time playful and tenacious about the face.

Though she is dignified, even regal, she is, unlike Hatshepsut, essentially feminine. Political ambitions would weigh far lighter with her than religious sentiment. We can well understand from the portrait the influence which Tyi exercised from the beginning over her husband, and which moulded the whole career of her son.

For two generations the ancient honour of Amen was subverted, and the religion of Egypt, officially at least, was the far more abstract worship of the Aten, the disk of the sun, which Tyi brought from her Syrian home and in which she trained her son to a like devotion. Even in the lifetime of Amenhetep the new idea shows itself in little by-ways, such as the name of the royal pleasure-boat—Aten-neferu, the beauties of Aten.

[*] Petrie, 'History of Egypt,' vol. ii., p. 182.

Amenhetep was perhaps the most magnificent king who ever reigned over Egypt; his works were great in design, and carried out with lavish splendour. The severe beauty of early Egyptian art, shown in the buildings of the Old and Middle Kingdoms, small in extent, yet strangely impressive in their massive simplicity; the grace and charm which the architects of Hatshepsut and Thothmes added to that early strength, pass under Amenhetep into a further form, full-blown and sumptuous indeed, but of yet undegenerate dignity.

To Amenhetep the original building of the temple of Mut has hitherto been ascribed. His was the earliest name to be seen there; it appeared many hundred times on the lion-headed statues of Sekhet ranged round the courts, and Mariette assigns to him the whole temple. But, as we have seen, it was Hatshepsut who commanded, and Sen-mut who raised its white colonnades for the Mistress of the Sacred Lake. Amenhetep undoubtedly added to the temple, besides bestowing upon it the hundreds of statues for the Ka of the goddess which give it individuality. His name appears upon the larger number of those remaining in the temple, as well as on those scattered about Thebes and in various European collections.

Three private statues of his reign were found in the temple. The first of these is a black-granite figure of the "royal scribe, the scribe of the recruits"

Men (Trench A, p. 331), who kneels, with his Hathor-headed shrine, praying that his Ka may be granted "choice breads and delicacies, and all things good, pure and cool." In addition to his work as scribe of recruits he seems to have held a special office in the service of the goddess, for he declares: "I am the herald of the mistress. I come upon the road. I listen to their petitions."

The second statuette is that of a "ha-prince of the southern town" (i.e. Thebes) named Maÿ (Trench A, p. 333). No king's name appears on it, but the material of which it is made, a fine crystalline limestone, dates it with sufficient near-ness, for this stone was not used except in the time of Amenhetep III. and his son Akhenaten. Maÿ calls himself superintendent of the granaries of Amen, and his brief prayers are offered to Mut for "a good life in her house for his Ka."

The third is but a fragment of a double statuette, representing a fourth priest of Amen and his wife standing side by side; but the figures have been almost entirely broken away and all that remain are some lines of hieroglyphics on the back of the base (plan no. 9, p. 335).

Of Amenhetep's building at Karnak one or two small temples remain, and the foot of a colossus still stands before a pylon, hence called by the Arabs the "temple of the great foot." But at Luxor the greater part of the splendid temple he founded remains; the great colonnade, the wide, beautiful cloistered court with its papyrus columns, the pillared halls and inner chambers leading to and surrounding the finely sculptured shrine.

On the western bank of the river the finest of his works, the great and rich house which he built for his Ka, has been swept away by the reckless barbarism of Merenptah, who plundered and ruined it in order to obtain material for the building of his own temple a little further west. At this temple of Merenptah excavation* has brought to light the fine decorative work of Amenhetep, the sculptures and sphinxes with his face, broken up and used as material for filling-in or for foundations. Even the great black-granite stela of the king had not been spared; his inscription was erased and the unused side was roughly smoothed to record the triumphs of a decadent successor. Though the site of the temple of Amenhetep can be roughly traced in the fields of to-day, all that is visible of it are two of the great figures of the king—the so-called "Colossi"—which once sat before the first pylon.

But when the temple stood in the days of its builder, an avenue of sphinxes, jackal-headed, and each holding before his base a statue of the king, led up from the river across the green plain to the gates, and behind them the columns and massive walls of the great temple looked as imperishable as their back-

* Petrie, 'Six Temples at Thebes,' pp. 11 ff.

ground, the broad-shouldered Theban hills. Of that huge wreck these two mighty figures are the sole survivors, and terribly defaced though they are, it is with a serene and most moving majesty that they sit, the green corn or the broad waters of the inundation round their feet, looking towards the distant columns beyond the river which still keep the name of their maker in the mouths of men.

The contribution of Akhenaten (Amenhetep IV.) to the temple of Mut was of an actively negative kind. To his reign must no doubt be ascribed the erasure of the name of Amen in many of the inscriptions, notably in that of Sen-mut. The reason of these erasures is to be found in the religious history of his reign; and there is no group of people more interesting than Akhenaten, his mother, and his wife—no part of Egyptian history more attractive than the record of their eager devotion to a purer faith. *B.C. 1383–1365.*

Though the reign of Amenhetep III. had been so long his son was too young at his accession to assume full power, and for some short time the government was in the hands of Akhenaten's mother Tyi; and even after he took up the affairs of the kingdom her influence in politics was very marked. This was natural both on account of her own personality and her connection with Northern Syria. Indirect evidence of this as of many points in the reign of Akhenaten is found in the series of cuneiform letters from Syria found at Tell el Amarna,

and belonging for the most part to his time.*
Those from Dushratta, the King of Mitani and
Akhenaten's father-in-law, written at the beginning
of the reign, all allude to Tyi as knowing every
detail of political negotiation, and indeed in one
or two instances are addressed to herself as
ruler.

Tyi had trained her son zealously in her own
religion brought from her Syrian birthplace, and
the mind of the prince, so like her own, was a fruitful soil for the growth of a higher theology than
Egypt knew.

Akhenaten while still a boy married a North
Syrian princess known in Egypt as Nefert-iti, who
was of the same race and family as Queen Tyi, and
who, like her, brought hereditary rights to her
husband through a royal Egyptian mother. Nefert-
iti's religion was of the same type as Tyi's, and
Akhenaten's single-hearted devotion to her, added
to the power of his mother's influence and his own
character, assured the success of the new faith while
he lived.

The open repudiation of the ancient religion took
place soon after his marriage, while the king was
still probably under twenty. But the change was
purely official ; the king only took his court and
immediate surroundings with him. The people
continued unmoved in the easier and grosser
beliefs, and the priests of the dishonoured god

* Petrie, 'Syria and Egypt' (" The Tell el Amarna Letters ").

clung the more tenaciously to his worship and
bided their time.   But the far more abstract and
philosophic faith must have appealed to others of the
new type of Egyptian who, like the king, were half
Syrian.

Akhenaten left Thebes, proscribing the very name
of Amen and the old gods, devoting himself by
change of name not now to Amen, but to the
Aten ; and on the plain at Tell el Amarna founded
a new capital with a new art and a new religion.
Here a great temple was raised to the honour
of the Aten—the sun's disk—typifying that radiant
energy of the sun which is at once the source
and the support of all life, and which was symbolised on the walls by rays emanating from the
disk, each ray ending in a hand which bestows life
upon the worshippers.

It was the Ideal—of which the radiant energy distributed by the sun's rays was the material Reality—
that Akhenaten worshipped.   Of all the old gods of
the land, he retained only one—the goddess Maat.
But she is no longer a goddess, but merely the
symbol of abstract Truth, when he calls himself
" Living in Truth."   The splendid Hymn to the
Aten may with some reason be attributed to him.
With the same sense of the poetry of the natural
every-day life of men which later inspired the author
of the 104th Psalm he celebrates the daily course and
workings of the sun and his revelation of himself
to his son Akhenaten and to the great royal wife,

his beloved, the lady of both lands Neferneferu
Aten (Nefert-iti).

Thy appearing is beautiful in the horizon of heaven,
The living Aten, the beginning of life:
Thou risest in the horizon of the east,
Thou fillest every land with thy beauty.
Thy beams encompass lands which thou hast made,
Thou art the sun, thou settest their bounds,
Thou bindest them with thy love.
Thou art afar off but thy beams are upon the land;
Thou art on high, but the day passes with thy going.
Thou restest in the western horizon of heaven,
And the land is in darkness like the dead.
They lie in their houses, their heads are covered,
Their breath is shut up and eye sees not to eye,
Every lion cometh forth from his den,
And all the serpents then bite;
The night shines with its lights,
The land lies in silence;
For he who made them is in his horizon.

    *   *   *   *   *   *

The land brightens, for thou risest in the horizon,
Shining as the Aten in the day;
The darkness flees, for thou givest thy beams,
Both lands are rejoicing every day,
Men awake and stand upon their feet,
For thou liftest them up.
Throughout the land they do their labours,
All the flocks leap upon their feet,
The small birds live when thou risest upon them,
The ships go forth both north and south,
For every way opens at thy rising.

    *   *   *   *   *   *

How many are the things which thou hast made.
Thou createst the land by thy will, thou alone,
With peoples, herds and flocks,
Everything on the face of the earth that walketh on its feet,
Everything in the air that flieth with its wings,
In the hills from Syria to Kush, and the plain of Egypt,

Thou givest to everyone his place, thou framest their lives,
To everyone his belonging, reckoning his length of days.

    *   *   *   *   *   . *

When thou hast made the Nile beneath the earth,
Thou bringest it according to thy will to make the people
    to live,
Even as thou hast formed them unto thyself,
Thou art throughout their lord even in their weakness,
Oh lord of the land that risest for them.

    *   *   *   *   *   *

Thou makest the seasons of the year to create all thy works:
The winter making them cool, the summer giving warmth.
Thou makest the far-off heaven that thou mayst rise in it,
That thou mayst see all that thou madest when thou wast
    alone.

    *   *   *   *   *   *

The land is in thy hand even as thou hast made them.:
Thou shinest and they live, and when thou settest they die;
For by thee the people live, they look on thine excellencies
    until thy setting.
They lay down all their labours when thou settest in the west,
And when thou risest they grow . . . .
Since the day that thou laidest the foundations of the earth.*

At Tell el Amarna a new art sprang up at once, whose duration was as short as that of the new religion. These two in Egypt were closely bound together, and the new art, which shook off convention and represented animals and birds and vegetation with a most spirited realism, died with the more spiritual religion after the king's influence was withdrawn, under the irresistible pressure of ancient tradition.

Akhenaten was a poet and had a genius for religion but no genius for kingship. While he

* Petrie, 'History of Egypt,' pp. 215 ff. Translation by F. Ll. Griffiths.

built his new city, broke the bonds of art, and eagerly followed out new religious ideas, the great empire won by his fathers was falling from him. The kings and chiefs of Syria and Mesopotamia soon found that the heart of the new ruler was given to far other things than war and conquest.

The first series of the Tell el Amarna letters relate indeed to peaceful times at the beginning of the reign, when the *status quo* was yet maintained, and are chiefly concerned with the giving and receiving of presents.

But before long it was found that rebellion went unchecked and unpunished; so the fire spread by degrees from the Euphrates to Southern Syria. By the end of Akhenaten's reign the more distant conquests of the Thothmes were lost, never again to be recovered, and Egypt's grip on Southern Syria loosened. So firm a hold could not entirely give way at once, but no king of Egypt could ever again, like Amenhetep III., keep the peace of the empire from Abyssinia to the great river.

Those towns and districts which remained faithful to their allegiance were either conquered or yielded in despair when their appeals for aid remained year after year unanswered.

One letter may be quoted as typical of the state to which Akhenaten's neglect of politics had reduced his subjects.

"People of Dunip to the king. Who would formerly have plundered Dunip without being plundered by Manakhbiria

[Thothmes IV.]? The gods of Egypt dwell in Dunip. But we now belong no more to Egypt. For twenty years we have sent messengers, but they remain with the king. . . . Azira has captured people in the land of Khatat. Azira will treat Dunip as he has treated Nii; and if we mourn, the king will also have to mourn. And when Azira enters Tsumuri, he will do to us as he pleases, and the king will have to lament. And now Dunip your city weeps, and her tears are running, and there is no help for us. For twenty years we have been sending to our lord the king, the king of Egypt, but there has not come to us a word from our lord, not one." *

But to the king it was important that the true religion should be made supreme, not that the empire should be kept inviolate.

Akhenaten died while yet only thirty-four years of age. He is a unique figure in the history of Egypt. The glories of war and of conquest were worthless to him ; the establishment of a new idea everything. The fervour of devotion with which he set himself to carry out this work, and his intense appreciation of the beauty of religion, mark him as a man born to the wrong place. A reformer on such lines is an incongruous figure in the roll of Egyptian kings, but the Hymn to the Aten has its own place among the poems of the world.

Akhenaten left no son. Two of his daughters successively brought the throne to their husbands. The second of these kings was Tutankhamen.

The name of Tutankhamen seldom occurs. A well-known tomb at Thebes belongs to his reign, but of his own work there are few or no remains.

B.C.
1353–
1344.

* 'Syria and Egypt,' p. 88.

He added something to the temple of Mut, as is
shown by his cartouche on a block of rose granite
there (plan no. 7), and his name also occurs in
the temple of Amen.

As his name implies, it was during his reign that
the new religion of the " heretic" disappeared even
officially, and the king again acknowledged the
claim of Amen and the old beliefs to their ancient
honour, and restored Thebes to her place as the.
capital city.

The statue of the king who sits in the second
court of the temple of Mut is possibly that of Tutankhamen (plan no. 15, pl. XV.).   The pleasant
face of the king is somewhat mutilated, and the
cartouche upon his shoulder and the long inscription down the block at his back have been most
carefully chiselled out.   It may seem strange that
this should be so in the case of a man who
abjured strange doctrine and whose very name
testified to his orthodoxy.   But he had touched
the accursed thing, lived in the palace and married
the daughter of the heretic—though indeed her.
name too had been changed from Ankh-sen-pa-
aten to Ankh-sen-amen; and the priests of Amen
could not wipe out completely enough all traces
of so monstrous a heresy.   Therefore the names
of Tutankhamen the son-in-law and of Aẏ the
official of Akhenaten are frequently erased, though
both of them abandoned the faith they served in their
youth, and returned to the old worship of Egypt.

PLATE XV.

TUTANKHAMEN.

The "divine father" Aŷ, who succeeded Tutankhamen, was a priest who had held high office under
Akhenaten. Why he should have obtained the
throne does not seem clear ; his wife was probably
of royal descent, and he no doubt secured his
position still further by a close adhesion to the
orthodox religion of Egypt. One statue found in
the temple of Mut may belong to his reign. It is a
small figure of a scribe named Thuthà (Trench A,
p. 337), who is represented sitting on a square seat,
dressed in a long kilt, and its style would lead one
to assign it to the end of the 18th dynasty. The
name of Thuthà is very rare, and seems to be some
foreign name transcribed into hieroglyphics. The
stela of a certain Thuthà is in the British Museum,
but he was a chamberlain of Aŷ, whereas this
man describes himself not as chamberlain, but as
" doctor, inspector and scribe." He held however
high office in the household of whatever king
he served, for he was a hereditary and *ha*-prince
and calls himself "the royal friend, great of love."
He says : " I am cool of his [the king's] town, I
am silent in his house, I keep the fear of the
god in my heart, and of the king in my heart,
and the reverence of my lord in my limbs, until
I reached the good old age which they [the
gods] gave." What the expression "cool of his
town" means is a mystery, unless one can take it
to be a way of saying that Thuthà was a person
of a dispassionate temper who never allowed him-

B C.
1344–
1332.

self to be carried away by his feelings in delivering judgment.

Thuthá is both detailed and comprehensive in his desires for offerings. After specifying all the usual things, including fine linen and wax, he concludes with a prayer for " all that which heaven gives and earth produces and that which is brought by the river from its cavern," so that his **Ka** might suffer from no possible omission.

There is also in the Louvre the stela of a scribe called Thuthá, having the cartouche Hormenka, but as the king's name on the Mut statue has been destroyed it is impossible certainly to identify this Thuthá with either of the two others.

B.C. 1332– 1328. The last king of the 18th dynasty, Horemheb, appears like Aŷ to have been a sort of makeshift and to have succeeded to the throne when well on in life. He is almost certainly the same man as the well known general Horemheb, and at the death of the " divine father " was strong enough to step into his place. The great conquests of the earlier part of the dynasty had made the army and its leaders so powerful and important that a soldier could match himself with a priest, and the claim of Horemheb, who had married a royal wife, was not disputed. With the reigns of Aŷ and Horemheb the greatest of the dynasties trickled to its close.

CHAPTER XII.

NINETEENTH DYNASTY.

WITH the 19th dynasty we come to the beginning of the decadence of Egypt. In the reign of Akhenaten, as we have seen, the dismemberment of the empire had begun; now through the tumult of loudly-praised wars we can trace its decline, and can see no less surely the gradual degeneration of art in temple-building, which had never been so profuse and gorgeous as now.

Yet the 19th dynasty did not altogether loose its hold on the power of the past; we find in its time some of the finest and some of the grandest work that Egypt possesses—work that will vie with Hatshepsut's at Deir el Bahari, and work which in colossal grandeur has no equal.

The dynasty opens with a twin reign. Rameses I., the father of Seti, and reputed first king of the dynasty, celebrated even on a monument of his second year his son as co-regent. Elsewhere also, on the walls of the hypostyle hall of Karnak, at Seti's temple of Abydos, they appear together. The temple at Gurneh, the dedication of which was enlarged when the builder changed, was begun by

B.C. 1328.

B.C. 1327– 1275.

P 2

Seti in honour of his father, and Rameses I. was worshipped here with divine honours.

The first public act of Seti's single reign was the beginning of a war against the tribes of Syria, who though tributary to Tutankhamen and Horemheb, rebelled against Rameses I. Some of the tribes submitted, but the campaign left a doubtful victory over the tribe of the Kheta, later enemies, and subsequently allies, of Rameses II. The victorious armies were met at the Sweet Water Canal by the princes of the people, and ascended the Nile to celebrate the victory at Thebes.

But the great contribution of Seti to Egypt lies in his buildings, in which a note of perfection is touched again before the greatness of Egypt passes. He did much at Thebes; he went on with the hypostyle hall of Karnak which his father had begun; he restored Deir el Bahari; below a spur of the Libyan hill which runs out eastwards he founded the Temple of Gurneh, "the Temple of Millions of Years," * and dedicated it to his father; and if his temple at Abydos is his greatest work his tomb at Thebes takes rank among the finest monuments of Egypt.

The temple at Abydos is of the white limestone made famous at Deir el Bahari; its work is not less delicate, though it can boast no such situation as Hatshepsut's temple, with its terraces and rampart of golden rock. The tablet of Abydos, naming a

* Murray's 'Handbook' to Egypt, p. 854.

series of seventy-six kings, forms the great historical interest of Seti's temple. They begin with the Mena till lately supposed to be of traditional fame. Yet the results of the last few years of excavation, culminating in the discoveries at El Kab, Negada and Abydos, seem to promise that the veil of oblivion shall again be lifted, showing us a vista beyond that point where Seti himself reckoned that history began.

In the arid valley of the tombs of the kings Seti dug his grave. Through the rude wooden door which guards it one descends into a fairyland of splendour, passage and staircase, chamber and chapel, hewn out of the solid rock, and painted with the scenes of the soul's journey into immortality, following the sun god. Serpents, sometimes winged, sometimes with legs of men, writhe about the walls ; on the square-hewn pillars the king meets the god face to face. In the second hall the drawings are unfinished, and one can see the black chalk of the master correcting the red outline of the draughtsman.

In death Seti's name was changed to Hesiri-i, vowing him to Osiris, the righteous judge of the dead, not to Set, the evil one. His tomb had been already robbed when the Ramesside inspectors visited it ; his sarcophagus, exquisitely carved in alabaster, is in the Soane Museum in London ; his mummy was found at Deir el Bahari wreathed with flowers. He was succeeded by his son.

Rameses II., formerly called the Great, is a monument to all time of successful vanity. Even B.C. 1275- 1207.

the present generation, which yearns to abase him and delights to expose the emptiness of his boasts, must find amazement almost changed to admiration at the very mightiness of self-glorification.

The Greeks belauded further his self-laudations, calling him Sesostris, the world-conqueror. But he named himself Conqueror of Asia before his victories over the Kheta; called himself Conqueror of the Negro and of Kush in virtue of successes that did not even extend his border line; and history knows nothing of his boasted defeat of the Libyans.

It is indeed over the Kheta that his most important victories were achieved. The Kheta, a tribe probably identical with the Hittites, had joined in a conspiracy against Egypt. The confederacy, under the headship of the hereditary prince of the Kheta, was a serious danger to Egypt, and threatened invasion. In his fifth year Rameses, hearing that they lay near Kadesh, marched against them and, deceived by lying spies who had fallen purposely into the Egyptians' hands, separated his army in two parts and formed a camp under Kadesh. In the Ramesseum the scenes of the war are given with great detail: we are shown the *testudo* of joined shields, the turned-up shoes, originally snow-shoes, of the Kheta; we find the scaling-ladder in use.

The Kheta, who lay in ambush, took the army at a disadvantage; Rameses boasted that, divided from his soldiers, he achieved single-handed, but with

the divine assistance of his father Amen, prodigies
of valour, and regained his forces. The victory was
for the Egyptians, and in another engagement was
made decisive, and "the vile Kheta," as the
Egyptians designated their enemies, entered into
alliance with Egypt. Rameses celebrated the conquest, and especially his own valour, by carving
the scenes and engraving the Epic of Pentaur,
duly appreciative poet laureate, on temple walls
at Karnak, at Luxor, at the Ramesseum and
elsewhere.

The treaty, for defensive purposes, between
Kheta-sar, "vile prince" of the Kheta, and Rameses,
is one of the oldest known. Its terms are child-like
in their simplicity, lawyer-like in their sufficiency.
The treaty confirms and renews pacts before
existing; "the great prince of the Kheta" and the
great King of Egypt conclude "a sweet peace and
sweet fraternity for all time"; they will make no
inroads on each other, they will defend each other
from external enemies and from disaffected and
traitorous subjects.

"If an enemy approaches the countries of
Rameses II., the great king of Egypt, he shall
send to the great prince of the Kheta, saying,
'Come and make me stronger than he is'; the
great prince of the Kheta shall come and the great
prince of the Kheta shall defeat his enemy. But if
the great prince of the Kheta does not come, then
he shall send his soldiers and his cavalry and they

shall defeat his enemy."* The great king of Egypt
was similarly bound. The alliance was further
secured by the marriage of Rameses to the eldest
daughter of the prince.

We find something more substantial in the fame
of Rameses when we come to his temple-building.
If he carved his name on the works of his predecessors, if his restoration showed rough against
finer work of better days, yet he was not backward
to build and to rebuild. So vast was his greed of
monumental fame that, as Wiedemann declares, his
aim seems to have been to show that all temple-
building throughout Egypt was due to him.† From
end to end of Egypt, from the cities of the Delta
to Abu Simbel above the first cataract, he built
temples and restored sanctuaries that had been
broken down.

At Abu Simbel he built one temple, his queen
another; at Thebes there was hardly one to which
he did not put his hand, though he must prepare
there his own funerary temple, the Ramesseum,
ornamenting its roof with a picture of the firmament
less conventional than the usual starred blue of
Egyptian ceilings.

In no form of monument was he so profuse as in
colossal statues of himself. At Tanis his figure—
close upon one hundred feet high with its pedestal

* 'Aegyptische Geschichte,' by Professor Wiedemann, vol. ii.,
p. 439.
† Ibid., vol. ii., p. 441.

and crown—must have stood like a tower above
the temple buildings and town;[*] at Memphis we
climb a ladder to look on the face of one of his
prone colossi. The half-destroyed colossus of the
Ramesseum must have weighed a thousand tons;[†]
before his great temple of Abu Simbel he hewed
four out of the living rock; two sat, six stood
before the pylons of Luxor; parts of eleven are
already uncovered in his court there.

Among other places, the Temple of Mut received
a certain attention. The wall which, starting from
the second court, engirdles the smaller chambers of
the temple, is of Rameses' time, and bears on the
outer surface of its eastern side the cartouches of
his wife Nefertari Mert-en-Mut, and of his son
Rameses Meri-Tum. There are some half-destroyed
lines of inscription which appear to refer to the
erection of statues of the gods.[‡] Nefertari was
probably the chief wife of Rameses. She was
associated with him in the foundation of the smaller
temple at Abu Simbel, and a relief there shows her
with him in an attitude of adoration. Elsewhere
also she appears, and after her death was adored
with divine honours.

But we have also more personal records of the
reign. The lower part of a very large Sekhet

---

[*] 'Tanis,' by Professor W. M .F. Petrie. Egypt Exploration
Fund, 1885, part i., p. 22.

[†] Murray's 'Handbook' to Egypt, p. 784.

[‡] 'Recueil,' xiii., p. 162; Bouriant, 'Notes de Voyage.'

statue in the outer court has a broken cartouche
which seems to be that of Rameses II. (plan no. 3).
This is rendered more likely by the fact that other
such statues in the Louvre, at Gizeh and at Turin
bear his cartouche.   The hotel garden at Luxor has
a small broken lion with his name; this probably
came from our temple, and affords us reason for
thinking that a part of a similar limestone lion
found in 1896 was also of this time.   The tame lions
of Rameses appear in reliefs of his campaigns.

Finally we found, most characteristic work of all,
a rose-granite seated statue of the king (plan no. 11,
pl. XVI., p. 43).   The face was little injured, the
cartouches quite clear.   The inscription on the
back is much destroyed and seems to give only
the usual titles.

Our temple has one other link with this reign, in
the statue of Bak-en-Khonsu, priest of Amen, who
was one of the architects of the Ramesseum and of
the building of Rameses at Karnak.   On a statue of
Bak-en-Khonsu in the Munich Museum the architect
describes the main features of the building :—" I
performed the best I could for the people of Amen
as architect of my lord.   I executed the pylon
of Rameses, the friend of Amen. . . . I placed
obelisks at the same made of granite.   Their height
reached to the vault of heaven.   A propylon is
before the same in sight of the city of Thebes, and
ponds and gardens, with flourishing trees.   I made
two great double doors of gold.   Their height

PLATE XVI.

Photograph by H. B. Gourlay.   *To face p. 218.*

RAMESES II.

reaches to heaven. I caused to be made a double pair of great masts. I set them up in the splendid court in sight of his temple." *

In front of these pylons was set up an avenue of sphinxes leading down, as the late French excavations have shown, to the quay.

Of the architect of all this magnificence we must speak more fully later, for this remarkable man was only in the zenith of his career under Rameses II., though he had begun official life under Seti.

But there was growing up under the shadow of the throne a man of a destiny greater far than Baken-Khonsu's, for it was probably about this period of Egyptian grandeur, when the seeds of ruin and decay were only beginning to take root, that there was born among the obscure race of their slaves the man who should be not only ruler and deliverer of his own tribe but world-prophet and lawgiver.

M. Naville's discoveries at Tell el Maskhutah † in 1883 have established the site of Pi-tum or Pithom, the fortified store city of Rameses II. built by the Israelites.

We cannot perhaps lay great stress on Miss Edwards's ‡ observations of the bricks with straw, the bricks with stubble, and the unqualified brick, used in the buildings, but there seems no doubt

* Murray, ' Handbook ' to Egypt, p. 843.
† ' The Store City of Pithom and the Route of the Exodus,' by Ed. Naville. Egypt Exploration Fund, 1885.
‡ ' Pharaohs, Fellahs and Explorers,' by Amelia B. Edwards, pp. 49, 50.

that Thuku or Succoth and Kes, the chief town of
Goschen, have, as well as Pithom, been identified.
And M. Naville suggests a very probable reason
for the oppression described in the book of Exodus,
in the spread of a subject and possibly disaffected
race over all the region where the Gate of Arabia
gave a possible entrance to the foes of Egypt and
the best road for the projected campaigns of
Rameses.

It was probably for the provision of desert
expeditions that the store city was built.

There have been traditions and speculations, none
worthy of credit, about which daughter of Rameses
it was who, bathing in the river, drew out of the
bulrushes the little papyrus bark sanctified by the
act of Isis against the bite of the crocodile.* She
called the baby Mesu, "a man child," but the
shibboleth of his people changed it to Mosheh,
"drawn out of the water."

As son of Pharoah's daughter Moses would be
brought up as soldier or priest.

Of the elder sons of Rameses, about whom we
have an unusual amount of information, one Kha-
em-uas was a priest, though he like the rest had
fought in the field. Kha-em-uas seems to have
shared in the king's essential priesthood, to have
celebrated for the family at great festivals, to have
taken part in the burial of the Apis. His name is
preserved in the story of "Setna and the Magic

* Wiedemann, 'Religion,' p. 278.

Book,"* for we read : " The mighty king Usr-
Maat-Ra" (Rameses II.) "had a son named Setna
Kha-em-uas, who was a great scribe, and very
learned in all the ancient writings."

Like Kha-em-uas, Moses was "learned in all
the wisdom of the Egyptians"; and his intimate
knowledge of ritual, of the priests and of the shrine
which they carried evidences still further that he
was brought up in Egypt as a priest.

While the Israelites still groaned under the hard
bondage of the complacent king his long reign
came to an end.

He had ruled for sixty-seven years. While the
empire was going to pieces he lauded his victories
or imaginary world-conquests on the innumerable
temples where art was as surely ruined, and on the
usurped works that better men than himself had
founded.

Whether he imposed as much on his own time as
on himself and on posterity seems doubtful. He
worshipped himself as divine in many temple
scenes, but comparatively few in Egypt paid him
divine honours. He patronised the very gods,
claiming a too special protection, and speaking of
" Sutekh of Rameses " or " Amen of Rameses."†

He went to the grave full of years, of which he
must have numbered at least eighty ; full of honours,
which he had rendered to himself ; surrounded by

* 'Egyptian Tales,' vol. ii., p. 87.
† 'Bubastis,' by Ed. Naville, vol. for 1889-90, p. 42.

descendants, for he had nearly two hundred children.*

If the finger had already written on the wall he saw it not, nor knew that his kingdom was divided and he himself found lighter than the feather in the balances.

He could hardly descend to the dust like simpler men, for the Ramesside inspectors examined as his a grave another than that which Champollion discovered, and the evidence of a papyrus indicates still a third place of sepulture.

His body, found in a tomb at Deir el Bahari, lies to-day exposed to public gaze in the Museum of Gizeh, and Egyptologists are still attempting to expose the bare character and doings of the man free from the ornaments and wrappings of a fictitious fame.

We have, as has been said, an unusual amount of information about the elder sons of Rameses.†

The eldest, "Amen wields his sword," was plume bearer and first general of infantry in the lists of the Ramesseum; the second, Rameses, was a general of infantry; the third, "Ra is on his right," held a lower office over the infantry, and was chief of chariots and first cavalry officer. Kha-em-uas was fourth son. "Mentu wields his

* One list of his children gives 162, of whom 111 are sons, 51 daughters; another gives 8 more daughters. *Cf.* 'Aegyptische Geschichte,' vol. ii., p. 462.

† 'Bubastis,' pp. 43 ff.

sword" was fifth; the "Beloved of Ptah" was but thirteenth.

But the chances of war and fate removed most of the twelve; the priestly call eliminated Kha-em-uas, and on the later inscriptions of Bubastis, Merenptah son of Hes-t-nefer stands as heir presumptive.

The most pressing affair for Merenptah on his accession was to gather up and consolidate the remains of empire, which during a long reign had been slipping from his father's hand.

B.C.
1207-
1187.

The great and decisive victory of the new reign was that over the Libyan invasion which threatened in his fifth year.

In 1896 Professor Petrie discovered that a temple on the edge of the Libyan desert which had been attributed to Amenhetep III. and lay behind the funerary temple of that king, was in truth the funeral temple of Merenptah.* A portrait statue of Merenptah himself, and a stela which gives the most complete account of this war, † were the great yields of the site.

The statue of Merenptah is carved in grey granite, and the face and head still retain some colouring. The painting of the eyes gives them a strange intent expression, which is increased by the slight stoop of the head. The brow is receding, the lower part of the face heavy and somewhat

* Petrie, 'Six Temples of Thebes,' pp. 11 ff.
† There is a duplicate inscription at Karnak, nearly half of which is destroyed.

animal; the lips are pushed forward. The whole effect is of a personality forcible but not exalted, impressively handsome but unpleasing.

Merenptah had not inherited from his father any reverence for the work of his predecessors. The temple of Amenhetep III. had been ruthlessly pulled to pieces to furnish building material, and the great inscription of Merenptah is inscribed on the back of a beautifully worked and polished stela of Amenhetep.

"The beloved of Ptah" was warned in a dream by his patron divinity that the Libyan invasion was in preparation, and he gathered all his forces to meet it. His preparations were so complete that when it took place he fell on his enemies and utterly defeated them. It is on the completeness of this defeat and the subsequent security of Egypt that the inscription is eloquent:

> "They were come their face in front *
> They were turned backward
> Their legs did not stay firm, but fled,
> The archers threw their bows away,
>
> *   *   *   *
>
> The wretched conquered Prince of Libya fled,
> Under the protection of the night,
> Alone, without the plume on his head.
>
> *   *   *   *
>
> The Lord of the All says:
> 'Give the sword of victory
> To my true-hearted, good and mild son Merenptah,'
>
> *   *   *   *

----

* 'Six Temples of Thebes,' pp. 26 ff. Dr. Spiegelberg's translation.

> The cities closed shall be opened again,
> He shall free many enchained in each district
> And give sacrifices to the temples (again)."

Still more vividly is the security pictured :

> "One is talking:
> Come far out upon the roads,
> There is no fear in the heart of men,
>
> *   *   *   *
>
> The wells (are) opened (again),
> The messengers return home
> The battlements lie calm in the sun,
> Until their guards awake.
> The soldiers lie in sleep
>
> *   *   *   *
>
> By night resounds not the cry:
> 'Stop!' or 'Come, come!' in the mouth of the people.
> One goes with singing
> There is no more the lament of sighing man."

The hymn ends with a record of defeats—Tehenu, Kheta, the Kanaan, Askelon, Gezer, Yenoam ; then we read :

> " *The people of Israel* is laid waste—their crops are not,
> Khor (Palestine) has become as a widow for Egypt."

Here for the first time then was found the name of Israel on the monuments. The most attractive interpretation of this, that it was an account of the killing of the male children or a record of the flight of the Israelites garbled as Rameses' son must have known how, must be rejected. From the position of the mention of Israel—named between Yenoam, a town near Tyre, and Palestine—Professor Petrie decides that the allusion is to some defeat of the

Q

Israelites in Palestine.   Merenptah is in all probability the Pharaoh of the Exodus; if the children of
Israel passed out of Egypt under him they did not
as a body enter Palestine until after the invasion of
Rameses III.   Therefore it is concluded that those
whom Merenptah defeated were either Israelites
who had not gone down to Egypt or some branch
which had re-entered Palestine after the famine was
over or shortly after the Exodus.

When the Exodus itself took place we cannot tell,
but M. Naville's researches at Pithom and survey
of the region throw much light on the route probably
taken.*   The start was made by the southern road
which would have taken them round the northern
shore of the Arabian gulf, but this was abandoned
on the rumour of pursuit; and they turned back,
the great multitude encamping between Migdol,
the watch-tower, and the sea, near Pi-Hahiroth,
Pharoah's farm, which M. Naville identifies with
Pikeheret.   It is probable, as M. Naville shows,
that an arm of the Red Sea ran up with shallows to
Lake Timsah, and the water could here be driven
back by a strong wind, as it is to this day in parts
of Egypt.   The fact that this was liable to happen
here explains, as he conjectures, the position of the
watch-tower.

The first station, Etham, M. Naville identifies
with Atuma, the place to which Sanehat had fled,
and whence the nomad tribes about this time asked

* 'Pithom,' by Ed. Naville ("The Route of the Exodus").

leave to pass that they might pasture their flocks by the farm of Pharaoh.

Here then the history of the subject race parts company with that of their masters ; the fates cross again later in less intimate manner, in alliance, in commerce, in war, but the discipline of Israel in Egypt was over; the rise of Israel, the fall of Egypt had begun.

Merenptah left no remains in the Temple of Mut though stones bearing his name were found near the temple.[*]

Seti II., who succeeded Merenptah, seems to have combined Rameses' power of self-laudation with infinitely less intrinsic title to fame. He calls himself at Abu Simbel "gallant and victorious as the god Mentu," the god of war[†]; he borrows a poem from Merenptah to celebrate victories which he had never achieved. Even his buildings are insignificant. The Temple of Mut, however, owes to him a part of its gateway (Pylon I.). The additions of the Ptolemies built up into perpendicular lines the pylon of Seti, which was of the ordinary pyramidal shape. Seti's cartouches are still distinguishable, though two later Rameses, with the dynastic gift of plagiarism, have written their names and titles more largely and prominently on the edifice.

The papyrus of " The Two Brothers," containing

B.C. 1187–1180.

----

[*] 'Aegyptische Geschichte,' vol. ii., p. 478.
[†] *Ibid.*, p. 481.

strangely familiar elements of other fairy tales, was composed for Seti when he became crown prince.

B.C. 1180– 1175. We do not wonder, when the boasts of the family sank down to such a level of futility, that an alien should have grasped at the sceptre of Egypt, and Amen-meses, successor of Seti, seems to have been a usurper. He does not appear (as indeed ten other kings do not) in the procession of kings in the temple of Medinet Habu.

Professor Petrie's excavations of 1896, in yielding information about his successors, have indirectly strengthened the theory of his usurpation.

B.C. 1175– 1168. These excavations revealed temples of the queen Ta-usert and of the king Siptah, last king of the dynasty. A rock inscription at Assouan of a court official Bai, records that it was Bai who secured to the king Siptah the throne of his father Seti.

Siptah married Ta-usert; but as the foundation deposit of Ta-usert's temple contained only her own scarabs and plaques, while those of Siptah's yielded also a scarab of Ta-usert, Professor Petrie argues that Ta-usert's had precedence in point of time. Thus Ta-usert, when building her funeral temple, was probably reigning in her own right, and Siptah, aided by Bai, established himself on the throne, legitimatising his position by marrying her.

Thus this evidence also confirms the idea that

there had been a lapse in the direct succession, and that it was the usurpation of Amen-meses which led to the fact that he was unnumbered by Rameses III. among the kings of Egypt. Siptah, "established for all years," as his scarabs named him, was the last king of the declining dynasty.

The Temple of Mut yielded two other records of this dynasty, which we cannot with certainty assign to any reign.

In the south brick wall the fragment of a statue representing the royal scribe Rŷ was discovered. The statue is in the usual squatting position (plan no. 22, p. 340). We feel that Rŷ may have been somewhat affected by the spirit of the 19th dynasty, so sure is he that the gods have but sent him the due reward of his deeds :

"I was just and free of evil. . . . I reached a good old age with daily favors and an excellent heart and pure hands."

The inscription is of more general interest as containing an exhortation to worship Amen, Khonsu, and Mut, who is called "Mut the great, fair of face, and rising in gold."

The base of a double statue representing a *uab*-priest of Amen, Sa-Mut, and his wife, may belong to this dynasty or the next (Trench B, p. 347). The wife's name was Baky, and she was a songstress of Amen. All that is left of the prayer is the ordinary petition for the supply of the Ka, namely, for "thousands of all things good and pure that issue before the Mistress of Asher."

Another still more broken statue, of the same limestone and bearing the name of Sa-Mut, in all probability represents the same man (Trench B, p. 347).

CHAPTER XIII.

TWENTIETH DYNASTY.

IN the declining times of the 20th dynasty there is one king who stands out above the rest— Rameses III.—whose justly won honours have been absorbed by the semi-mythical Sesostris.

The dynasty opened with troublous times; there is evidence that the reins of government were but loosely held. A Syrian, "a man of Khal," by name Arisu, tried to seize sovereign power and to extort tribute from the people. The very gods were neglected, and their offerings not rendered; it is probable that in these times of internal contention the temples were broken down, for the manner of their building made them suitable or even destined them for fortresses.*

In these times the gods established their son Set-nekht, who restored peace and the offerings of the gods.

B.C. 1168.

Among the few remains that have been found of Set-nekht, it is interesting that the temple of Mut retains a gateway (plan no. iii.) in which he is appropriately called "beloved of Mut."

---

* 'Bubastis,' vol. for 1889–90, p. 4.

But Set-nekht's greatest claim to remembrance is in his being father of Rameses III., whom he made co-regent with himself, as it appears, from almost the beginning of his reign.

Such an arrangement succeeded, as indeed it was probably calculated to do, in bringing about the peaceful accession of Rameses on the death of his father.

If Set-nekht had been able to restore tranquillity within the country, Rameses had a far more diffi- cult task in safeguarding Egypt from dangers without. The disintegration of the empire, which had begun under Akhenaten and proceeded with great strides under Rameses II., had proceeded until as we have seen it threatened the unity of Egypt itself. New enemies were rising up without ; but the power of ancient enemies had not wholly de- clined. While the Libyans were, as ever, the traditional foes of Egypt, a new Asiatic tribe coming south overthrew the Kheta and constituted a fresh danger to Egypt.

The first victories of Rameses were over the Libyans. For a long time they had held the west bank of the Nile from Karbana to Memphis. The result of his campaign was to recover this, the western boundary of Egypt.

In his eighth year Rameses began to wage his most important campaign against the new foe— the confederacy of Asiatic tribes. Assembled in the country of the Amorites, these prepared to

PLATE XVII.

FIG. I.—RAMESES III.

FIG. 2.—(20TH DYNASTY).

To face p. 232.

descend on Egypt, and warfare was waged by land and water before Egypt was victorious. The prisoners taken in the war were vowed to the great gods of Thebes and presented as slaves in their temples.

The building of the funerary temple of the king proceeded step by step with his campaigns; the temple at Medinet Habu grew court by court as his achievements and victories gave subjects for the decoration of its walls. The only representation of naval warfare given to us by Egyptian art is that which commemorates, on the walls of this temple, the victories against the Asiatic tribes.

But the temple records not only these campaigns on the east and the west; victories in the north and the south, in Palestine and Ethiopia, have at least a brief mention here.

We said that the decadence of art, as of empire, had begun in the time of Rameses II.; but this process too was gloriously if briefly suspended by his worthier successor.

If the later temple of Medinet Habu has not the exquisite proportions, the delicate simplicity, of the so-called Thothmes temple, if it has not the perfection of finish that Deir el Bahari exhibits, nor the splendour of Amenhetep's temple—ruthlessly destroyed—it has a grandeur of its own, in its own way perhaps unsurpassed.

The gateway tower was for long a puzzle to archæologists. It has been called the palace of the

king; but for this it is, as Wiedemann points out,
too small, too little capacious; and most of the royal
palaces were on the other bank of the Nile. It has
been thought to be a fortress, but the subjects of
interior relief are intimate and domestic—the king
with his harim, playing draughts with wife or
daughter.

Wiedemann suggests that these are rooms for
the royal family on festal occasions, or for ceremonies of the king's robing; and Professor Maspero
proves * what Mariette had before indicated † that
the form of architecture, otherwise unknown in
Egypt, the straight tower, with its gateway,
rooms and wings, is copied from the Canaanitish
migdol, or watch-tower, seen by the king on some
of the Canaanite campaigns.

The late Government excavations ‡ have given a
more commanding height to the tower, have shown
up too in quite new proportions the porters' lodges
at the entrance. From here one gets the superb
vista of the temple. Between the gateway and the
temple there is a broad open space where now is
discovered on the one hand the temple of
Ameneritis and on the other the eye can rejoice
itself in the 18th-dynasty temple free from the

---

* 'Histoire ancienne des peuples de l'Orient classique.' G.
Maspero. Vol. ii., pp. 127 ff.

† 'The Monuments of Upper Egypt' (translation of the
Itinéraire de la Haute Égypte') of Auguste Mariette-Bey, by
Alphonse Mariette, pp. 208, 209.

‡ Carried on by M. Daressy, 1896, 1897.

earth banks which hid its beauty. Through the great pylons of the temple itself, where of old the giant flagstaffs flew their banners, one sees across the outer court, where steps lead through another gateway and across another colonnaded hall. Beneath the colonnade is a raised cloister, as there was in the second court of the Mut temple. Beyond this again a gateway leads to the smaller chambers.

The walls are emblazoned with the king's victories, his lion hunts, his festivals. Much colour is left in some of the courts, till, looking on it, one is led to think that no one, who has not seen Egyptian sky and the roof of Medinet Habu, knows what blue is.

The "Sesostris" of the Greeks was nourished on the glories of Medinet Habu. To this temple the tale of the treasury of Rhampsinitus owes its origin, as the story of the all but successful treachery of the brother of Sesostris may be traced, according to Wiedemann, to the conspiracy of State officials and of the harîm against the life of Rameses III.

Round the precinct runs a later wall, which includes, besides the greater and lesser temples, two tanks, one open, one covered, which probably served, but less grandly, much the same purposes as the Lakes of Karnak and of Asher.

This superb temple did not exhaust the building energies of the king. He built another temple at Tell el Yahudiyeh. At Thebes, chief scene of his

activities, we find his hand at Deir el Bahari, at
Gurneh, at the temple of Karnak, and at the other
temple of his founding, the temple of Khonsu. The
French excavators at Karnak have cleared the little
temple of his building which breaks the southern
wall of the great court of the temple of Amen ; the
ruins of another temple lie at the north-eastern end
of the lake of Asher.

Neither did Rameses forget the temple of Mut,
though his gifts there are not of great importance.
Two small defaced cynocephali in sandstone were
found in the outer court in the excavation of 1895,
having the cartouches of Rameses III. on the back.
These were left in the temple, but, all fragmentary
as they were, the Arabs stole them.

A more important find in 1896 was of fragments
of the small black-granite sphinxes of the king.
One of these included a defaced head and shoulder
bearing the cartouche ; the other was a similar head
with the face fairly perfect, and evidently a portrait
(plan no. 6, pl. XVII., fig. 1).

The clay mould of a seal found in Trench C
gives the first name of Rameses.

Finally we have a private monument of great interest belonging to this reign—the white limestone
statue of Bak-en-Khonsu (plan no. 16, pl. XVIII.,
p. 343), who, as we have mentioned, was the architect of Rameses II. The face and carving of the
statue seem to have been purposely injured ; but,
like the statue of Sen-mut, it was too large to be

easily destroyed, and was therefore thrown out of the temple at the same time as the other and found immediately under it.

Bak-en-Khonsu was, as we read on this statue, "son of the doctor and superintendent of recruits of the temple of Amen, Amen-em-apt."

The Munich statue tells us that Bak-en-Khonsu was steward of Seti I. ; then priest of Amen ; then successively divine father, third prophet, and second prophet of Amen. He was architect under Rameses II., and finally he became high priest of Amen. On this statue he is called hereditary and *ha*-prince, the *sem-ur* priest ; he calls himself "opener of the doors of heaven in order to see her statue" (presumably the statue of the goddess), and "chief of the secrets in heaven." The usual prayers are added.

Mr. Newberry's calculation on the basis of these facts (p. 346), shows that Bak-en-Khonsu must have been no less than one hundred years old when the statue was executed. Since, moreover, he was then still living, we may be amply reassured as to the robustness of the Egyptian constitution. We marvel that Pitt entered on public life at twenty-two and was prime minister before twenty-five ; Bak-en-Khonsu —with in some ways a more comprehensive education, for he was steward, priest, and architect—took his official position still earlier ; he allowed himself, as we see (p. 345), only four years for his "extreme infancy," and twelve years

of youth ; and thus became a public official at the
age of sixteen.   But the Greeks and we are more
cynical about the life-gifts of the gods than were
the Egyptians, and the days of the years of the
life of Pitt would have seemed an unloving reward
to Bak-en-Khonsu.

The statue bears the cartouches of Rameses III.
One of the last of Egypt's great kings, he succeeded, so papyri of his reign emphatically tell us,
in establishing peace and tranquillity.   His last act
and deed, given in presence of his officials, contains,
besides bequests to the gods and a sketch of his
wars, certain civil provisions.

To Rameses III. belongs the beautiful grave
discovered by Bruce, popularly known through its
paintings of the blind harpers.

Of his less illustrious successors we have little to
say.   That one or two stand out above the rest is
but faint praise.

Rameses IV., made co-regent with his father,
walled in the second court of the Temple of Mut.
His inscription runs round the west, north and east
sides.   He also inscribed his name on the sloping
ends of the pylon of Seti II.   There are comparatively few monuments of this reign left in
Egypt.   Rameses IV. boasts, in the manner of his
greater predecessor, of power which he probably
never possessed, of actions which he probably never
accomplished.   He prays for a like reward—a reign
of sixty-seven years.   As his boasts were emptier

PLATE XVIII.

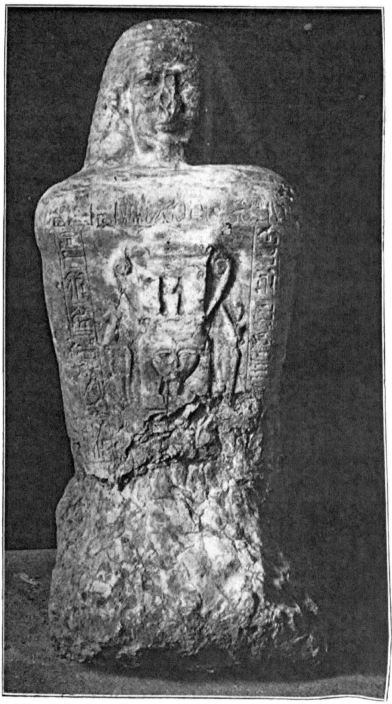

BAK-EN-KHONSU.

than his predecessor's his reward was in all probability less substantial.

Rameses VI., a son of Rameses III., appears   B.C.
1125.
from the evidences of his reign found in the Delta
to have been one of the greater kings of the dynasty.*
At Thebes he built the engirdling wall of Medinet
Habu, but his finest monument is the grave which
he stole from his predecessor and re-decorated. It
is in character with this that the contributions he
made to the temple of Mut are the carving of
his name on the pylon of Seti, and an alabaster
base found in 1896 (plan no. 8) bearing his
cartouches.

Rameses IX. shows a piety not too often remarked,   B.C.
1120.
in his Commission instituted to inquire into the
spoliation of the graves of the Pharaohs. The
royal Commission did not wholly succeed in stopping
the plunder, which appears to have been carried out
by organised bands of thieves. More efficient safeguarding was found necessary as time went on.

We have from the temple of Mut but one other
monument of the dynasty, and that undated. This
is the broken statuette (Trench B, pl. XVII., fig. 2,
p. 349). The principal figure represented is nameless, but she is the mother of the man standing by
her side, who is called "her son, her beloved one,
the sculptor Bak-en-Amen."

The statue, indeed, was probably a double one
representing both parents of the sculptor. On the

* 'Bubastis,' vol. for 1889–90, p. 46.

side of the seat three figures are incised. Over
one, a woman, is written "Asti"; the second and
third, two men, are called Nefer-mennu and
Aa-em-ab. There is a vacant space at the end
where a figure seems to have been sketched, and
over it is written: "To the Ka of the favoured of
the place of his heart Nekht-Amen."

Thus the representation is probably of a family
group—originally giving both parents seated, the
most distinguished son, possibly the sculptor of the
group, standing in front, and portraits of the other
children incised at the sides.

The Ramessides have been numbered up to the
XIIIth, but investigation has lately shown that one
of those, called the XIIth, is a wholly fictitious
character. With the last Rameses the dynasty
closed. He contributed a few monuments to Egypt,
at Memphis, Abydos and Thebes; but at the
Temple of Mut he left no record.

CHAPTER XIV.

TWENTY-FIRST AND TWENTY-SECOND DYNASTIES.

WITH the next two dynasties we come in a sense to a new era in Egyptian history. The founders of the 22nd dynasty were not native to Thebes; and neither dynasty probably had any right through the male line to the throne.

The theory in Egypt had always been, as we have seen, that inheritance came through the female line, and that sovereignty was conferred by the wife. This in effect however usually resulted in a dual determination of sovereignty, the king's son succeeding and determining his right by marrying the king's daughter. Certain isolated rulers had no doubt been brought in by the single right of their wives; but here, on the other hand, we reach a time when the whole rights of the dynasty rest on the queens, and one king confirms his own right again and again by marriage with every heiress.

But though the kings of these two dynasties were not of the old royal line it is still questionable whether their accession was by violent usurpation or the peaceful accession of the most powerful

R

class and family in the State through rights of
marriage. The first dynasty was of priests, the
second of soldiers. The two most powerful classes
in early times were always the military and the
sacerdotal; the kings of Egypt in virtue of their
office were priests, in virtue of their position must
be warriors.

In both the 21st and 22nd dynasties the first
rulers were the most powerful, and the dynasty in
each case disappears in comparative obscurity.

On the authority of Manetho the rulers of the
21st dynasty were supposed to be Tanite; but the
names he gives cannot be paralleled with those of
the priest-kings whom we know from the monuments,
and must therefore be those of a contemporary line
of princes in the Delta.

The figure of Herhor, the first king of the
dynasty, appeared in conjunction with that of the
last Rameses on the walls of the temple of Khonsu.
Before the death of this king he had already taken
titles practically royal, and monopolised the chief
offices of state. He was not only, as the other kings
of the dynasty, high priest of Amen, but com-
mander-in-chief, superintendent of both lands, and
first architect; he was represented moreover with
the uraeus, symbol of the divinity of royalty. But
the power which he had absorbed as high priest
was probably only in the second degree the
cause of his kingship, as placing him in such a
position that he might aspire to the hand of a

king's daughter and claim the rights conferred by marriage.

Herhor's chief architectural work was done in the temple of Khonsu, but it is not mainly through this that his name is remembered.

The plundering of kings' graves, into which the Commission of Rameses IX. had inquired, had been ineffectually dealt with. Herhor devised a more practical plan of safeguarding by burying the mummies in a common tomb at Deir el Bahari, which could be more easily watched. The work of searching out the bodies of the kings, transporting, re-burying with certain new wrappings, new dates and inscriptions, and translations of inscriptions, went on under his successors. Many of the kings of this dynasty were buried in the same place, and some of those of the 22nd dynasty. Thus the tomb discovered in 1881 opened a large region of new knowledge to the Egyptologist.

Herhor was succeeded by his grandson.

B.C.
1080.

There has indeed been some little confusion in the evidence on the subject, arising from the fact of the discrepant genealogies ; from the discovery of the mummy of a high priest Pi-netem, as well as of a king of that name ; and from the absence of the cartouche in most of the inscriptions of the king. But the whole mass of evidence appears to make it clear that Pi-netem, high priest in his turn and king in right of his wives, was the son of the high priest Piankh, who was a son of Herhor. The omission

R 2

of the cartouches appears to come from the fact that Pi-netem reigned emphatically only as being the husband of the heiress.

His first wife was Hathor-tai-Hent-taui (or otherwise given as Hathor-sa-t-Hent-taui). She was the daughter of Tent-Amen, a "royal daughter," and Nebsenui. It is an interesting point to notice, as bearing on the absence of caste in Egypt, that Tent-Amen, who, being a "royal daughter," conferred royal rights on her daughter, herself married successively two commoners, for neither Nebsenui nor her other husband Khonsu-Mes appear to have been of royal rank, though the bodies of both her husbands and of Khonsu-Mes's daughter Tauhert were found in the shaft at Deir el Bahari.

The daughter of Pi-netem and his wife was called Ramaka, "royal daughter, royal wife, lady of both lands." On the pylon of the temple of Khonsu Amen is said to have given the sovereignty to Ramaka. It appears, then, to have been in order to legitimatise more securely his own position, to exclude all possible pretenders to the throne, that Pi-netem made his own daughter royal wife.

The body of Ramaka was found in the royal tomb at Deir el Bahari. At her feet was the mummy of an infant. Yet the baby must have lived, and its mother must for a short time have survived its birth, for there is at Marseilles a statue of the two, with their cartouches. And the king had time to name this infant of days with full titles, "royal daughter, great royal wife, lady of both lands Mut-em-hat."

The temple of Mut contains a memorial of Pi-netem's first wife Hent-taui, which was visible before the late excavations. On the east side of the outer court there is a Sekhet statue somewhat differently carved from the rest (plan no. 2). It is headless and shows no inscription in front, but a shaft up the back is engraved with the cartouche of the queen, who erected the memorial when the king "Ra-Kheper-Khā" (Pi-netem) brought gifts to the temple of Amen.*

After Pi-netem the dynasty sinks into comparative obscurity.

The daughter of one of the later kings became the wife of Solomon, and under his rule Solomon traded with Egypt and brought up the forbidden strength of war.

The last king of the dynasty was Pasebkhanu II., whose daughter formed the necessary link with the rulers who followed.

During the decay of the 21st dynasty a new family had been rising into power, whose names show them at once to be not native Egyptians, but of foreign origin. A theory, now generally surrendered, was that they were of Assyrian origin, and this was supported by the apparent parallelism of the names Nemart, Usarken and Tekelet to Nimrod, Sargon and Tiglath. It was further

* Lepsius, 'Denkmäler,' iii. 249 f.

adduced in support of the theory that the family call themselves great princes of Mā and that Mat is the Assyrian word for land.

But the parallelism is more attractive than etymologically correct or historically supported ; a sounder explanation of the title is found in its being an abbreviation of Mashwasha, the name of a Libyan tribe—a name indeed which seems to require abbreviation for ordinary use ; and this hint of origin is further supported by the fact that the first name known in the family is unquestionably Libyan.

There is much historical significance in the succession of the princes of Mā. The old Egyptian royal line had passed away ; the native priests had had their turn of sovereignty ; the downfall of a country is imminent when its army is recruited from foreign mercenaries ; and the seal is set on its destruction where, as here, the commanders of the mercenaries, princes of ancient enemies of the land, possess themselves of the sovereign power.

The 22nd dynasty is called Bubastite ; their chief remains are in the Delta, and during the successive reigns of their kings the centre of gravity of the empire tended more and more to transfer itself to the north, while Thebes was being abandoned to the rule of the priests.

Although it was their position as commanders of the troops which practically raised the Bubastites to the sovereignty, they did not fail to legitimatise their position by marriage.

The first king of the dynasty is Sheshanq. His B.C. 960–93 grandfather, another Sheshanq, had married into the royal line of Thebes, and the king further strengthened his position by marrying his son to a royal daughter of the last king of the 21st dynasty.

On another side too they were not backward to strengthen their position. In a paper in the 'Recueil,' * M. Daressy has traced the alliance between the Bubastite kings and the priests of Memphis, showing that the latter emphasise the alliance by a succession of names parallel to those of the royal house.

It is indeed this "moral support" of the priesthood of Memphis that, according to M. Daressy was decisive in the rise of the Bubastites.

As they stood, racial princes of the mercenary troops allied by marriage to the Theban and the Memphite priesthood, the position seemed strong. But there were elements of weakness. The dynasty was not Egyptian nor bound by long course of time to the people, and with the move of the seat of government to the north the hierarchy of Thebes tended to become independent, thus splitting the kingdom in two.

That their kings did not wholly relinquish the southern capital is evident; although the great buildings of the dynasty are in the Delta, Sheshanq and his successors added to the temple at Karnak

* 'Recueil,' vol. xviii., pp. 46 ff. "Inscriptions Inédites de la XXII⁸ Dynastie." G. Daressy.

and recorded their victories on its walls. A relief giving the names of one hundred and thirty-three conquered towns commemorates the great event of Sheshanq's reign, the war against Palestine at the time of Rehoboam.

Solomon, like Sheshanq, allied himself, as has been said, with the kings of the 21st dynasty, but enmity with Egypt must have arisen later, possibly on the accession of Sheshanq; for Jeroboam's refuge from the wrath of Solomon was with Sheshanq king of Egypt.

No lasting bond was formed however between Jeroboam and the king, for the list on the wall of Karnak includes conquered towns in the northern as well as in the southern kingdom of Palestine.

The raid on Palestine was completely successful. Sheshanq conquered Jerusalem and plundered the temple, bringing away the golden shields, which the braggart son of Solomon replaced with brass.

In the temple of Mut, Sheshanq dedicated a large number of the Sekhet statues. For the most part these are of the same size as those of Amenhetep III., but the work and the engraving of the cartouche on the front are less careful. The one exception is the large Sekhet statue in the colonnaded court (plan no. 5, pl. XIX.) which stands ten feet high, and, instead of bearing on the head the disk with the uraeus in front, has a complete crown of uraei, formerly surmounted by a disk. The inscription on the front of the seat in this case

PLATE XIX.

hotograph by J. F. Vaughan. *To face p. :*

SEKHET OF SHESHANQ I.

is well and deeply cut, instead of being simply scratched on the granite.

There was also an alabaster statue of Sheshanq in the temple, for we found in 1896 (Trench A) a shoulder and part of an arm of a statue, about half the size of life, the latter fragment being inscribed with the name of Sheshanq's eldest son Uapt, called "justified son of the Lord of the two lands Sheshanq beloved of Amen" (p. 349).

From other sources it appears that Uapt was "high priest of Amen-Ra" and "general of the soldiers" (p. 350), being thus strengthened in his position as king's son by holding high military rank and the chief sacerdotal office at Thebes.

Of most of the later kings of the dynasty we know little. Though several left records at Karnak their building activities were mainly occupied in the Delta, and especially centred on their own city Bubastis, where the festival hall of Usarken witnesses, by the fragments of statues built into its walls, the ruin of earlier days.

With Sheshanq IV., last king of the 22nd dynasty, B.C. 789. we find some revival of the martial spirit, but his campaigns in the south and in Asia could not save the doomed dynasty. The dismemberment of the empire had laid it open to attack, and it was from the south that the conqueror came.

.

CHAPTER XV.

TWENTY-THIRD TO TWENTY-FIFTH DYNASTY.

IT is almost impossible to unravel the history of
the chaos into which Egypt fell during the 23rd and
24th dynasties, if indeed the lines of petty kings,
who fought for portions of the dismembered kingdom, can be dignified by the name of dynasties
at all.

Egypt was becoming hardly pressed by two
powers, by the Assyrians on the north and by the
growing strength of the Egypto-Ethiopian kingdom
on the south. Caught between these two irresistible
forces, which slowly approached one another, the
Egyptian princes and chiefs scrambled for a share
of all that was yet unabsorbed, and no less than four
of them claimed the right to wear the royal uraeus.
Such supposed rights however now seemed likely
to be swallowed up by the overmastering claim of
the king of Ethiopia.

Ethiopia, since the days of the 12th dynasty,
had been a dependency of Egypt. Its ruler was
a viceroy appointed by the king, whose official title
was " King's Son of Kush."   In early days this title

did not necessarily imply that he should be literally
a king's son, but later the vice-royalty became the
monopoly of the princes of the royal house. The
principality was always ruled in exact accordance
with Egyptian custom. The increasing weakness of
Egypt from the time of the Ramessides onward
made it easily possible for these princes to establish
a line independently hereditary, to push forward
their boundaries into Upper Egypt, and to take
the title of king of Kush. Though a national
kingdom was thus established it was carefully
framed on Egyptian lines. The names of the
kings, originally of pure Egyptian race, were always
formed on the old pattern, and written in the same
manner with the royal cartouche. The names of
the queens, which are evidently foreign, appear as
freely on the monuments as those of the royal wives
of Egypt. To women was accorded the same important position, and inheritance through the wife
and mother held good in Ethiopia. The language
—though in course of time it differentiated—the
writing, the architecture, and above all, the religion,
were those of Egypt. The capital of this kingdom
was Napata, and there, in the temples of Mount
Barkal, as in Thebes itself, were honoured the gods
of Thebes, "Amen, lord of the thrones of the world,
and Mut, Lady of Asher."

Piankhy-meri-amen, king of Ethiopia, and later
of all Egypt, was descended directly from the
Theban priest-kings of the 21st dynasty. During

the 22nd dynasty, although the throne had gone from them and the seat of sovereignty had moved northward with the Bubastites, this royal and priestly caste retained a great measure of their power and influence at Thebes. Piankhẏ had thus ground for his claim to the throne of the whole country, and with Upper Egypt practically in his hands he despatched an expedition against the weakened and divided powers of Middle and Lower Egypt, which had rebelled against his authority. This threat to their independence forced the little kings to forego their quarrels and to unite under Tef-nekht, prince of Saïs, to rid themselves if possible from the danger of a new and masterful overlord.*

To take and spoil Thebes was for the army of Piankhẏ a mere form without any violent reality, as they had special orders to honour Amen there, but further north they suffered a defeat at the hands of Nemart, the local king of the " Hare-city." †

This check roused Piankhẏ, and, " raging against his defeated army like a panther," in the twenty-first year of his reign he undertook the conquest of the country in his own person.

748? The whole story of his invasion of Egypt is told with picturesque detail on the great stela at Gebel

* Note the identity of some of the names of these rebellious princes, Nemart, Sheshanq, Usarken, with those of the 22nd dynasty; names repeated also in the families of the Memphite priesthood. The descendants of this dynasty had become local kings of towns and provinces.

† Hermopolis.

Barkal which he placed in the temple there to commemorate his victory. Piankhŷ delayed at Thebes on his march north to be present at the chief yearly festival of Amen.

"I will sacrifice to my father Amen in his beautiful festival : He will lead me in peace to see Amen in the good feast of the festival of Apt : I shall bring him forth gloriously in his divine form unto Southern Apt, in his goodly feast of the feast of Apt at night-time;* . . . and I will bring him forth gloriously to his own house to rest upon his throne on the day of making the god to enter,† and on the second day of Athyr I will cause the land of the North to taste the taste of my fingers."

His beaten soldiers, hearing how his Majesty raged against them, tried hard to redeem their honour, and took three or four towns, sending him a message each time to announce their success, "but his heart was not appeased thereby."

When Piankhŷ had duly honoured Amen he sailed down the river to the "Hare-city," and besieged Nemart there. He took the city after three days' fighting, and Nemart, after prudently sending his queen and sisters and daughters to intercede with the harĭm of Piankhŷ on his behalf, made his submission to the king, bringing gifts and "a horse in his right hand."

* Torchlight procession from Karnak to Luxor with the image of the God.

† Return procession from Luxor to Karnak.

Piankhỷ pardoned him, warning him that "the heart is a rudder that wrecketh its owner in that which concerneth the will of God."   After the king had sacrificed to Thoth he visited the royal stables, and found that the horses had been neglected and starved, a neglect which angered him a great deal more than resistance to himself. "As I live, as I love Ra, as my nostril is refreshed with life, very grievous are these things to my heart, the starving of my horses, more than any ill which thou hast done in the fulfilling of thine own desire. The fear which thy surroundings have of thee beareth witness to me of thee."

Thereupon Piankhỷ assigned all Nemart's wealth to the treasury and his granary to the god Amen.

Then he went his way northward, summoning each city to open its closed gates. "If a moment passes without opening, behold ye are reckoned as conquered—and that is painful to the king. Do not love death and hate your life." "Open and ye live, close and ye die. My Majesty passeth not by by a city closed."

Such hints were enough for all the cities of Middle Egypt, and the march to Memphis was bloodless. So religious a king was most anxious to spare so sacred a city as the ancient capital of the Old Kingdom, and he besought it to open its gates and let him enter in peace to sacrifice to its gods. "For His Majesty loveth the . . . Be safe and sound, that even the children weep not."

PLATE XX.

To face p. 254.

PIANKHÝ BLOCKS.

1

Photograph by Brugsch Bey.

Memphis, very strong and well stored for a siege, refused to yield. It was the time of the inundation, when boats could be moored to the houses, and Piankhŷ made a furious assault from his ships on the river side of the city, and carried it "as by a flood of water." He was careful to protect the chief temple, and his first action on entering the town was to purify himself and sacrifice to the great god Ptah.

While at Memphis, Piankhŷ satisfied his religious instincts by a pilgrimage to Anu * (Heliopolis), the ancient centre of the worship of the sun-god, Ra. " His Majesty proceeded to the camp which was on the west of the Atiu Canal :—he was purified in the midst of the Cool Pool, his face was washed in the stream of Nu,† in which Ra washes his face. He proceeded to the sand-hills in Anu ; he made a great sacrifice on the sand-hills in Anu before the face of Ra at his rising, consisting of white bulls, milk, frankincense, incense, all woods sweet-smelling. He came, proceeding to the house of Ra, he entered the temple with rejoicing. The chief lector praised the god that warded off miscreants from the king. The rites of the Chamber of Early Morning were performed, the cloak was put on, he was purified with incense and cold water, flowers for the Hat Benben‡ were brought to him. He took the

---

* On.

† The rising Nile.

‡ House of the Benben. The Benben was probably a small obelisk or pyramidal stone sacred to Ra.

flowers, he ascended the staircase to the great window to see Ra in the Hat Benben. The king himself stood alone; he put the key into the bolt, he opened the double doors, and saw his father Ra in the Hat Benben. He sanctified the Madet * boat of Ra, and the Sektet * boat of Tum. The doors were shut, clay was applied, and sealed with the king's own seal, and the priests were charged: 'I, I have examined the seal ; let none other enter therein of all the kings who shall exist.'" After the capture of Memphis, Piankhy advanced into the Delta, where he met little opposition. The *erpa*-prince, Pediast, prostrated himself, promising "gold unto the limit of thy desire, malachite heaped before thy face, horses many of the best of the stable, the leaders of the stall." Tef-nekht of Saïs himself, the head and front of the offending, fled to the marshes, and after his troops had been defeated sent abject messages of submission. "I am afraid of thy mighty spirit on account of that saying, 'The flame is my enemy.' Do not cut down the grove to its roots. A year hath cleansed my Ka and purified thy servant from his wickedness." He offered all his treasure to the conqueror, and "the best of the horses accoutred with everything."

The four kings, "two rulers of the north and two rulers of the south," who claimed the right to wear the uraeus, acknowledged his supremacy, and Pi-

* Here the morning and evening bark of the sun. Elsewhere the Sektet is the morning boat.

PLATE XXI.

2

Photograph. by Brugsch Bey.   3   *To face p. 256.*

PIANKHŶ BLOCKS.

ankhỷ treated them all with royal liberality, but only
Nemart of the Hare city might be admitted to eat
in the king's house, because he alone was clean ;
the others were all eaters of fish, and therefore
ceremonially impossible.*

Thus Piankhỷ triumphed over Egypt, and returned
to Thebes with great rejoicing and a heavy tribute
to bestow upon his father Amen the best of his spoil,
and to pay due honour to Mut, the Mistress of the
Sacred Lake.   For Piankhỷ, "beloved of Amen,"
was a devoted son of the Theban gods, as became
the descendant of the priest-kings of Thebes.
Mention has already been made of the great temple
to Amen at Mount Barkal, where now his stela of
victory was set up, but early in his reign, Upper
Egypt being virtually in his hands, he had added to
the temple of Mut in Asher, and on the walls of a
chamber he built there inscribed the record of a
peaceful expedition to bring, like that of Hatshepsut,
the precious things of the south to Thebes.   The
ships of the expedition were sculptured row above
row on the walls, each with its name and measurements, and a list of its cargo, as is shown by the five
blocks (plan no. 12, pl. XX., XXI., XXII., pp. 370-
379) which alone remain of the whole chamber.   On
these are pictured a few of the ships and their
contents.   The first boat—as was seemly—was

* All the quotations from the stela of Piankhỷ are from an
unpublished translation by F. Ll. Griffith, and used here by his
kind permission ; see p. 137.

S

called the "vessel of Amen," and was laden with
gold; the next was the "great vessel of Saïs," and
had on board a general, Tef-nekht himself, who
apparently acted as admiral, and is described as the
"great one of the fleet"; the third was the "vessel
of Piankhÿ," and was about seventy-five feet long;
and another served as the harîm boat. The reverse
sides of some of the blocks were also sculptured,
but the scenes remaining are disconnected and much
destroyed. One of them probably represented the
departure of the fleet from the quay at Karnak
(pl. XXII., block 5). But only half the scene remains;
half the quay, with a tree to represent those growing
on the fertile soil beside the water, an obelisk, pylon,
and sphinx to express the great temple and the
sphinx avenue which lead up the quay, are without
their corresponding pairs. On the quay stand
figures to speed the departing boats, which have
just pushed off, while the steersman guides them
forward.

The expedition, which may have been to the
country south of Khartûm, seems to have been led
by Piankhÿ in person, and it is interesting to find
that Tef-nekht of Saïs, who afterwards headed the
rebellion in Lower Egypt, went with the king as
second in command. It would seem therefore that
even during the first twenty years of Piankhÿ's
reign he claimed the throne of the whole country,
and that this claim was not at first disputed, since
Tef-nekht was evidently on the most friendly terms

PLATE XXII.

4

with his overlord. . It was, then, rather the suppression of a revolt than the conquest of new dominions that brought Piankhŷ into the lower country in later years. The addition of this sculptured chamber to the temple of Mut must also have been made in these years, before the revolt broke out.

Although this dynasty is called Ethiopian, Piankhŷ was by descent of the true royal Egyptian stock, and his claim to the red crown, as well as the white, was by right as well as by might. He must have ruled more than twenty years over Egypt after he had pacified it, for mention is made, in an inscription, of his forty-sixth year.   B.C. 729?

The history of the years following his reign is in hopeless confusion. The king Bakenranf, who was   B.C.
traditionally supposed to be the son of Tef-nekht,   720?–714?
appears in the 24th dynasty, while the successors of Piankhŷ, Shabaka and Shabataka, are placed in the 25th dynasty. From the best dating which it has been possible to evolve, it is clear that there were several parallel reigns in the upper and lower countries, but complete certainty is out of the question.

An interest attaches to Bakenranf in that he was considered by the Greeks to be a great law-giver, and there is also the tradition that the penal code attributed to him was incorporated by Cæsar into Roman law; but the Greek legends of Egyptian kings are inconceivably fictitious. He probably made an attempt to re-assert the complete indepen-

S 2

dence of Lower Egypt, for a fresh invasion from
Ethiopia took place towards the end of his reign.
It is not certain whether this conquest was the last
act of Shabaka, a king whose name appears at
Karnak, or the first of his successor, Shabataka, but
it appears to have settled the question of the over-
lordship of the lower country; though, as the
Ethiopian kings were more Egyptian than the
Egyptians, they naturally ruled the country after
the strictest native fashion, and as far as possible
through the local princes and governors.

As this southern dynasty had again brought the
whole Nile valley under one rule, it was inevitable
that it should come into collision with the power of
Assyria, which was pressing steadily nearer Egypt.
Sennacherib, having conquered Judæa, turned his
eyes upon the Delta, and all Egypt united to resist
a like fate. Already, in B.C. 706, the young
Ethiopian prince Taharqa had been general of the
Egyptian forces in Palestine, and he was again
called upon to meet the Assyrian nearer home.
His task of driving the invaders out of the Delta
was an easy one, helped as it was by an epidemic
which fell upon the army of Sennacherib and
practically destroyed it—the disaster recorded by
the Hebrew chronicler which led to the raising
of the siege of Jerusalem.* Such plain intimations
of fate were not to be disregarded, and the Assyrian
danger was averted for thirty years.

* 2 Kings xix., 2 Chronicles xxxii.

PLATE XXIII.

MENTU-EM-HAT.

Taharqa, who is described in the Assyrian annals
of the time as " King of Kush," returned to
Ethiopia, where he ousted Shabataka from the
throne, claiming a superior right to it through his
mother, according to the Egyptian law of inheritance. His years of leadership in Lower Egypt had
smoothed his way, and he became also, without resistance, the acknowledged king of the whole country. B.C.
He fell upon evil times. The success of his early
career passed out, and a night of defeat settled upon
Egypt. Taharqa was the last ruler who was an
Egyptian king in spirit as well as in name. The
life of the nation was drained to extinction in the
struggle with Assyria, which filled the last part of
his long reign. The power of empire had departed
from Egypt and had been given to another.

Taharqa's first care was to find allies. He made a
federation with the strong and wealthy kingdom of
Phœnicia, a kingdom which included the island of
Cyprus. This island, lying in the ordinary route
from Egypt to the coast of Phœnicia, was inhabited
by a race half Phœnician and half Greek, who were
called Takhara, and are identified with the Teukri.
To this people, as we shall see, it is probable
Taharqa owed a good friend. Two statues of the
man whom he appointed governor of Thebes were
found in the temple of Mut. The name of Mentu-
em-hat has long been familiar, but he has never been
known by face before. The first of these statues
(plan no. 24, 25, pl. XXIII., p. 350) is in the usual

squatting position, and unfortunately headless, but
it bears the name and the titles of Mentu-em-hat
already known, adding those of "*heq*-prince of the
hills" (or desert), and superintendent of the
frontier. Of the second statue the head and
shoulders remain (plan no. 25, pl. XXIV., p. 357);
most of the inscription, including the name of the
subject, is gone, but fortunately the titles are preserved. As both statues are similar in workmanship, belong to the same period, and, above all, as
the titles on the second coincide with those of the
first, and include the very rare one of fourth priest of
Amen, there is no manner of doubt that this remarkable face is that of the *ha*-prince of Thebes, Mentu-
em-hat. The face of this statue is a portrait most
true to life. The arrangement of the hair, which is
otherwise quite unknown, only adds to its conviction,
though no detail is needed to assure of its verisimili-
tude. The very man himself looks from the stone, and
the best explanation of his career is found in his face.

That face is quite un-Egyptian; the flat upright
forehead and the long upper lip, giving an unusual
length of line from the eye to the corner of the
mouth, are features difficult to assign to any known
type. Professor Petrie conjectures that he might
have been by origin a Cypriote, as the nearest
parallel in face and expression is to be found in the
heads of these Takhara or Teukri of Cyprus.*

* Max Müller identifies the Takhara with the Philistines
inhabiting the coast opposite Cyprus ('Asien u. Europa,' p. 389).

PLATE XXIV.

Photograph by Dr. Page May.

Photograph by J. F. Vaughan. To face p. 262.

MENTU-EM-HAT.

In such times of difficulty and danger it is far
from impossible that Taharqa should have chosen
from among his new allies a man of strong
character to be governor of Thebes.   It lessened at
once the danger of disaffection in Egypt itself, and
cemented his bond with a friendly people.   He had
need of such men, in spite of the twenty years of
peace granted to him after his accession.

Esarhaddon was now king of Assyria.   He and
his son Assurbanipal conquered Phœnicia, the ally
of Egypt, making of it a tributary state, and the way
to the Delta lay clear before them.   The first con- _{B.C.}
quest was not far-reaching, but a second, under-
taken by Assurbanipal, brought ruin to the king
and the country.   Taharqa defended Memphis in
vain ; the city was taken and he fled to Thebes, only
to be followed and driven to the southern bounds
of his kingdom.

Thebes fell into the hands of the Assyrians, to
be sacked and plundered, its temples wrecked and
their treasures spoiled.   The victory was so complete that Assurbanipal is described in the Assyrian
annals as " King of Egypt, Thebes and Ethiopia."
The country was divided into many little princi-
palities governed by satraps, who were chosen for
the most part by the victor from the native Egyptian
princes, as a means of assuring the submission of
his new subjects.   On a cylinder of Assurbanipal
a list of these satraps is given ; among them are
the names of Nekau of Saïs, of a Tef-nekht, a

Sheshanq, and of *Manti-me-anhi* of Thebes. The identification of this satrap of Upper Egypt with Mentu-em-hat, prince and governor of the Thebaïd, admits of no doubt, and the likelihood of the appointment is obvious. Although he had helped Taharqa to defend Thebes, his position was confirmed by the new authority, and the withdrawal of the Assyrians left him free for the work on which he was set. Mentu-em-hat was as devoted a servant of the gods of Thebes as Piankhy himself. The inscriptions he has left at Medinet Habu and at the temple of Mut, dated in the reign of Taharqa, set forth in minute detail his pious labour in the restoration of the ruined temples and plundered desecrated shrines.

The inscription * on the walls of that small chamber in the temple of Mut generally called the "Taharqa Chamber" (plan, a) is the record by Mentu-em-hat of this work of purification and restoration. "I have purified the temples of all the gods in the nomes of the whole of Upper Egypt as they ought to be purified after [profanation]." † The inscription is much broken, but enough is left to show that Mentu-em-hat cleansed the temples of many gods, repaired their breaches, replaced the sacred vessels and treasure which had been stolen, and restored the rites of the gods and the "festivals of

* Translated by M. de Rougé. 'Mélanges d'Archéologie,' tome 1er, 1er fascicule.
† From M. de Rougé's translation.

Thebes" in their due order.   On one of the statues
found in the temple he calls himself "a perfect
noble and true veteran in the service of the gods of
Thebes," and his works justify his words that he
"was great of monuments in Thebes, and great of
glory in the southern country."   On the same
statue he mentions that he "restored the temple
of the goddess Mut, Lady of Heaven, in good
white limestone—made great her altars, spread her
fire (?) and provisioned her house in all good
things."

The remains of Mentu-em-hat's work have long
since disappeared in native lime-kilns.   The only
limestone remaining in the temple is the lowest
course of the walls of one small inner chamber
(plan, h).   As the sandstone walls outside it bear
19th-dynasty names, it is clear that the Assyrian
destroyers did not raze the temple to the ground
—for restoration is the burden of Mentu-em-hat's
inscriptions—but only plundered and wrecked it.
It is possible therefore that these few blocks of
limestone are the sole survivors of that temple
which Pu-am-ra "saw erected in good white stone"
by Sen-mut in the far distant days of Hatshepsut.

Mentu-em-hat had the full consent of the king in
all his works, for Taharqa too served the gods of
Thebes, as the great rock temple to Amen and Mut
at Mount Barkal bears him record.   Besides this
great work in his native capital, Taharqa inscribed
his name on buildings at Memphis, Tanis and

Thebes, and there remains also an Apis stela dated in the twenty-sixth year of his reign. Afterwards the legend that he was a great conqueror was current among the Greeks, and his conquests were said to extend from the Pillars of Hercules to India. This fame was easily earned by the transference to a statue of Taharqa of a base of Rameses II. sculptured with a list of conquests. This base, in its turn, had been transferred from the statue of one of the 18th-dynasty conquerors, according to the simple and direct method of attaining reputation practised by Rameses. The list included Naharaina (Mesopotamia) and other distant places where Rameses had never set foot.

After a few years of apparent quiescence Taharqa gathered Egypt together for a last effort to shake off the Assyrian domination. His effort, in which Mentu-em-hat was his faithful helper, was successful, but it brought down retribution tenfold upon the country.

c. 655? Assurbanipal prepared a fresh invasion; while it was preparing Taharqa died, and the flood descended on his successor Rudamen. Thebes was devastated a second time, with a still more terrible completeness, in which the careful and splendid labours of Mentu-em-hat were swept away.

The vengeance of Assurbanipal made a deep impression on the minds of the surrounding peoples. "Art thou better than No-amon," says the Hebrew prophet Nahum, in his bitter invective against

Assyria, whose hand then lay heavy upon Palestine. "Art thou better than No-amon, that was situate among the canals, that had the waters round about her; whose rampart was the Nile, and her wall was the waters? Ethiopia and Egypt were her strength, and it was infinite. . . . Yet was she carried away, she went into captivity: her young children also were dashed in pieces at the top of all the streets: and they cast lots for her honourable men, and all her great men were bound in chains." *

Of the close of the career of Mentu-em-hat there is no record; there is nothing to show whether he was one of those honourable men who went into captivity, whether he survived the overthrow of his life-work and painfully attempted a second restoration, or whether his life too came to an end with that of the dynasty he had served.

* Nahum iii. 8–10, R.V., and *cf.* marginal readings.

CHAPTER XVI.

DYNASTY XXVI.

WITH the downfall of Taharqa, the national life of Egypt in any true sense came to an end. Her remaining history is merely the history of exhaustion before inevitable death. For seven hundred years her powers had been on the decline, the normal waning of a vigorous vitality past its prime. But the wounds of the Assyrian invasions drained dry that splendid spring of life which had sustained the nation through its unparalleled course of five thousand years, and had already assured its influence on future civilisations.

The attempt of the kings of the 26th dynasty to revive a spirit already extinct only hastened the end; there is no trace of Egyptian feeling in the Hellenised Egypt of the last few centuries B.C. 655. before Christ. These kings, though un-Egyptian in mind and method, were of native birth. Psamtek I., son of a prince of Saïs, claimed his throne through his wife, daughter of Ameneritis and an Ethiopian prince Piankhý. Ameneritis was the sister of Shabataka, of the 25th dynasty, and therefore

PLATE XXV.

SER (SAÏTE PERIOD).

a royal heiress. Psamtek's reign seems to have
been parallel with that of Rudamen at Thebes
for a brief interval, but Rudamen, thoroughly dis-
heartened by the Assyrian destruction of Thebes,
withdrew altogether to Ethiopia, leaving Upper
Egypt to become part of the kingdom of Psamtek,
whose name is found at Thebes in B.C. 665.
Ethiopia henceforth remained separate, holding
friendly relations for the most part with Egypt,
but maintaining its independence until Roman
times.

Psamtek was free from the Assyrian danger.
The death of Assurbanipal, which followed hard
on the second invasion of Egypt, marked the
beginning of a rapid failure in the power of the
empire, and Babylonian victories shortly put a term
to its existence. Psamtek therefore was left in
peace to get the better of the twelve princes or
satraps between whom the country was divided, and
to attempt the hopeless task of raising up a living
and united Egypt. The means by which Psamtek
and his successors tried to reinspire the country was
by the infusion of the young and vigorous life of
Greece, then in the height of its efficiency. Greek
soldiers fought the battles of the Saïte kings,
Greek merchants and sailors guided their commerce, Greek settlers farmed the rich lands of the
Delta. The capital was established in the midst
of them at Saïs; and Thebes, the embodiment of
the spirit of ancient Egypt, was deserted, silent,

ruined. Egypt passed from the old to the modern world.

The period of this dynasty has been called a period of renaissance in art, because in its work the forms of the great art of the early kingdom were reproduced. The style of the 4th dynasty was faithfully copied, but the spirit which informed the result was wholly different in kind. The head of the princess Nefert of the 4th dynasty, and the head of a woman of the 26th, found in the temple of Mut (Trench A, pl. VI.), are alike in simplicity of arrangement and style, but the one is not the lineal descendant of the other, she belongs to a different world.

Greece brought back to the country where she had learned her rudiments an art developed and transformed by the genius of a wholly different type of mind.* The history of the dynasty makes this abundantly clear.

Psamtek, having by means of mercenary troops established his authority over his fellow-princes, opened the country to that stream of Greek immigration and adventure which has not ceased to flow, so that to-day the " Greek shop " is, in the life of many a native village, the sole hint of the existence of Europe.

* M. Daressy, in the 'Recueil' (vol. xviii., pp. 46 ff., " Inscriptions Inédites de la XXII° Dynastie "), hints that evidence is forthcoming to show that much work has been ascribed to the Saïte which is the product of the 22nd dynasty.

That stream had long before reached the out-
skirts of Egypt. For a thousand years, since indeed
the days of the 18th dynasty, little colonies of
Greeks and of the inhabitants of the islands and the
shores of Asia Minor had fringed the Egyptian sea-
board and the Libyan borders, but now they
penetrated to the very heart of the country. A
little settlement of Greeks had, during the 23rd
dynasty, established itself for trading purposes in
the Western Delta. It was this place that Psamtek
chose for a great military settlement of his mercenary troops, and beside the fortified camp grew
up that famous mercantile city known as Naukratis.
A large scarab factory existed here, and scarabs of
Psamtek and other Saïte kings are found, but no
later name than that of Apries.

The remainder of his mercenaries Psamtek placed
at Defeneh (Daphnae) on the eastern frontier,
building there too a great fortified camp, thus
providing himself with a bulwark on either hand,
against Asiatic invasion from the east and on the
west against that long-lived foe of Egypt the tribes
of Libya.

Greek legend and tradition clustered thickly round
the kings of the 26th dynasty ; for the first time the
intimate life of the Egyptian court was open to that
restless curiosity, ever eager to hear and to tell some
new thing. To Psamtek and his contemporary
princes was ascribed the Labyrinth of Amenemhat III., and he was credited with a taste

for scientific experiment, though, judged by the
well-known story of his attempt, by means of two
infants, to discover the language of the primeva
race, it was not thought at all necessary to attribute
intelligence to his methods.   With the establishment
of the capital at Saïs under these new conditions,
the gods of Thebes were not presented to the
outer world as supreme.   In Egypt the Osirian
triad was worshipped in the Delta, and thus
was prominent in the Greek writings which informed the world of the history and customs of
Egypt, and these deities received the worship of
successive conquerors, willing to propitiate the gods
of the land.   Psamtek built largely at Saïs ; his
work is also found at Memphis and Abydos, and he
lived too near the traditions of the 25th dynasty
not to leave his name at Thebes.   The stones
of a small temple of his were found by M. de
Morgan in the Sacred Lake at Karnak, and the
little "temple of Ameneritis," in the great court
before the temple of Rameses III. at Medinet
Habu, was his acknowledgment to the heiress of
the 25th dynasty through whom he claimed his
crown.

It is possible that the statues of Mentu-em-hat were
placed in the temple of Mut at the beginning of his
reign.   In style and workmanship they belong to
the Saïte period.   If this were so, Mentu-em-hat
must have survived the second Assyrian destruction
of Thebes, to have made such life-like portraiture

PRIEST (SAÏTE PERIOD).

To face p. 272.

possible.   The dating, which would have contained
the king's name, is broken away, but Psamtek's name
occurs at Thebes in B.C. 655, and it is not unlikely
that a king who claimed descent from the 25th
dynasty should pay tribute to the devotion of the
adopted son of Egypt, Taharqa's faithful servant.
On the other hand it is possible that even in the
stress of the time between the first and second
sacking, the governor's own energy placed in the
newly restored temple the *Ka*-statues which also
commemorated his piety.*

Several other statues of the Saïte period besides
those of Mentu-em-hat were found in the temple of
Mut, and we may therefore infer that the temple
was not so ruined but that it was still in use, and
that *Ka*-statues could still be placed there.   None
of these figures unfortunately retain their date, so
that they cannot be assigned to any particular
reign, and only on three is the name preserved.

The first of these is a standing figure of a priest
of Amen in Karnak and Erment, called Ser
(Trench A, pl. XXV., p. 361).   He wears a wig
of the Saïte period, and a kilt, held in place by
an inscribed girdle.   On his right shoulder is
incised a tiny figure of " Khonsu the child," and on
his left the name of Mut the Great, Mistress of
Asher; on the back of his wig is a fantastic picture

* It is probable that the fragment of a black-granite statue
found in the same wall (at plan no. 23) as statues XXVI. 1 and 2
is part of yet a third figure of Mentu-em-hat, since it is of the same
period and bears the same unusual title " fourth priest of Amen."

of the bark of the sun, rowed by birds. The inscription on the supporting column at the back contains priestly titles; on the side of it is incised a figure of " his wife, and mistress of his house," the " sistrum-player of Amen, Sa-naïâ-nub." Another priest of Amen in Karnak is shown in pl. XXVI. (Trench A, p. 361). His name is broken away, but he wears the tunic of a vizier, and holds a small statuette of Sekhet in front of him.

Only the lower half of a figure of Ser-Tahuti (Trench B, pl. XXVII., fig. 4, p. 360) is preserved. He was a scribe of the treasury in the temple of Amen, and is represented kneeling, clothed in a long garment, and holding a shrine. The figure of a woman, a " follower of the Goddess Mut " called Mut-sepi, is shown in pl. XXVII., fig. 1 (Trench A, p. 359). The inscription says she came to the temple court " to bow down [literally, to smell the earth] before the Mistress of Heaven," and also gives the name of her son " Horuza, who makes to live her name." He was high priest of Mut, " opener of the two doors of the house of gold of Mut," and no doubt placed the figure of his mother in the temple. In front of her Mut-sepi holds a small figure wearing the double crown. She may perhaps have been a royal nurse, but any explanation the inscription may have contained of her relation to the little king is broken away. A clumsy little figure represents a divine father and priest of Amen, whose name is lost

PLATE XXVII.

SER-TAHUTI.

SAÏTE FIGURES.

MUT-SEPI.

To face p. 374.

(Trench C, pl. XXVII., fig. 5, p. 366). He was the son of a high priest and of a sistrum-player of Amen, and he addresses his prayers to Amen, Osiris and Seker. He holds before him a small figure of Imhetep, a divinity just then in fashion, on whose knees lies a scroll. Besides these figures there was found the woman's head (pl. VI.) just referred to, whose sculptor had yielded himself to the inspiration of the New Art ; but the exquisite work in very hard stone is obviously also a life-like portrait of a new type in Egypt. Another portrait of the time is that of the old man—the supposed Philistine — probably another foreign official in Egyptian service (pl. VII.). Its truth as a portrait need not be pointed out. At some period during the 26th dynasty it is probable that the brick wall round court A of the temple was built. It is of excellent masonry, and the courses are laid in curved lines. A gate in the east side (i) opened on a narrow paved path leading up to a little shrine on rising ground beyond the lake.

Psamtek was succeeded by Nekau,* who continued B.C. the attempted fusion of Greek with Egyptian, and who tolerated the worship of the gods of Greece. His reign presents a series of ambitious failures. He tried to make Egypt a sea-power by beginning the creation of a fleet, and he tried to join the Red Sea with the Mediterranean by digging a canal which was never finished. Tradition assigns to

* Called Pharaoh Necho in the Old Testament.

T 2

him one successful undertaking—the sending out of a Phœnician expedition to circumnavigate Africa, which was accomplished in a voyage of three years. On their return they asserted that on the voyage back the sun rose on their right hand; but what is the proof of their success to us, was to their contemporaries only an unusually incredible traveller's tale.

But Nekau's chief ambition lay in Asiatic conquest. In spite of a defeat by the Babylonians, he made his way as far north as Karkhemish, in a campaign wholly indecisive, but tempered by a wayside success in Palestine. On the march north he met Josiah on the old battlefield of Thothmes III. at Megiddo, and the king of Judea was killed.[*] On the way back to Egypt, he besieged and took Jerusalem and dethroned its king. But a second expedition to the Euphrates ended for Nekau in utter rout, and Nebuchadrezzar chased the flying Egyptians as far as Pelusium, on the threshold of Egypt. The news of his father's death recalled Nebuchadrezzar to Babylon, and the country was saved from the horror of another invasion.

The successor of Nekau, Psamtek II., was called upon to defend his southern boundaries against the Ethiopians, who then broke peace with Egypt. To restore his frontier and punish the invaders he was obliged to have recourse to the help of a large body of Greek and Phœnician mercenaries, who, camping at Abu Simbel, on their passage up the river, scribbled their names and comments all over the

* 2 Kings xxiii.; 2 Chron. xxxv.

colossi of Rameses II. which are seated before the rock-cut temple.

Psamtek was active in building; he restored many temples both in Egypt and Nubia. He built at Thebes, and both there and elsewhere wrote his name somewhat indiscriminately on the works of others.

The succeeding king, Uah-ab-ra, called Apries by the Greeks, made one last attempt to measure the strength of Egypt against Babylonia. He invaded Phœnicia—then with Cyprus a province of Nebuchadrezzar—and destroyed the Cypriote fleet. But he was not able to carry his success further, and was effectually driven back by the Babylonian troops. Egypt forthwith gave up the unequal contest, and the king had to content himself with the puny revenge of opening the country to refugee Jews, who were also on the watch for opportunities of annoying the common enemy.

Apries perforce turned his attention to his western boundary, where in the disputes between the Libyans and the Greek settlers of Cyrene he thought he saw a chance of playing the part of the fox in the fable. In this venture too he was unlucky, for though the Libyans accepted his offers of protection, the issue of the struggle went against him.

. The name of "Uah-ab-ra" is found scattered all over Egypt as far as the first cataract, and a base with his name found at Corinth witnesses to the close relation of the country with Greece.

B.C. 589.

The story of the connection of Apries with Aahmes his successor is overlaid by a swarm of wholly untrustworthy Greek legends. Aahmes, the hereditary general of the Egyptian army, apparently owed his chance of royalty to the favour of the native Egyptians, and it seems probable that after some defeat of Apries by the Babylonians or by the Cyrenian Greeks the king was forced to accept him as co-regent. Aahmes then legitimised himself in the orthodox manner by marrying the sister of Apries, the daughter and heiress of Psamtek II. A proof of the joint reign is found in the name of a private person compounded with both cartouches, Uah-ab-ra-Aahmes.

During the joint reign, Nebuchadrezzar paid his debt to Egypt by an invasion which carried him as far as Syene, at the first cataract. There he met the Egyptian army under the well-known general Neshur (Hor), but without any decisive result, for the imperative summons of trouble with Persia called Nebuchadnezzar back to Babylon before he could make his conquest in any way effectual. The destruction of his kingdom rapidly followed, and Egypt was freed from one danger only to fall into a greater. If Babylon were the devil, Persia assuredly was the deep sea.

570.   Aahmes had won the throne by popular favour; to retain that popularity he was obliged to redress the great native grievance, Greek commerce. He destroyed the camp at Defeneh, removing and

scattering its inhabitants, and restricted the landing
of Greek merchandise to Naukratis alone.   Defeneh
ceased to be, after an existence of only one hundred
years, but Naukratis survived through its commerce
till the founding of Alexandria took from it its
mercantile pre-eminence, and then, robbed of its
military strength and its material prosperity, it became the town of the scholar and the retreat of
the philosopher.

Aahmes nevertheless is the central figure in
the Greek traditions of Egypt.   The ancient secrets
of the land were more easily exploited by inquisitive
interest in his reign than at any time before, and
Greek authors delighted to prove that the elements
of their philosophies were drawn straight from the
fountain-head—"the wisdom of the Egyptians."   A
hundred Greek stories of Egypt connected themselves with "Amasis."

The power of Persia had by this time engulfed
Babylon, and the smaller states of Asia Minor and
Syria cast about for some means of saving their
independence.   A confederacy, of which Crœsus of
Lydia was the head, was quickly demolished by
Cyrus, and Aahmes, finding the conqueror at his
gates, gave up a resistance which had become futile.
While the borders of Persia still marched with those
of Egypt, Aahmes occupied himself in the west with
the affairs of Cyrene.   He entered into a treaty
with the people, and made a princess of Cyrene his
second queen.

So long and peaceful a reign gave the busy
Greeks full opportunity to develop the resources of
the country, and it is recorded that at this time
there were no less than twenty thousand inhabited
places in the valley of the Nile. Aahmes also pro-
fited by his immunity from invasion to build in
many places. His name occurs at Karnak, but is
only found in Egypt proper. For in his days Egypt
slipped back to the dimensions she had at the time
of her birth as a country; her conquests, which
began with the 12th-dynasty annexation of Nubia
and spread into the empire of the 18th over the then
civilised world, had fallen gradually from her, and
the boundaries of the last king of Egypt were like
those of Mena—the first cataract and the eastern
desert.

c. 526.
c. 525.
Near the end of his reign Aahmes associated his
son Psamtek with him as co-regent, and soon after the
unfortunate prince entered on his full heritage of
trouble.

A few months after his accession, Kambyses entered Egypt, his army guided over the desert route
by a Greek deserter from the court of Aahmes.
The Egyptians made their stand near their eastern
boundaries, but were swept aside, and the capture
of Memphis made Kambyses master of the Delta.
He arranged for its government in the usual fashion
by making Psamtek satrap, and went south to over-
run the upper country, and even to make his way
into Ethiopia. Thence, tradition asserts, he re-

turned a furious madman to wreak destruction on
the temples he had spared, and to do despite to the
gods whom he had previously delighted to honour.
Among the others, the temple of Mut suffered at his
hands, chiefly no doubt by the destruction of the
statues ranged so thickly round its courts, which
formed so obvious and tempting an outlet for rage.
But it is not possible to prove that the wholesale ruin attributed to him was really the result of
his fury.

Psamtek was no sooner established in the office
o Persian satrap than he began to plan a revolt
which should restore freedom to the country
and himself. His designs were betrayed, and
Kambyses at once put him to death. Henceforth
Egypt ceased to exist as an individual country; the
position which she in old days had imposed upon
other kingdoms became hers, to be a conquered
and tributary state, a mere province of the empires
of Persia, Greece and Rome, to give all and receive
nothing.

For three hundred years after the conquest of
Kambyses, Egypt remained practically a Persian
satrapy; the frequent revolts of the native princes
had but short-lived success, and were, in spite of
help from Greece, invariably crushed out. When
the Persian empire flew to fragments under the
blows of the Macedonian Alexander, he was hailed
as a deliverer in the Delta, and the country submitted itself willingly to his indulgent rule. The

policy of the 26th dynasty saved Egypt now from
being treated as an ordinary conquest, and the
succession of Ptolemies who ruled for three hundred
years after Alexander's death adopted wholesale
the national usages. To give some semblance of
reality to their kingship they played the Pharaoh in
architecture, religion and outward observance, but
their assumption of the Egyptian manner is merely
a fancy dress, and carries no conviction. From an
archaeological point of view the adjective " Ptolemaic" withers an Egyptian building. These Greek
princes built largely throughout Egypt proper, and
the best-preserved temples now existing—Denderah,
Edfu, Philae—are their work. Careful copies of
Egyptian temples, they are elaborate, magnificent,
and dead.

Three of the Ptolemies made small additions to
the temple of Mut, in such a way as to show that it
was standing intact in their time. At the southern
end Ptolemy Philadelphus built against the outer
wall a small shrine of three tiny chambers, which
jutted from the main building, and had a flight of
steps leading down to the lake (plan x, y, z).
He also lengthened the gateway of Seti II. before
the first court (Pylon I.).

B.C.
286-247.

Philadelphus seems to have been truly Greek in
his desire for learning. He caused the Egyptian
priest known as Manetho to compile a history of
Egypt from all the records then existing. Of this
unique book only a few fragments, containing

PLATE XXVIII.

Photograph by J. F. Vaughan.   SHRINE OF PTOLEMY PHILADELPHUS.

To face p. 282.

however lists of kings and dates, are known.   In the first flush of the discoveries of modern Egypt-ology many of the assertions of Manetho were condemned as purely legendary and untrustworthy, but later monumental evidence tends more and more to prove this condemnation hasty and rash, and to show that in spite of his hardly recognisable Hellen-ised names there is more fact and less fiction in his history than has been supposed.   The "mythical" king Mena, with whom he begins, at all events seems to have been human enough to require a tomb.   The finding of a copy of Manetho's history is one of the great things still to be hoped for from Egyptian research.   Tradition has it that during the reign of Ptolemy Philadelphus seventy scholars began the translation of the Jewish Scriptures, which resulted in the Greek version of the Old Testament known as the Septuagint.

Ptolemy VII., whose career even for those times was chequered, also repaired or added to the gateway of the first court of the temple of Mut (Pylon I.), and made a tiny chamber in the thickness of the eastern wall (plan *k*).   His reign, which began when he was six years old, was spent in ascend-ing and re-ascending the throne, being alternately driven off it by a foreign prince or by his own family, and reinstated by the Roman senate. The brother who ousted him, Ptolemy IX., with his wife Cleopatra III., have left their names also on the gateway of the outer court, where

B.C.
182–146.

B.C.
146–117.

they apparently continued the addition of Philadelphus.

The rare figure of the ancient and uncouth little
god Bes, with his lion-skin, was repeated four times
on the wall of Ptolemy IX., and the long "hymn to
Mut" (plan XX, YY) sculptured on this pylon is
also of Ptolemaic times, but the inscription is too
much damaged to make a satisfactory translation
possible.*

One of the Ptolemaic princes also added the engirdling brick wall which, meeting the Saïte wall
round the outer court, completed the circuit of the
temple. This was laid, in the manner of the time,
upon a single course of stone, and any large
fragments of statues which the Persians had
shattered were unceremoniously taken to eke out
the brickwork, while four piers which buttressed the
wall on the south side were also built up of stones
from the temple and portions of both statues of
Mentu-em-hat. On the western side, nearly opposite the middle of the temple, there are, in the high
bank of earth sloping up from the lake, some other
stone beams and blocks of Ptolemaic work, which
may have belonged to a shrine on the west side like
the shrine of Philadelphus on the south ; but the bank
has not been sufficiently cut down to show whether
they are the remains of building, or merely tumbled
stones.

* "Notes de Voyage," 'Recueil,' xiii., p. 163.

CHAPTER XVII.

CONCLUSION.

WE have but isolated bits of evidence for the subsequent history of the temple.

It is difficult to found any conclusion on the few remains of true Greek work which we found in the temple.

These bring us at once to the modern world—the foot in Pentelic marble, the arm in bronze, with thumb and first finger lightly touching, are, in all their free curves and living reality, as different from the studied Egyptian work of Ptolemaic times as the fossil or skeleton from the breathing animal. The pure idealism of earlier days had become stark and dead. In these fragments of Greek art we see the new birth of the modern world.

When and why these were brought into the temple we cannot tell. It is tempting to think that the statue to which the beautiful marble foot belonged was placed in the temple among the *Ka*-statues of the old world, for we found with this a piece of the robe, showing in all probability that the statue had been broken in the temple.

During the time of the Saïtes, Greek settlers

came as far north as Aswân, so that some considerable time before the end of the Ptolemaic dynasty the statue might have been placed here. The style of the fragment shows that it belongs to about the third century B.C.

The other remains of the Greeks include the leg of a small bronze figure, less finely worked than the bronze arm, and fragments of dishes in steatite. These show the same lightness of artistic touch, in strange contrast to the Egyptian's conscientious workmanship.

In B.C. 27 there occurred a great earthquake, mentioned by Strabo and Eusebius.* It is conjectured that it may have done great damage in Thebes—that this was, in fact, the first great agent of destruction, laying the temples open to spoliation, and to the ravages of time and peoples. It will be seen that the fall of the many and heavy statues in the temple of Mut, as well as of roofs and walls, would make destruction very complete.

Thus the temple may have been, even in Roman times, to a great extent destroyed, and the Roman things found in the temple seem to have no essential connection with it. Several Roman pots were found ; a stone mortar in the outer court ; a bronze lamp, a tray, and a tall candlestick, on which the lamp was probably placed ; as well as pottery lamps ; and a second small marble foot seems to be of Roman workmanship. The only find of Roman times which

* *Cf.* Murray's 'Handbook' to Egypt, pp. 779, 780.

possessed any real interest was the pot with coins of Nero (plan no. 26, p. 381).

These coins, though not by any means uncommon, possess a certain interest in the light of contemporary events. They were all struck between 64 A.D. and 68 A.D.; and the designs and inscriptions show a strong Hellenistic tendency. The inscriptions are in Greek; one of them bears the head of Hera, so named; another that of Asclepius, named according to the Greek form.

In 66 A.D. Nero went to Greece with the intention of becoming a victor, by force or fraud, in the Olympian games. From Greece he intended to go to Alexandria, but the intention was never carried out.

The coins appear to have been struck at Alexandria in anticipation of his visit; some of them, dated 66 A.D. and 67 A.D., show symbolic heads of Alexandria, and all bear the impress of Nero's Hellenistic leanings acording to the current direction of his megalomaniac tendencies.

As there are no coins later than 68 A.D., we may conclude that the pot was deposited shortly after that date. It was buried, with every evidence of deliberation, in earth which was above the pavement level. Thus the temple must then have been in a ruinous condition.

The only evidences of early Christian times were two small pottery lamps. One had a curious cross traced on the back of it. Each arm of the cross ended in a circle; in each angle made by the arms a small circle was traced.

From this time we lose every evidence of the history of the temple up to nearly the middle of this century. But Mr. Newberry drew our attention to an extract among some manuscript notes by James Burton, in 1840,* and to two manuscript maps, in the British Museum, the one by Burton,† and the other by Hay.‡

The extract runs as follows :—

"A letter from M. Prisse at Thebes to Sir G. W[ilkinson] which he showed me on 23rd July, 1840, mentions the demolition of the ancient remains that had taken place at Thebes by permission of the Pasha's" (probably Mohammed Ali) "government . . . . A few small temples about the horse-shoe lake temple had been taken away to build a saltpetre manufactory. The first pylon S. of the great temple had been destroyed and Prisse was present at the demolition of the third."

Thus the temple which Sen-mut designed for Hatshepsut, which has held the records of the Pharaohs and the statues of their subjects, from the "great ones of the great" to the unknown and untitled, was carried off, by the orders of a barbaric pasha, to build a saltpetre manufactory. Doubtless the Arabs shared in the spoils, carrying off "the good white stone of Anu," and the marble of the Greek, polished stela and finely-sculptured statue, to burn for the enrichment of their fields.

The two maps are of great interest. Burton's

* Additional MS. 25,639, f. 43 (The Burton Papers).
† *Ibid.* 25,645, ff. 162, 163.
‡ *Ibid.* 29,825 B. (The Hay Papers.)

is the more complete and correct, therefore presumably the earlier. Hay makes the same error as Mariette in showing no gateway on the south of the three-chambered Ptolemaic building; otherwise all that he gives of the plan closely resembles Burton's. One must suppose that his plan was executed later than Burton's, when the pasha had demolished some of the remains of the temple. If otherwise, one can only think that the ruin caused by the earthquake obscured some points that the pasha's demolition made subsequently clear. Both maps were executed probably between 1830 and 1840.

There is still a fourth map, that of Lepsius,[*] drawn before Mariette's excavation, and referred to by him.

Burton's map is extremely interesting, and most careful. From this map we have taken in our own the position of the pillars of the outer court.

Burton shows no gateway (i) through the eastern brick wall of this court; this was probably blocked up. He marks the brick also as "crude brick."

The walls in the thickness of the eastern part of the second pylon he gives very much in the same way as Mariette, except that whereas Mariette marks the doorways of the two chambers which we have lettered *k* and *j* opposite to one another, Burton more correctly marks that of the chamber *k* as nearer to the great court.

He shows a door leading out of the north-western

[*] Lepsius, ' Denkmäler,' i. 83.

U

end of the longer chamber (*j*) into the great court. This Mariette and Hay also give, but we cannot substantiate it. As Hay's plan is however discrepant with the others in respect of the size of this chamber, and the door on passage-way (ii); as Lepsius does not give the door on to court A; and as at least two or three courses of the wall still exist above pavement level, we conclude that Mariette, Hay and Burton must have misinterpreted some indication of an opening other than a door higher up in the wall. It may be that the wall was too far destroyed to exhibit this when we came to excavate.

The western part of the same pylon Burton shows by dotted lines, marking a passage-way through it. This was where we found the air-bricks. This wall had been so completely destroyed that we had hesitated before rendering it by a solid line. On the evidence of Burton's map we have changed this to a dotted line, as we cannot consider its plan as certain.

Burton correctly shows that the parts of the pylon walls which are on the inside of the second court are of different building to the rest.

The interior of the second court and of the hypo-style hall is left unfinished; so far as it is done, it appears to correspond with our own; but the plan of this part was less evident than any other. Hay's plan is also doubtful here; those of Mariette and Lepsius incorrect. Burton's plan of the chambers in the upper part of the temple agrees with our plan, not with that of Mariette. The Ptolemaic building he leaves indefinite towards its northern end, correctly showing the two southern chambers and the gateway.

The sanctuary with its adjoining chambers and the colonnade that surrounds them, as well as Hay's and Lepsius's plan of the same part, are very much in accord with our own: Lepsius and Burton indicate, but doubtfully, a door in the southern wall of the colonnade, but Burton gives this as a mere guess. based on the conjectured use of the colonnade as a passage to the outer air so that the priests might perform their ablutions without passing through the sanctuary. There is no trace however of such a door, and the chamber z, which is backed against this wall, shows still the feet of figures in relief at this place.

Burton's plan of the surrounding temples gives one very interesting explanatory point. On the sandhills to the east of the temple, and almost opposite court A, where only one small painted chamber can now be seen, he indicates the plan of a temple of not inconsiderable size, having steps leading down towards the Temple of Mut. There is little doubt that these steps would lead to the sloping paved way and the gate (i) on the east of court A, which however Burton does not mark. What the date of this temple was, and the reason of its being in such close communication with the Temple of Mut, remains at present a mystery.

It is no doubt the demolition by the pasha which rendered the map made by Mariette so incorrect; when Hay and Burton planned the temple the walls were probably standing above ground. The demolition would reduce them to ground level, and Mariette had no time to excavate. What was of importance, he says, was to find out the plan accurately. Mariette evidently did not realise that the excavation he was able to do was insufficient for that purpose, but it is curious that he does not, like Burton and Hay, leave indefinite that which he had not time to ascertain. All is drawn out as if it were complete and certain.

Nevertheless, Mariette regrets that more excavation was not possible.

"The Temple of Mout," he says, in the 'Monuments of Upper Egypt,'* "has suffered more than any of those previously described, and we cannot help feeling a still deeper regret at the ruined state to which it has been reduced when we reflect that here we have an entire temple, with its surrounding wall, its pylons, sphinxes and sanctuary, and even its lake. . . ."

Bouriant, in his " Notes de Voyage," † says very plainly that any excavation would not be worth while. He deprecates the idea that even an approximate restoration can be arrived at, and adds that it would be necessary to " faire des fouilles assez coûteuses, et, à part le plan lui-même, ces fouilles ne donneraient que peu de résultats."

* 'The Monuments of Upper Egypt,' p. 185.
† 'Recueil,' xiii., p. 161.

But the results of the excavation—unforeseen indeed — must answer for themselves, and we at any rate did not find them unrewarding.   Although a complete examination, which should include the underpinning of walls for foundation-deposits, would be a costly business, our results— the clearance of the temple, the discovery of its real date, and of so large a number of statues—were obtained by a comparatively small expenditure of money, of time, and of labour.   The time spent on the work was less than six months, and our work-men were few indeed compared to the staff em-ployed on a professional excavation.

The little intimate touches of everyday life which so many of the inscriptions afforded, were a dearer remuneration of our work.   Throughout many cen-turies of the history of Egypt, during her strenuous rise, her magnificent empire, her painful decline, there were placed in this little temple statues of kings, princes, priests, ordinary citizens, whose inscriptions, formal and conventional though they are, often contain a touch of personal revelation. It is such hints of personality that focus clearly for us who look back at them across the ages, the figures of these distant pioneers of civilisation.   Whatever helps us to realise the primal influence of the world is of peculiar interest, for we know that in Egypt we stand at the source of western civilisation and of an influence that lies across our lives to-day.

In a hundred ways the Egyptian race has moulded

the things we see and hear.   The very "rudiments"
—στοιχεῖα, as the Greeks say—of life and language
flow from them.   Their fundamental ideas of art
are manifest in the forms with which the Greek has
clothed them.   Through the Israelite, their religious
language and symbols are in daily use, and the
children of Europe have their part in the inalienable
inheritance—stories of the tests of princes, of escapes
of a shipwrecked sailor, and of the blessings and
curses of fairy godmothers.

Truly the Egyptian has built for himself an
"eternal habitation" other than he designed, and
his Ka has still an embodiment more lasting than
sculptured granite, and a dwelling wider than tomb
or temple.   Of old, foundation - deposits — the
"ideas" of the building—were buried deep below
the temple, that the Kas of the builders might
rejoice in their work ; but to-day, not in temples
made with hands, not in the white courts and
colonnades of Sen-mut or Mentu-em-hat, not in the
mighty wreck of Apt and the ruins of Asher, do
the Kas inhabit—"why, where's the need of
temple when the walls o' the world are that"—
for in the life of the races that come after them
is their enduring home and monument—

>. . . . Monumentum aere perennius
>Regalique situ pyramidum altius
>Quod non imber edax, non Aquilo impotens
>Possit diruere, aut innumerabilis
>Annorum series et fuga temporum.

PART V.

INSCRIPTIONS.

I.

LOWER part of a seated figure of [hieroglyphs] Sa-Ra-Amen (? Amenemhat I.).* He sits upon a cube, wears a short tunic, and the hands are laid upon the knees. Upon the right side of the seat are four lines of hieroglyphs giving the *De ḥetep seten*† formula to Osiris that he may give *per-kheru* offerings for the *Ka* of Sa-Ra-Amen :—

(1) [hieroglyphs]

(2) [hieroglyphs]

(3) [hieroglyphs]

(4) [hieroglyphs]

Below this inscription is a roughly incised figure

---

* *Amen*, as a personal name, occasionally occurs as an abbreviated form of Amenemhat. See Newberry, 'Beni Hasan,' I., pl. viii., l. 3 ; *cf.* also *idem*, p. 25, note 3.

† Professor Erman has pronounced this formula to be unintelligible ('Grammar,' p. 40*), but on this and the group *per-kheru*, see Griffith, 'P.S.B.A.,' 1896, Nov., pp. 196 *et seq.*

of a man standing, and similar figures are incised upon the front of the seat on either side of the legs of Sa-Ra-Amen. A prayer to Anubis is inscribed upon the lap of the figure :—

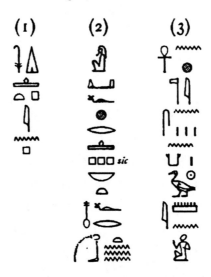

The figure and hieroglyphs are very rudely executed, and there can be no doubt that this statue dates from the early Middle Kingdom. Height, 1 foot 8 inches. Limestone. Found 1897, Trench B.

II.

Fragment of the base of a statuette, inscribed on the upper part with the name and titles of a certain *sem*-priest named Amen-

* The *sem*-priest, whose distinguishing garment was a leopard skin, officiated at funereal ceremonies. See 'Beni Hasan,' I., pls. xvii. and xxxv., upper row.

emhat-ankh.* 12th dynasty. Height, 3 inches.
Black granite. Found 1896, Plan no. 17.

III.

Lower part of a group of two figures (husband
and wife), seated side by side on a low chair. The
man is on the left side, and the inscription gives the
usual *De ḥetep seten* formula to [Amen ?] that he
may give *per-kheru* offerings for the benefit of the
Ka of . . . . † The inscription runs: [hieroglyphs] The female is named Aahmes, and upon her garment is
a line of hieroglyphs giving the *De ḥetep seten*
formula to Mut, Lady of Asher : [hieroglyphs] Early 18th
dynasty. Height, 10 inches. Limestone. Found
1897, Trench B.

IV.

Lower part of a small seated figure of the
goddess Mut (?), with a male child [cartouche]
Amenhetep I., seated upon her lap. On the chair
on either side of her feet are incised two vertical lines of hieroglyphs—that on the left giving

* Names compounded with the cartouches of Middle-Kingdom
monarchs are rare.
† The name is destroyed.

the prenomen of Amenhetep I. and "loved of Rannut, Lady of Heaven":— [hieroglyphs] [hieroglyphs] That on the right gives the nomen of Amenhetep I. and "beloved of Mut, mistress of the two lands":—

[hieroglyphs]

On the right side of the chair is, in incised relief, a seated figure of Queen Aahmes Nefertari. She wears a feathered crown with uraeus and is clad in a long skirt. In her left hand she holds the *uas* sceptre [symbol], in her right the symbol of life [symbol].

In four vertical lines above her is an inscription giving her name and titles:—

(1) [hieroglyphs]   (2) [hieroglyphs]

(3) [hieroglyphs]   (4) [hieroglyphs]

"The divine wife, and great royal consort, Aahmes Nefertari, beloved of Amen-Ra, living eternally."

On the left side of the chair is a figure of Princess Sat-Amen, similarly clad, and holding the same symbols. The inscription before and above her reads: [hieroglyphs] [hieroglyphs] "The royal daughter and royal sister, the divine wife, Sat-Amen, beloved of Mut, Lady of Asher, living eternally." Upon the back of the seat were several horizontal lines of hieroglyphs,

the six bottom ones alone remaining.   These give
the names of Amenhetep I. and the usual prayer or
wish for life, stability, etc.

Read :

Amenhetep I.   Height, 5 inches.   Limestone.
Found 1897, Trench C.

V.

Statue of Sen-mut, architect and favourite minister
of Queen Hatshepsut. The figure is represented
kneeling, holding before him a Hathor-headed
shrine. . The upper surface of the knees and
arms, both sides of the statue, the back, and

pedestal, are covered with inscriptions giving prayers for the deceased, his biography, with full titles, parentage and name. The hieroglyphs, which are incised, were filled in with red paint. The statue is 5 feet 2 inches in height, and is of red crystalline sandstone from Gebel Ahmar. Above the knees and arms are eleven lines of hieroglyphs reading as follows :—

(1) " Presented by favour of the Queen, the hereditary prince [the royal chancellor Sen-mut, justified].

(2) " Steward of the USERT-KAU, he who is within the heart of the Queen in Thebes, establishing their monuments,

(3) " to eternity, firm of favours before them daily,

(4) " the overseer of the fields of Amen, Sen-mut, justified.

(5) " The overseer of the garden of Amen, Sen-mut.

(6) " The overseer of the heifers of (7) Amen, Sen-mut, justified.

(8) " Chief steward of (9) Amen, Sen-mut, justified.

(10) " Chief steward of the Queen, Sen-mut, justified.

(11) " Chief over the slaves of Amen, Sen-mut."

On the back of the statue are twenty-two horizontal lines of hieroglyphs reading :

(1)

(2)

(3)

(4)

(5)

(6)

(7) [hieroglyphs]

(8) [hieroglyphs]

(9) [hieroglyphs]

(10) [hieroglyphs]

(11) [hieroglyphs]

(12) [hieroglyphs]

(13) [hieroglyphs]

(14) [hieroglyphs]

(15) [hieroglyphs]

(16) [hieroglyphs]

(17) [hieroglyphs]

(18) [hieroglyphs]

(19) [hieroglyphs]

(20) [hieroglyphs]

(21) [hieroglyphs]

(22) [hieroglyphs]

(1) "[Presented by favour] of the sovereign, the queen of Upper and Lower Egypt, RA-MAAT-KA, giving [life eternally].

(2) "[The hereditary prince], royal chancellor and friend, overseer of the house of Amen, Sen-mut, in order that he may be before

(3) "[Mut, Mistress of the] Sacred Lake, and in order that he may receive the offerings presented before the goddess [according to ?]

(4) " . . . the favours of the queen who lengthens the duration of time to eternity so that his memory might be good [before]

(5) "[the people] after years as they come, for the hereditary prince and overseer of the granaries of Amen, Sen-mut, justified.

(6) "[Praising] the chief steward Sen-mut, the architect of all the works of the queen in Karnak, in Erment, [in]

(7) "[Deir] el Bahari, in the temple of Mut in *Asher*, and in Luxor [before]

(8) " [the majesty] of this goddess, in establishing the monuments of the mistress of the two lands and in making great and establishing

(9) "the works; not was he deaf to the orders of the palace L.P.H.: what was commanded of him came into existence

(10) "immediately . . . the place of the heart of her majesty,

(11) "truly; there was not his equal; strong of heart without fainting upon the monuments of the gods, the royal chancellor and priest of Amen,

(12) "Sen-mut, he says: I am the great one of the great in the land to its extremity . . . steward of Amen,

(13) "Sen-mut, justified. I filled the heart of the queen in very truth, gaining the favour of his mistress daily, the overseer of the cattle of Amen, Sen-mut. I

(14) "was upright, not giving to one side, and the mistress of the two lands was pleased by that which came forth from her mouth, the *ari-nekhen* and Priest of Truth, Sen-mut. I entered in

(15) " . . . in praise and made wide the heart of the queen daily, the friend and regulator of the palace, Sen-mut. I made to flourish

(16) "the storehouses of the divine offerings every ten days, the overseer of the granaries of Amen, Sen-mut. I was leader of the guides

(17) "of the gods daily, the chieftainess L.P.H., the steward of Amen, Sen-mut. I was chief architect upon

(18) "all [the works] of the royal house, guiding all the handicrafts, and superintendent of all the priests of Mentu-em-Ant, Sen-mut.

(19) "The affairs of the two lands were reported to me, and I wielded the north and the south . . .

(20) " . . . I knew her (*i.e.* the queen's) comings in the royal house, and was beloved truly of the ruler, the overseer of the garden of Amen, Sen-[mut].

(21) "O ye who live upon the earth, ye hour-priests of the temple, when ye see my statue . . .

(22) "[repeat ye a prayer for funereal offerings] . . . "

On the left-hand side of the statue are fourteen lines of hieroglyphs giving prayers for the deceased, and reading:

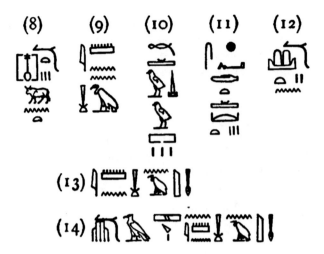

(1) "[May she (*i.e.* the goddess Mut) give] offerings of fine bread within the south to the *Ka* of the Great one of the Southern and the Northern Tens, Sen-mut.   May she give

(2) "delicacies within the northern country to the *Ka* of the Great one of the Great, the Noble of the Nobles,

(3) "Sen-Mut.   May she give all that which appears upon her altars in Karnak and

(4) "[in] the temples of the gods of the south and north to the *Ka* of the Chief over the secrets in the temples,

(5) "Sen-mut.   May she give mortuary gifts of bread and bees, oxen and wild-fowl, and draughts of the

(6) "pure water from mid-stream to the *Ka* of the chief steward of Amen, (7) Sen-mut, justified.

(8) "The overseer of the heifers of (9) Amen, Sen-mut,

(10) "who fills the storehouses (11) and replenishes the granaries,

(12) "the overseer of the granaries of (13) Amen, Sen-mut, justified.

(14) "The overseer of the gardens of Amen, Sen-mut, justified."

On the right-hand side of the statue are fifteen lines of hieroglyphs, giving titles of Sen-mut, together with his parentage and a prayer for a good burial in the western hill.

(1)

(2)

(3)

(4)

(5)

(6)

(7)

(8)　(9)　(10)　(11)　(12)　(13)

(14) 　　(15)

(1) . . . "the chief of the land to its extremity, the steward of Amen, Sen-mut, justified.

(2) "The chief steward of the queen, Sen-mut, devoted towards the great god

(3) " . . . Hathor, Chieftainess of Thebes, Mut, Mistress of the Sacred Lake,

(4) " . . . , Chieftainess L.P.H., the queen of Upper and Lower Egypt, RA-MAAT-KA, living eternally,

(5) "[Grant that they may give] a good burial in the western hill

(6) "[for the devoted] one towards the great god, for the *Ka* of the chief over the secrets in the great house, Sen-mut,

(7) "glorious in heaven, (8) strong on earth,

(9) "for the *Ka* of the Overseer of the temples (10) of Neith, Sen-mut,

(11) "made of Ra-mes, (12) born of Ha- (13) nefer,

(14) "Sen-mut, justified.

(15) "Overseer of the husbandmen of Amen, Sen-mut, justified."

On the upper surface of the pedestal are five lines of hieroglyphs, one on either side of the figure and three in the front. Those in the front of the figure read :

(1)

(2)

(3)

(1) " . . . before the people, the steward of Amen, Sen-mut, that it may be granted that he go forth

(2) "a living soul to smell the sweet scent of the north wind to the *Ka* of the steward of Amen, [Sen-mut,]

(3) "receiving . . . upon the altar of Amen in every festival of the [heaven and the earth?]."

On the left-hand side we read :

"May she grant a coming and a going in the divine land according to the following of truth to the *Ka* of the reporter, mouth of the King of Lower Egypt, glorious friend of the King of Upper Egypt."

On the right-hand side we read :

"To the *Ka* of . . . , strong of right arm, follower of the King upon the countries of the south, north, east, and west . . . , receiving the 'order' of the gold of favour."

Around the sides and front of the pedestal is the following line of hieroglyphs :—

"Sen-mut issuing forth as a living spirit, he follows each god . . . "

Queen Hatshepsut.   Height, 5 feet 2 inches.
Sandstone.   Found 1896, Plan no. 15.

Sen-mut was already known to Egyptologists
from other monuments.   His tomb in the Sheikh
Abd el Gurneh at Thebes was discovered by
Professor Steindorf and the present writer in the
spring of 1895 ; a famous statue of him is preserved
in the Berlin Museum, and an inscription cut on a
rock at Aswân records that it was he who directed
the work of cutting the two great obelisks afterwards
set up by Hatshepsut at Karnak.   His funereal
stela, also at Berlin, shows that he had charge of
the sacred cattle.   A cylinder with his name and
titles is at University College.   His staff, a limestone vase belonging to him, five glass beads
bearing his name, and several funereal cones from
his tomb are also preserved.   His portrait occurs
on one of the walls of the Southern Speos at Deir
el Bahari.   From the above-mentioned remains we
can glean many interesting facts relating to the life
of Hatshepsut's remarkable favourite.

The earliest of these monuments are the statue
at Berlin and the Aswân inscription.   The former
mentions him as being " Chief tutor of the royal
daughter Ra-neferu," the eldest child and heir of
Thothmes II. by Queen Hatshepsut ; the latter,
written about the sixteenth year of Hatshepsut's
reign, states that Sen-mut was then " Keeper of
Ra-neferu's palace."   The Berlin statue further
records that the names of Sen-mut's ancestors were

not then in writing—in other words, that he was of humble origin ; his parentage, however, is given on his later monuments, namely on his tomb, on his stela, and on the Benson statue. The Aswân inscription states that he went to the granite quarries to superintend the cutting of the two great obelisks at the express desire of the queen. The inscription on the Berlin statue, written in the first person, says : " I was a noble who loved his lord,* and I gained the favour of the mistress of the two lands. He exalted me before the face of the land to the rank of overseer of his house and purveyor of the land. I was chief over the chiefs, superintendent of the overseers of the works. I executed his orders in this land, I lived under the lady of the two lands, the Queen of Upper and Lower Egypt,. Ra-maat-ka, living eternally." Other titles which he held are given on his funereal cones, among them being " Priest of Amen," " Overseer of the cattle and fields of Amen," " Steward of the divine wife Hatshepsut," and " of the royal daughter Ra-neferu." A variant of the title " Overseer of the overseers of the works " is given in the inscription on the Benson statue. Sen-mut is there called " Regulator of the regulators of all the royal buildings," and the buildings themselves are further mentioned as being at Karnak, Erment, Deir el Bahari, the temple of

---

* The inscription, like many others of this reign, speaks of the queen sometimes in the masculine and sometimes in the feminine gender.

Mut in *Asher*, and the temple of Luxor.   Like the
architects of the Middle Ages he was a skilled
workman himself, and "he guided all the handicrafts."   He was not, however, merely architect
and engineer, but also confidential adviser and
magistrate, "not giving to one side [more favour
than to the other side]."   Although he is nowhere
expressly mentioned as being vezîr of the queen,
the titles *ari-nekhen* and "Priest of Truth," found
in the Benson statue, would seem to imply that he
held that much coveted position.

VI.

Standing figure of the 𓏞𓀭𓈖𓏌 "High priest
of Amen," 𓂝𓅯𓏏𓆇 Hapu-senb.   He is represented wearing a short kilt; the left leg is thrust
slightly forward, and the arms are pendant, with the
hands flat on the thighs.   Upon the base or pedestal
are incised six lines of hieroglyphs, one horizontal,
the rest vertical, giving the *De ḥetep seten* (1) to
[Amen,] "Lord of the thrones of the two lands,"
(5) to [Mut, "Lady of Asher]u," to Sekhet-aat,
"Mistress of the two lands," and to Bast, "Mistress
of Ankh-taui," that they may give *per-kheru* and
other offerings for the benefit of the *Ka* of Hapu-
senb.   The inscription runs:

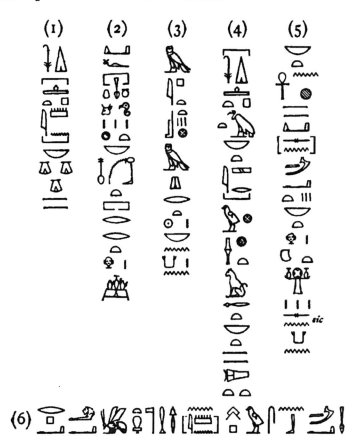

The figure is supported at the back by a slab of stone, cut like a stela, and inscribed with fifteen horizontal lines of hieroglyphs giving the name and titles of Hapu-senb. The defaced cartouche in l. 11 is undoubtedly that of ⬭ Ra-maat-ka, Queen Hatshepsut.*

* Upon a squatting statue of Hapu-senb in the Louvre is the cartouche of ⬭ Thothmes II., but upon his cenotaph at Gebel Silsileh (see Griffith, 'P.S.B.A.,' 1889, p. 108) is the cartouche of Ra-maat-ka. His tomb is in the Sheikh Abd el Gurneh at Thebes, and several funereal cones from it are preserved (cf. Daressy, 'M.M.F.,' viii., Fasc. 2, No. 230).

The back of the statue, shaped to represent a
stela, is inscribed with the following text :—

Queen Hatshepsut.   Height, 2 feet 9 inches.
Black granite.   Found 1897, Trench B.

VII.

Kneeling figure of the 〖hieroglyphs〗 "second priest
of Amen," 〖hieroglyphs〗 Pu-am-ra,* son of the 〖hieroglyph〗
doctor 〖hieroglyphs〗 Pu-am.   He is represented clad in
a short tunic, with the arms resting upon the thighs,
and holding in his upturned hands small ♉-shaped
vases.   Down the centre of his skirt is a vertical
line of hieroglyphs giving his name and titles,
reading :

〖hieroglyphs〗

On the upper surface of the pedestal, in front of
the figure, is an inscription also giving the owner's
name and titles :

(1) 〖hieroglyphs〗

(2) 〖hieroglyphs〗

* Pu-am-ra, whose statue is here dated in the reign of Hatshepsut, lived on into the reign of Thothmes III.   His tomb,
discovered by Dümichen in the Assassîf at Thebes, contains

The continuation of this inscription is found on the front and two sides of the pedestal. It records that he superintended (1) the erection of a "great ebony shrine inlaid with electrum," and (2) the building of a chapel (?) "in good white limestone," both given by Queen Ra-maat-ka (Hatshepsut) in honour of "her mother, the goddess Mut, Lady of Asheru." The inscription runs:

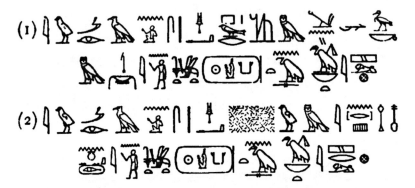

The back of the figure is supported by a slab of stone inscribed with three vertical lines of hieroglyphs giving the *De ḥetep seten* formula to Amen, "Lord of Heaven," and Mut, "Lady of Asheru," that they may give "all that which appears upon their altars and their daily favours" for the *Ka* of Pu-am-ra.

———————

some of the most beautiful sculpture to be found in Egypt. It has been copied and will shortly be published by the present writer. A fragment of a statue of the same individual is also preserved at Florence.

(1)   (2)   (3)

Queen Hatshepsut. Height, 1 foot 8 inches.
Black granite. Found 1897, Trench B.

VIII.

Statuette of a [glyph] "Superintendent of
the inner chamber" (? "cabinet") named [glyph]

Min-hetep, son of ⟨hieroglyphs⟩ Bethu. The figure
is represented squatting, with the arms crossed over
the knees, and the name of the ⟨hieroglyphs⟩
"divine wife Ra-neferu,* living," is incised upon
the wrists. Down the front of the legs are one
vertical and seven horizontal lines of hieroglyphs
giving the *De ḥetep seten* formula to Mut, "that she
may give all that appears upon her altar and all
fine breads and delicacies" for the benefit of the *Ka*
of Minhetep :—

(1) ⟨hieroglyphs⟩

(2) ⟨hieroglyphs⟩ (9) ⟨hieroglyphs⟩

(3) ⟨hieroglyphs⟩

(4) ⟨hieroglyphs⟩

(5) ⟨hieroglyphs⟩

(6) ⟨hieroglyphs⟩

(7) ⟨hieroglyphs⟩

(8) ⟨hieroglyphs⟩

* The Princess Ra-neferu was the eldest daughter of Thothmes II. and Hatshepsut. She must have died young, before the
adolescence of Thothmes III. Her portrait at Deir el Bahari has
been recently destroyed, but a drawing of it was made by Champollion in 1828, and published by him in his 'Monuments.'

† ⟨hieroglyph⟩ occasionally occurs as a monogram for ⟨hieroglyphs⟩
Cf. 'Beni Hasan,' I., pl. xxvi., l. 188.

Upon the right side of the figure is incised [hieroglyphs] "The superintendent of the inner chamber, Min-hetep, son of Bethu, justified." On the left side is recorded the name of his mother [hieroglyphs] Abu, [hieroglyphs] Two vertical lines run down the back of the statuette, but the upper parts of both are destroyed:

(1) [hieroglyphs]   (2) [hieroglyphs]

On the base of the statuette the names of Min-hetep's mother and father are again given: [hieroglyphs] "his father Bethu, justified," and [hieroglyphs] "his mother Abu, justified."

Queen Hatshepsut. Height, 9 inches. Black granite. Found 1896, Trench A.

IX.

Lower part of a statuette of a [hieroglyphs] "Superintendent of the treasury," named [hieroglyphs] Senemaah,† son of the [hieroglyph] "doctor," [hieroglyphs] Uazmes.

* Cf. the common formula, 'Recueil,' vii. 127, and Brugsch, 'Wortb.' Sup. 88.

† The tomb of Senemaah, the son of Uazmes by the lady Aahmes, is in the Sheikh Abd el Gurneh at Thebes. The sculpture is of a very fine order; and an inscription in it states that it was executed by his son Pïaay, "chief sculptor of the temple of Amen," and completed early in the reign of Thothmes III.

The figure is represented in a squatting posture, with the hands crossed over the knees. Down the front of the legs are seven horizontal lines of hieroglyphs giving the *De ḥetep seten* formula to Khonsu of Thebes, "that he may give all that which appears upon his altar" for the *Ka* of Senemaah :—

(1) [hieroglyphs]

(2) [hieroglyphs]

(3) [hieroglyphs]

(4) [hieroglyphs] *sic*

(5) [hieroglyphs]

(6) [hieroglyphs]

(7) [hieroglyphs]

Around the pedestal or base are two inscriptions, both beginning from the front, one reading from right to left, the other from left to right. The right line (1) gives the *De ḥetep seten* formula to Anubis, "that he may give glorification, power, and justification" to the *Ka* of Senemaah. The left line (2) gives the same prayer to Osiris, "That he may give all that which appears upon his altar."

(1) [hieroglyphs]

(2) [hieroglyphs]

Thothmes III. Height, 1 foot 1½ inches. Black granite. Found 1896, Trench A.

X.

Statuette of a [hieroglyph] "superintendent of the granaries," named [hieroglyph] Min-nekht.* The figure is represented sitting on a plain seat and clad in a long kilt reaching to the ankles. On the right-hand side of the seat are five vertical lines of hieroglyphs giving the *De ḥetep seten* formula to Khonsu, that he may give food for the *Ka* of Min-nekht.

* Of Min-nekht several monuments are known. His cenotaph, dated in the reign of Thothmes III., is at Gebel Silsileh (*cf.* 'P.S.B.A.' 1889, p. 104), and his tomb is at Thebes. Another statuette of him is preserved at Gizeh, and two pallets bearing his name are known : one is at Gizeh, the other was formerly in the Hay collection. Several funereal cones from his tomb are also preserved. His name occurs several times in a papyrus now in the Louvre, dated in the twenty-eighth to thirty-fourth years of Thothmes III.

(1)	(2)	(3)	(4)	(5)

On the left side of the seat are likewise five vertical lines of hieroglyphs, also giving the *De hetep seten* formula to Khonsu :—

(1)	(2)	(3)	(4)	(5)

Upon the pedestal or column supporting the figure at the back is a vertical line recording two titles of Min-nekht: the one, "the eyes of the king in the south country"; the other, "his ears in the districts of the north."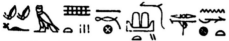

Thothmes III. Height, 1 foot 2 inches. Black granite. Found 1896, Trench A.

XI.

Group of two figures seated side by side on a low chair or cube. The right-hand figure is of a "doctor" named ⟨⟩ Tahuti-shera; the left figure, his wife ⟨⟩ Thent-nub. Both personages are clad in tight-fitting garments characteristic of the middle 18th dynasty. Upon the knees of the male figure is incised the name ⟨⟩; on those of the female ⟨⟩ ⟨⟩ The inscriptions on the right side of the chair are entirely defaced; on the left side are six vertical lines of hieroglyphs giving the *De hetep seten* formula (l. 1) to Amen-Ra, (l. 2) to Mut and "the gods and goddess within Karnak," that they may give *per-kheru* offerings for the *Ka* of Thent-nub. The last line records that the group was sculptured at the order of Thent-nub's son the *uab*-priest Aahmes.

On the upper side of the pedestal between the two figures and on the right-hand side of the same is a short inscription giving the *De ḥetep seten* formula to Amen and Mut, "that they may give thousands of all things" to the *Ka* of Tahuti-shera.

18th Dynasty {Thothmes III.? / Amenhetep II.?} Height, 1 foot 2½ inches. Limestone. Found 1896, Trench A.

XII.

Statue of the ⟨glyph⟩ "royal scribe" ⟨glyph⟩ Amenemhat, son of the ⟨glyph⟩ "royal scribe Antef" by the ⟨glyph⟩ "Lady of the house Mut-em-ua-sat." He is represented squatting, with the arms crossed over the knees, and in the right hand holds a lotus flower. Upon the right shoulder is incised the prenomen of Amenhetep II. ⟨cartouche⟩ and over the right breast his nomen ⟨cartouche⟩ Around the front of the statue below the knees are eight horizontal lines of hieroglyphs giving the *De hetep seten* formulæ : (1) to "Amen-Ra, king of the gods, that he may give a good life full of favours and a good old age" for the *Ka* of Amenemhat ; (2) to Tem, lord of Heliopolis ; (3) to Ptah ; and (4) to Osiris, that they may give him all kinds of offerings. The fifth line gives the *De hetep seten* formula to [Mut] in Karnak, that she may give offerings from " all her festivals of heaven and earth " for the benefit of Amenemhat's *Ka*. The whole inscription reads :

(2) [hieroglyphs]

(3) [hieroglyphs]

(4) [hieroglyphs]

(5) [hieroglyphs]

(6) [hieroglyphs]

(7) [hieroglyphs]

(8) [hieroglyphs]

Amenhetep II.   Height, 2 feet 8 inches.   Black granite.   Found 1895, Plan no. 1.

XIII.

Kneeling figure of the [hieroglyphs] "super-intendent of the cattle of Amen," [hieroglyphs] Amen-

Ḳen. He holds before him a small shrine with

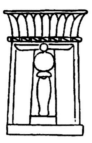

elaborate cornice, and bearing an inscription on
either side of the shrine entrance (1 and 2) giving
the cartouche and titles of Amenhetep II. :—

Upon the right side of the figure are five vertical
lines of hieroglyphs giving the *De ḥetep seten* to
Mut-urt, "Lady of Asheru and mistress of all the
gods," that she may give "her favours in the house
of the King" for the benefit of the *Ka* of Amen-
Ḳen :—

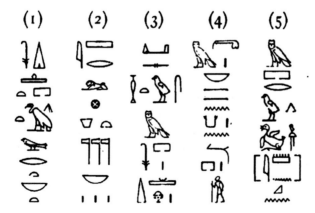

Upon the left side is a similar inscription to Mut,

" Mistress of heaven and of the two lands," that she may give "a good time within Thebes" for the *Ka* of Amen-Ḳen :—

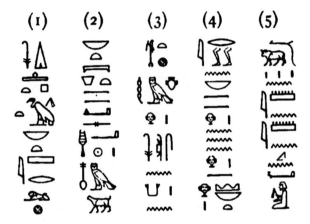

Amenhetep II.   Height, 1 foot 3 inches.   Black granite.*   Found 1897, Trench C.

XIV.

Statuette of the "king's son" Tahuti-mes.†   He is represented kneeling, and holding

* The tomb of Amen-Ḳen, situated high up in the southern slope of the Sheikh Abd el Gurneh at Thebes, contains some of the most elaborate and beautiful painting to be found in Egypt. Several scenes from it have been published ; notably the fine series of new year presents (L. D. iii. 63a) and the portrait of the young king Amenhetep II. seated on the knee of his nurse, Amen-Ḳen's wife.   Several funereal cones are known (Newberry collection).

† The small hard white-limestone statuette of the "Royal Son" Thothmes must date from the reign of Thothmes IV.   This prince is only otherwise known to us from a scarab in the Tyszkiewicz collection.   It is important to note as evidence of

before him a Hathor-headed shrine, upon the top
of which is inscribed :—

" All that which appears upon the altar of the Lady
of the [Sacred] Lake for the *Ka* of the king's son
Tahutimes."

Upon the pedestal of the shrine is the name of
the goddess Mut, Lady of Asheru, The base of the statuette is also inscribed.   The
name of Tahutimes and that of Heq-er-shu,
" the tutor of the royal children," are incised upon the
upper surface of it, whilst around the base are two
De ḥetep seten formulae, both to Mut, that she may
give (1) "life, prosperity and health," and (2) "a
watchful heart (?)" for the benefit of Tahutimes.
These inscriptions read :—

Upper surface of base : and

the date of this statuette that the "Tutor of the royal child,
Heq-er-shu," is named on the base of it : his name also occurs in
the tomb of Heq-er-nehêh, the tutor of the elder son of
Thothmes IV., Amenhetep, afterwards the great king Amenhetep III.

Around base :

(1) [hieroglyphs]

[hieroglyphs]

(2) [hieroglyphs]

[hieroglyphs]

Thothmes IV.* Height, 1 foot. Crystalline lime-stone.   Found 1896, Trench A.

XV.

Squatting figure of a [hieroglyphs] "super-intendent of the heifers of Anhur," named [hieroglyphs] Meryti.   He wears a kilt, and the arms are crossed, in the usual fashion of such figures, over the knees.   Upon the right shoulder is incised the cartouche [hieroglyphs] Ra - men - kheperu ;   upon the left [hieroglyphs] Tahutimes-Kha-khau (Thothmes IV.).   Across the front of the legs is an inscription, in five horizontal lines, giving the *De ḥetep seten* formula (1) to Amen-Ra, "lord of the thrones of the two lands," (2) to Mut, "Lady of

* See note (†) page 328.

Asheru," and (3) to "the cycle of gods of Karnak,"
for the benefit of Meryti.   It reads :

(1) [hieroglyphs]

(2) [hieroglyphs]

(3) [hieroglyphs]

(4) [hieroglyphs]

(5) [hieroglyphs]

Upon the right side of the figure below the knee
is a single line of hieroglyphs giving one of the
principal titles and name of Meryti, [hieroglyphs]
[hieroglyphs].   Upon the left side is a similar line
reading : [hieroglyphs]

The column supporting the figure at the back is
inscribed with the title of the high priest of Osiris (?)
and name of Meryti : [hieroglyphs]

Thothmes IV.   Height, 2 feet 1 inch.   Sandstone.   Found 1897, Trench B.

XVI.

Statuette of a [hieroglyphs] "scribe of recruits," named
[hieroglyphs] Men.   He is represented kneeling and
holding a Hathor-headed shrine, upon the top

of which is inscribed the prenomen of (image of cartouche)
Amenhetep III., and the name of the goddess
(image) Mut. Upon the pedestal of the shrine is
(image) "Mut, Mistress of Asher," and
upon either side of the same the inscriptions—

Around the base of the figure are two *De ḥetep seten* formulae, one (1) to Sekhet and Uazet, that they may give "offerings of food," the other (2) to Mut, "that she may give all that appears upon her altar daily," for the *Ka* of Men :—

(1) (hieroglyphs)

(2) .... (hieroglyphs)

Upon the pedestal supporting the figure at the back is a vertical line of hieroglyphs giving a *De ḥetep seten* formula "for thousands of all good and pure things" for "the royal scribe and scribe of recruits, Men." It reads :

Amenhetep III. Height, 1 foot 8 inches. Black granite. Found 1896, Trench A.

XVII.

Statuette of a "Prince of Thebes," named Maŷ. He is represented squatting, with the hands crossed over the knees. On the front of the legs are incised two vertical lines of hieroglyphs giving the name and titles of Maŷ :—

(1)   (2)

Upon the back of the statuette are two similar inscriptions :—

(1)   (2)

Around the base run two inscriptions, both beginning in front, one reading from right to left, the other from left to right :—

(1)

(2)

The first line gives the *De ḥetep seten* formula to Mut, "that she may give a good life in her temple daily" to Maŷ; the second gives the same formula "that she may give a good time in Thebes."

18th Dynasty (Amenhetep III. ?).   Height, 1 foot 1 inch.   Crystalline limestone.   Found 1896, Trench A.

XVIII.

Fragment of a double statuette of a "fourth priest of Amen" (cf. l. 2) and his wife (?). The figures were represented standing side by side, but only a small part of the centre portion of the statuette is preserved. On the back are the remains of thirteen vertical lines of hieroglyphs reading :

18th dynasty (? Amenhetep III.).   Height,
10 inches.   Crystalline limestone.   Found 1897,
Plan no. 9.

XIX.

Seated figure of a ⟨hieroglyph⟩ "scribe" named ⟨hieroglyph⟩ Thuthà. He is clad in a kilt reaching halfway down the leg, and the hands are laid flat upon the knees. The seat upon which he sits is plain. Supporting the back of the figure is a slab of stone inscribed with five vertical lines of hieroglyphs, giving in the first two lines the *De hetep seten* formula to Amen-Ra, "chieftain of the two lands, within Karnak," that he may give *per-kheru* offerings "of all good and pure things which heaven gives or the earth produces or which are brought down by the Nile from his caverns," for the *Ka* of Thuthà. In the third line Thuthà, speaking in the first person, says : " I am cool [in temperament?] of his [the king's] town and silent in his house ; I keep the fear of my god and the king in my heart, the reverence of my lord in my limbs until I reach the [good] old age which they [the gods] give." These five lines run :—

(1)	(2)	(3)	(4)	(5)

Two other prayers are given on the pedestal or base of the figure : that on the left side giving the *De ḥetep seten* formula to [Amen-Ra,] "king of the gods," and to Osiris, "Lord of Dadu"; that on the right, to Amen-Ra, "Lord of the thrones of the two worlds," and to Osiris, "Lord of Abydos." Both these prayers are for *per-kheru* offerings for the *Ka* of Thuthä.   These inscriptions read :

End of the 18th dynasty. Height, 1 foot. Limestone. Found 1897, Trench A.

The personal name Thuthà is very rare. There
is a stela of a scribe bearing this name preserved in
the Louvre (No. 414) and bearing the cartouche of

[☓☓☓] Hor-men-ka.   A chamberlain of Aẙ
(Stela, Brit. Mus. 211) also bore the name, and it
is probably to about this period, the end of the
18th dynasty, that the above statue belongs.

XX.

Lower part of a squatting figure of a [☓☓] "royal
scribe," named [☓☓] Rẙ. The arms are represented
crossed over the knees and the right hand holds a
leathern thong.   The head and part of the pedestal
are destroyed.   Around the front of the figure is
incised an inscription of seven horizontal lines of
hieroglyphs giving in lines 1–3 the *De ḥetep seten*
formula to "Amen-ra, Lord of the thrones of the
two worlds and of eternity, to Mut-urt, Lady of
Asher, beautiful of face and rising in gold, to Khonsu
of Thebes and all the gods and goddesses of Thebes,
to Osiris within the West, to Anubis within the
temple, and to the goddess Hathor, that they may
give thousands of loaves of bread and of all good
and pure things upon which the gods live," that they
may give these things "daily and on each monthly,
half-monthly and every other festival of heaven and
earth," for the benefit of the *Ka* of the "royal scribe
of the Lord of the two lands [the Pharaoh] Rẙ."
The inscription which follows is much mutilated ; it
apparently gives an exhortation (ll. 3, 4) to "all

people upon earth" to worship Amen, Mut and Khonsu (the Theban triad), and ends autobiographically (ll. 6, 7): "I was just and free of evil; .. I went out upon the ... of the gods; I reached a good old age with daily favours and an excellent heart and pure hands."

The seven lines of hieroglyphs run :—

(1)

(2)

(3)

(4)

(5)

(6)

(7)

19th dynasty.   Height, 1 foot 6 inches.   Black
granite.   Found 1897, Plan no. 22.

XXI.

Statue of a [hieroglyphs] high priest of Amen

named [hieroglyphs] Bak-en-Khonsu, son of the

[hieroglyphs] "superintendent of the recruits of

the house of Amen," [hieroglyphs] Amen-em-apt.

The figure is represented squatting
with the arms crossed over the knees.
Across the wrists are the cartouches
of Rameses III.   Around the knees
is a single horizontal line of hieroglyphs giving the name, titles and
parentage of Bak-en-Khonsu :

[hieroglyphs]

[hieroglyphs] Down the front of the legs are five

vertical lines of hieroglyphs giving (ll. 1 and 2) the
name and titles of Bak-en-Khonsu ; and (ll. 3–5) the
De ḥetep seten formula to "Amen-Ra, Lord of
the thrones of the two worlds, within Karnak, and
king of the gods, to Mut-urt, Lady of Asheru, to
Khonsu, of Thebes, and to Tahuti, Lord of the
Southern Ȧn, that they may give thousands of all
good and pure things" for the *Ka* of Bak-en-
Khonsu.

(1)   (2)   (3)   (4)   (5)

Rameses III. Height, 4 feet 4 inches. Lime-stone. Found 1896, Plan no. 16.

The statue of Bak-en-Khonsu is of great interest, and the fact that it bears the cartouche of Rameses III. is of importance. Bak-en-Khonsu was already known from other monuments. His tomb is preserved in the Drah abu'l Neggah at Thebes, and his sarcophagus is in the Liverpool Museum. A famous statue of him is in the Glyptothek at Munich, and on it is given a remarkably full record of his biography. From this inscription we read that he was "four years in extreme infancy," and "twelve years in youth," that he was then (at the age of sixteen) made a steward by Seti I. At the same time he was appointed priest of Amen, which position he held for four years, and was then promoted to the rank of divine father of Amen, a post which he filled for twelve years. The inscription further records that he was "third prophet of Amen" for fifteen years, "second prophet of Amen" for twelve years, and when the statue at Munich (dated by the cartouches of Rameses II.) was made he had been "first prophet" for twenty-seven years. Adding these numbers together we get a total of eighty-six years, at which age it would appear that the Munich statue was executed. Supposing therefore that he was made a steward by Seti I. at the age of sixteen and in the twenty-fourth year of that king's reign, the Munich statue must have been executed in the last

year of the reign of Rameses II.* Supposing
therefore that he was eighty-six years of age at the
time of Rameses II.'s death, we must add at least
another fourteen years† to bring him even to the
first year of Rameses III., the king whose cartouche
we find engraved on the Benson statue. This
would give him at the very least a total age of one
hundred. On the Munich statue he prays that he

---

* If Bak-en-Khonsu was made a steward by Seti I. after the
age of sixteen then the Munich statue would probably have
borne the cartouches of a later sovereign than Rameses II., for
from the time of his having been made a steward by Seti I. to the
time of the Munich statue we get seventy years, which is three
more years than the entire length of the reign of Rameses II. It
is more probable that he was promoted to the position of steward
three years before the death of Seti I. This would give the
following dates :—

8th Seti I.—born.

24th Seti I.—made steward and second priest of Amen.

27th—Seti I. dies and is succeeded by Rameses II.

1st Rameses II.—attains rank of divine father.

13th Rameses II.—is made third prophet.

28th Rameses II.—is promoted to be second prophet.

40th Rameses II.—attains rank of first prophet. (That he was
already "first prophet" in 46th Rameses II. is proved from a
papyrus; see 'A. Z.' 1879, p. 72.) This position he still held
when in the

67th Rameses II.—the statue was executed and Rameses II.
died.

† Rameses II. was succeeded by five kings who altogether
reigned fourteen years, perhaps even thirty years. Then came
Rameses III., whose cartouche is engraved on the Benson statue.
Fourteen years at least must therefore be added to the eighty-six
already attained by the veteran Bak-en-Khonsu at the death of
Rameses II., which gives his age, at the very lowest computation,
one hundred years.

might attain the grand old age of one hundred and ten years.* It is quite possible that this prayer was granted, for, as has been seen, he was still flourishing, at one hundred at the very least, when the Benson statue was executed.

XXII.

Group of two figures seated side by side ; in two fragments both very much mutilated. On the right side is the figure of a woman with a mutilated inscription down her skirt reading :

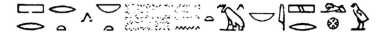

Upon the kilt of the second figure, a man, is another mutilated inscription giving his name  Sa-mut. The slab supporting the figures and seat at the back is almost entirely destroyed. Upon the base is given a prayer for "thousands of all good and pure things" for the *Ka* of the *u.ib*-priest Sa-mut :—

* This prayer is given in the inscription covering the lower part of the statue. It runs: "May he [*i.e.* Amen] bestow upon me a happy existence of one hundred and ten years."

By the side of the feet of the figure of the woman is her title ⟨hieroglyphs⟩ "chantress of Amen," ⟨hieroglyphs⟩ Baky.

20th dynasty.   Height, 1 foot 11 inches.   Limestone.   Found 1897, Trench B.

XXIII.

Mutilated double statue representing a man named Sa-mut, clad in long skirt, and at his side a female whose name is destroyed. Perhaps they are the same individuals as represented in No. XXII. The inscriptions are very much mutilated; down the skirt of the right figure was apparently a prayer for offerings, ending with the name ⟨hieroglyphs⟩ "Sa-mut, justified." On the left figure was a prayer to ⟨hieroglyphs⟩ "Mut, Mistress of Asheru."

19th dynasty (?).   Height, 1 foot 6 inches. Limestone.   Found 1897, Trench B.

XXIV.

Lower part of a seated figure of a woman (?). The feet, part of the legs, and right side of the seat are alone preserved. Upon the right side of the chair

are represented three figures in incised relief. Over
the first are three vertical lines reading :

"to the *Ka* of the favoured of the place of his heart,
Nekht-Amen." Over the second figure is the name
Nefermenu ; and over the third the
name Aa-em-ab. Space is left for a
fourth figure, but it was never finished ; only the
name, Isis, has been cut by the sculptor.

On the right side of the right leg of the seated
figure is a small figure in relief of a man represented
clad in a short tunic and holding a lotus flower over
his breast. The inscription above him reads :
"Her son, her beloved
one, the sculptor Bak-en-Amen."

20th or 21st dynasty. Height, 1 foot 5 inches.
Limestone. Found 1897, Trench B.

XXV.

Fragment of the arm of a statue of Uapt, son of
Sheshanq I. It bears a mutilated inscription which
may with certainty be restored thus :

" Uapt, justified, son of the Lord of the two lands Sheshanq I., beloved of Amen."

The titles borne by this prince were—

"High priest of Amen-Ra, king of the gods, general of the soldiers."

He is mentioned also in the temple of Karnak.

Sheshanq I. Length, 8 in. Alabaster. Found 1897, Trench A.

XXVI.

1. Squatting figure of the "fourth priest of Amen," and "*Ha*-prince of Thebes," Mentu-em-hat. The face and upper part of the head are destroyed, and the

statue is broken across immediately below the knees.
He is represented wearing a beard and elaborately
curled wig; his arms are crossed above the knees,
and across them is a single vertical line of hieroglyphs, recording that he "restored the temple of

Mut" : [hieroglyphs]   Before him he holds
a Hathor-headed shrine of the usual kind (cf. shrine
of the statue of Sen-mut), down which is incised
a prayer to Mut "that she may give a good life
and stability in her temple to the *ha*-prince of

Thebes, Mentu-em-hat" : [hieroglyphs]

[hieroglyphs]   Around the legs are incised twenty-two horizontal lines of inscription,
eleven on the right side and a corresponding
number on the left. Those on the right side give
the *De ḥetep seten* formula to (l. 1) "[Amen, ...]
Mentu, Lord of Thebes, Mut, Lady of Heaven,
Khonsu and [all the gods] (l. 2) within Karnak
that they may give all kinds of good offerings
for the benefit of Mentu-em-hat's *Ka*. In ll. 3
and 4 several important titles borne by Mentu-
em-hat are given, among them being those of

[hieroglyphs] "great chief of the Temple," [hieroglyphs]

"instructor of the priests," [hieroglyphs] "scribe
of the temple of the house of Amen," and "*Ha*-
prince of Thebes ([hieroglyphs]) to its entirety." In
ll. 5-8, Mentu-em-hat exhorts all "priests, divine

fathers, *uab*-priests and scribes" to repeat the
formula given in ll. 1-4. In ll. 9-11 he records
that he was a "perfect noble and a true veteran in
the service of the gods of Thebes," that he looked
after "the festivals of Thebes," and erected a
temple to the goddess Mut, Lady of Heaven,
"in good white limestone (?)."   This inscription
reads :

(1)

(2)

(3)

(4)

(5)

(6)

(7) [hieroglyphs]

(8) [hieroglyphs]

(9) [hieroglyphs]

(10) [hieroglyphs]

(11) [hieroglyphs]

Upon the left side is (ll. 1–3) the *De ḥetep seten* formula to " Mut-urt, Lady of Asher, Lady of Heaven, and Mistress of the gods," that she may give "*per-kheru* offerings at the monthly and half-monthly festivals, and at all festivals of heaven and earth daily." for Mentu-em-hat. Ll. 4–6 are much mutilated. Another prayer to Mut for " all good and pure things " is given in l. 7. Ll. 9–11 record that Mentu-em-hat " made great her (Mut's) altars, spread her fire (?), and provisioned her house in all [good] things"; that he was " great of monu-

ments in Thebes and great of glory in the Southern
Country" (Upper Egypt).   The inscription runs :—

(1) [hieroglyphs]

(2) [hieroglyphs]

(3) [hieroglyphs]

(4) [hieroglyphs]

(5) [hieroglyphs]

(6) [hieroglyphs]

(7) [hieroglyphs]

(8) [hieroglyphs]

(9) [hieroglyphs]

(10) [hieroglyphs]

(11) [hieroglyphs]

The pedestal or base upon which the figure squats is also inscribed. On either side of the feet are recorded the name and titles of Mentu-em-hat. The line on the right side gives the interesting title ⌐⌐ "*heq*-prince of the hills or desert"; that on the left ⌐⌐ "superintendent of the frontier."

Right-hand side :

Left-hand side :

Around the pedestal at the front and on either side of the statue runs an inscription giving the *De ḥetep seten* formula to "Amen, Mentu, Tem, Horakhuti, Mut, and the divine cycle of gods within the temple of Mut," that they may give "*perkheru* offerings" for the benefit of the *Ka* of Mentu-em-hat.

Front :

Right side :

Left side :

Reign of Taharqa.   Height, 3 feet 8 inches.
Black granite.   Found : Upper part, 1896, Plan
no. 24 ; Lower part, 1897, Plan no. 25.

Of Mentu-em-hat, the ⸻ " Prince of Thebes "
under Taharqa, several other monuments are
known.   His tomb, with massive crude brick pylons
and surrounding walls, is in the Assassîf not far
from the temple of Deir el Bahari (Schiel, 'M.A.F.,'
t. v.).   A fragment of bas-relief from one of its
walls is in the Florence Museum (Schiap., 'Cat.,'
No. 1590). Crude bricks stamped with his name and
titles still lie in hundreds about the Assassîf. Terra-
cotta cones with various inscriptions from the same
tomb are preserved in several of the principal museums
of Europe (Daressy, 'M.A.F.,' viii., Fasc. 2, Nos. 174,
175, 193, etc.).   A broken *ushabti* figure in blue
glaze, from Mentu-em-hat's tomb, is in the possession of Miss Gourlay, and another in greyish-green

granite is in Miss Benson's collection. A fragment
of granite bearing his name was in the Grant collection (*cf.* 'Rec. de travaux,' viii., p. 67). A statue of
him is in the British Museum, and an inscription
recording his restoration of the Theban temples is
incised upon the walls of a small chamber in the
temple of Mut (Mariette, 'Karnak,' pl. 47). He is
referred to among the vassal princes of Egypt on a
cylinder of Assurbanipal, and his name occurs in
an inscription at Medinet Habu (E. de Rougé,
'Mélanges d'Arch.,' t. i., pp. 19–21). From these
monuments we learn the following names of various
members of his family :—

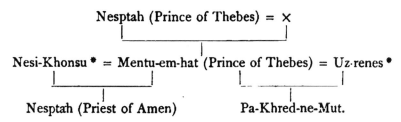

Nesptah (Prince of Thebes) = ×

Nesi-Khonsu * = Mentu-em-hat (Prince of Thebes) = Uz-renes *

Nesptah (Priest of Amen)   Pa-Khred-ne-Mut.

2. Head of a ⸻ "fourth priest of Amen,"
and ⸻ "*Ha*-prince of Thebes." Unfortunately, the name of this remarkable individual is
not preserved. The head, however, is undoubtedly
of the Saïte period, and from the fact that he bears
the rare title of fourth priest of Amen combined
with that of the *ha*-prince of Thebes, it is extremely probable that it represents the celebrated
Mentu-em-hat of the reign of Taharqa. (See *supra*,
No. XXVI. 1). The column supporting the figure

at the back is inscribed with six vertical lines of
hieroglyphs, giving the name, titles etc. of [Mentu-
-em-hat (?)].   The lines read :—

Left Side of Column.		Back of Column.			Right Side of Column.
1.	2.	3.	4.	5.	6.

26th dynasty.   Saïte.   Height, 1 foot 9 inches.
Basalt.   Found 1897, Plan no. 25.

XXVII.

Statuette of a 𓀀𓏲𓈖𓅓 "follower of the goddess Mut" named 𓐠𓅓𓏲 Mut-sepi. She holds before her a figure wearing the double crown 𓋖. At the back the figure is supported by a column upon which is inscribed a vertical line of hieroglyphs recording that Mut-sepi came to the temple-court to bow down before (lit. "smell the earth") the Mistress of Heaven (the goddess Mut). The line reads :

Upon the right-hand side of the column or pedestal is another vertical line of hieroglyphs giving the name of Mut-sepi's son "who made to live her name." He is called 𓅓𓃀𓏏𓀀 Horuza and was apparently a high priest of the goddess Mut (𓊪𓈖𓉐𓅓 lit. "Opener of the two doors of the house of gold of Mut"). His father's name 𓋹𓆤𓀀 Ankh-Hapi is also given ; he bore the title of the high priest of Amen. The whole inscription reads :

A corresponding inscription upon the left-hand side of the column reads :

(1) [hieroglyphs]

[hieroglyphs]

(2) [hieroglyphs]

(3) [hieroglyphs]

26th dynasty, Saïte. Height, 1 foot 2 inches. Basalt. Found 1897, Trench A.

XXVIII.

Statuette of a [hieroglyphs] "scribe of the treasury in the temple of Amen," named [hieroglyphs] Ser-Tahuti.

The figure is represented kneeling and wearing a long kilt. Below the girdle fastening the kilt are two lines of hieroglyphs recording his name and titles :—

(1) [hieroglyphs]

(2) [hieroglyphs]

Upon the column supporting the back of the figure is the lower part of a vertical line of hieroglyphs reading : [hieroglyphs]

26th dynasty, Saïte. Height, 9 inches. Alabaster. Found 1897, Trench B.

XXIX.

Upper part of a statue of a 𓉻𓏏𓊪 𓂝𓏠𓈖𓏤 "priest of Amen in Karnak" whose name is unfortunately destroyed. He is represented standing and wearing the long official tunic hung, like a vezír's garment, from the shoulders. Before him he held a small statuette of the goddess Sekhet. Upon the slab of stone at the back of the figure is a vertical line of hieroglyphs reading :

26th dynasty, Saïte. Height, 11 inches. Basalt. Found 1897, Trench B.

XXX.

Upper part of a statuette of the priest of Amen, Ser. The figure is represented standing with the left leg thrust forward and the arms with closed hands at the sides. He wears a kilt with inscribed

girdle-band and a full wig characteristic of the Saïte
period.   The legs are broken off from the knee.

On band or girdle-strap is the following inscription :—

" Priest of Amen-en-apet, [and of the Gods] within
Erment, the scribe of the offerings of Amen, third
Sa of Amen [?] Ser, son of the priest of Amen and
uab-priest À[rẏ]sep, justified."

On the right shoulder is incised—

" Khonsu-pa-Khred [Khonsu the child], son of
Amen."

On the left shoulder—

" Mut-urt, Mistress of Asher."

On the pedestal supporting the figure at the back
are five vertical lines of hieroglyphs, three on the
back and one on either side; that on the left side
reads:

Below this is incised a small figure of
Ser's wife with the right hand raised as
if in the act of adoration.   Above her is
"his wife and mistress of
his house."

In front of her is a vertical line reading:

"Sistrum-player of Amen, Sa-naïa-
nub, daughter of the priest of
Amen . . .'

On the right-hand side of the pedestal the vertical line reads :

"Priest of Amen-em-apt, the Osirian Ser, son of the priest of Amen-em-apt, the *hersheta*, Áry-sep, justified . . ."

On the back of the pedestal are given titles (including that of "high priest in Erment") of Ser etc.   The inscription reads:

(1)   (2)   (3)

26th dynasty, Saïte. Height, 2 feet 2 inches.
Black granite. Found 1897, Trench A.

XXXI.

Fragment of a statuette
of a  "divine father
and priest of Amen" whose
name is destroyed. He was
son of a "high priest of
Amen" named Un-nefer, by
a sistrum-player of Amen-
Ra," Nesheru - pa - Khred.
The head and legs are
broken off, but the priest
holds before him a small
figure of the god Im-hetep,
who is represented seated
and reading from a broken
scroll. At the back of the
figure are two vertical lines
of hieroglyphs reading :

This inscription gives the [*De hetep seten*] formula
to Amen (?), Osiris and Seker that they may give

per-kheru offerings in all good and pure things for the *Ka* of the Osirian, the "divine father of Amen in Karnak . . . [son of the] high priest of Amen, Un-nefer, born of the Lady of the house, the sistrum-player of Amen-Ra, Nes-heru-pa-Khred . . ."

26th dynasty, Saïte. Height, 11 inches. Basalt. Found 1897, Trench C.

INSCRIBED FRAGMENTS OF STELAE, ETC.

1. Fragment of a stela in limestone with an inscription giving the [*De hetep seten*] formula to Osiris that he may give *per-kheru* offerings daily for the *Ka* of an individual named 𓉔𓏏 𓅭 𓄿 Aah-mesu. The inscription runs :

2. Limestone fragment bearing the inscription 𓈖𓁐𓅭𓏏𓊃𓏏𓆑 "son * of the *Sedem-àsh* of the steward of [Amen ?].

3. Limestone fragment with inscription :

---

* Lit. "made of."

⬭ 𓏤 "son* of the scribe of the accounts of Amen . . ."

4. A similar fragment bearing the name of a person named 𓋹 Ankh.

5. Another fragment bearing the name of a "Lady of the house" named "Antef."

6. Fragment of a sandstone stela cut for an *uab*-priest and *amt-set* priest of the temple of Amen in [Karnak?] whose name is destroyed. A incised figure of the deceased, of which the hands only remain, was in an attitude of adoration before Ptah and Sekhet.

7. Fragment of a limestone stela originally representing Thothmes III. worshipping his ancestor Amenhetep I. The fragment shows underneath the vulture wings three lines of hieroglyphics with a head of Thothmes III. between the middle line and the two to the right. The inscription is as follows :—

"[Good] god, lord of the two lands, Teser-ka-ra" (Amenhetep I.).

* Lit. "made of."

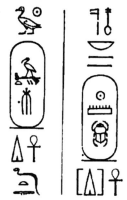

" Son of the sun, Thoth-
mes, giving life etern-
ally, good god, lord of the
two lands, Men-kheper-ra
[Thothmes III.], giving
life."

INSCRIPTIONS ON THE SEKHET STATUES.

The usual type of these inscriptions is as follows :

" The great god, Lord
of the two lands, Ra-maa-
neb, beloved of the god-
dess Sekhet, Lady of Amt,
giving life eternally, son of
Ra of his body, Amenhe-
tep III., Prince of Thebes,
beloved of Sekhet, Lady
of Amt, giving life eternally."

Variations of the inscriptions occur, the statues

2 B

being dedicated to Sekhets of different localities. The name (*nomen*) of Amenhetep is frequently erased. Some statues have no inscription. Many bear the cartouches and titles of Sheshanq I. ; one is dedicated by Pi-netem and one by Rameses II.

Blocks of Piankhŷ.

Five blocks of stone forming part of a wall of a chamber built by Piankhŷ in the temple of Mut. The blocks are sculptured on both faces and formed part of two scenes : the one representing Piankhŷ's fleet returning, heavily laden with all sorts of merchandise, from a great foreign expedition ; the other some religious ceremony connected with the Theban temple. The chamber to which these blocks belonged must have been erected some few years before the twenty-fifth year of Piankhŷ's reign, for Tai-ef-nekht (Tef-nekht, the Tnephachtus of classical writers) is represented on one of the blocks accompanying an expedition of which Piankhŷ was the leader. This Tai-ef-nekht, here described as "General of the soldiers of Herakleopolis," was afterwards "Lord of Saïs and northern Egypt," and the principal figure of the great rebellion against the authority of Piankhŷ, which is so graphically recorded on the celebrated stela from Gebel Barkal now in the Gizeh Museum.

The scene of Piankhŷ's foreign expedition is of great interest, it being otherwise unrecorded. It was to some country to the south of Egypt, for bundles of *nef*-plants and *dûn*-palm fruits in very great numbers were brought back; perhaps it was to the country beyond Khartûm. The length and breadth of each vessel are given in the inscriptions above the ships, together with a list of the merchandise carried in them. These lists apparently follow the same order in each instance; and the merchandise named comprised :—

(1)   "bundles of *nef*-plants." Piankhŷ's boat (Block I., ship 3) carries 6400 bundles; the harîm boat (Block II., ship 4) 2200; whilst two others (Block III., ship 1, and Block IV., ship 1) carry over 4000.* Bundles of *nef*-plants are represented in the tomb of Rekhmara among the tribute rendered by the chiefs of Nubia and the Sudân. The *nef*-plant is also mentioned in a late inscription at Philae as a product of   *Meḥŷ*, a district and town of Nubia to the south of Ibrim.

(2)   "*dûm*-palm nuts." Piankhŷ's boat is laden with 60,000, the harîm boat with 30,000. The hieroglyphs expressing the numbers carried by the other vessels are in

---

* The hieroglyphs expressing the hundreds, tens, or units, are destroyed.

each case destroyed. These nuts are the
fruit of the *dûm*-palm, *Hyphaene Thebaica*
(L.). It grows luxuriantly in Upper Egypt,
but no further north than Assiut.

(3) "turtle-doves." The harim boat contains 340. Two other vessels (Block II.,
ships 1 and 3) carry 240 each, and another
(Block IV., ship 1) 300. Piankhy's boat
carried 440.

(4) "ox-hide shields" (?). In the list of
contents of the harim boat but one shield is
mentioned ; the vessel immediately preceding
it contained two, and the first vessel upon
the same block two also. Two is the number
given for the ship (No. 1) on Block III.

(5) "leather or parchment rolls." The list
above the harim boat gives 12, that of the
vessel preceding it 15.

(6) "*pessa*-plants." The numbers recorded
are: Piankhy's vessel 20, harim boat 13;
Block II., boat 1, 12 ; Block III., boat 1, 12.
The word occurs in the Papyrus
Harris, and seems to mean there a measure
or bundle (*cf.* Papyrus Harris, Pl. 65*a*, l. 8;
74, l. 6, etc.). The *pessa*-plant has not been
identified.

(7) ⟨hieroglyphs⟩ "bundles of *zef*-reeds." The number given above Piankhŷ's boat is 300; above the harîm boat 300. 300 is also the number above boat 1, Block III.

(8) ⟨hieroglyphs⟩ "blocks of *bennu*-stone," a kind of precious stone used for inlay work. It is also mentioned in the Papyrus Harris I., pl. 74, l. 7. Twelve blocks were in the harîm boat and twelve in the vessel preceding it.

(9) ⟨hieroglyphs⟩ "staves (or wands ?) for the hour-priests." The harîm boat and the vessel preceding it contained 50 each. Fifty is the number also given over the first two vessels on Blocks III. and IV.

(10) ⟨hieroglyphs⟩ ? The determinative shows that it was some woven fabric or perhaps a ring (?). The numbers given are : Piankhŷ's vessel 50 ; the harîm vessel 50 ; Block II., ship 1, 50.

(11) ⟨hieroglyphs⟩ "bunches of *shut*" (?). Loret renders the word *shut* by *Andropogon Schoenanthus* (L.) (*cf.* his 'La flore Pharaonique,' p. 22). It formed part of the cargo of Piankhŷ's vessel. It is mentioned also in the lists above the first and second boats on Block II.

(12 and 13) ⟨hieroglyphs⟩ and ⟨hieroglyphs⟩ two kinds of linen (?) cloth, each occurring in most of the lists.

(14) ⟨hieroglyphs⟩ This is mentioned in one list only, that of the harîm boat. It is perhaps some kind of grain.

Block I.—From the uppermost row of a scene representing Piankhy's fleet. The first vessel, of which only about one half is preserved, is ⟨hieroglyphs⟩ "the vessel of Amen," and appears to have been laden with gold. The second ship ⟨hieroglyphs⟩ "the great vessel of Saïs," has on board the ⟨hieroglyphs⟩ "general of the soldiers of Herakleopolis," and ⟨hieroglyphs⟩ "the great one of the fleet," ⟨hieroglyphs⟩ Tai-ef-nekht, who is figured standing before a kind of deck-cabin. The fore part only is preserved of the third ship. It is called ⟨hieroglyphs⟩ "the boat of the King Piankhy." The inscriptions above it give its length as 43 cubits (a little over 75 feet), and a description of its cargo (⟨hieroglyphs⟩ "that which is in it"). The inscriptions read :—

Over the first vessel :

Over the second :

Over the third :

Block II.—From a lower row of the same scene. Parts of two boats are represented and the remains of four inscriptions preserved. The names of the first and second ships are unfortunately destroyed.

The length and breadth of the first were 45 cubits and 23 cubits respectively. The inscriptions above the two boats read :—

First boat :

Second boat :

In the row below were likewise two ships. The inscriptions above them record that the first was a vessel of Amen (?) some 45 cubits in length and 15 in breadth. The second was  "the ship of the harim of Amen,"

with a length of 45 cubits and a breadth of 15.
The inscriptions detailing the cargo run :—

First boat :

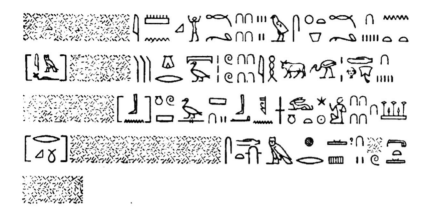

Second boat :

Block III.—From a row of the same scene.
One complete vessel is represented, manned by

ten oarsmen aside (twenty in all), a steersman and a "look-out." The name of the vessel is destroyed and only a fragmentary list of the cargo is preserved sculptured above the boat. This inscription runs :—

The upper part of a second row of ships is seen below this vessel. The inscription naming the boat and detailing its size alone remains :—

"The boat of the (?) and of the Hegatu Ua neb, length 45 cubits, breadth . . . . cubits."

Block IV.—From the same scene. Remains of two vessels are preserved together with very muti-lated lists of their cargoes; the whole stone indeed has been very much damaged by salt and consequent flaking.

Block V.—On this mutilated block is seen the prow of one of the ships of the expedition approach-ing what seems to be the quay at Karnak.

Three of the above blocks are also sculptured on
their reverse side with some religious scene, un-
happily too much disconnected to be of value
historically.   On the back of Block I. priests are
represented kneeling, and a date—
" the fourth month of the inundation season, the day
nineteen "—is given.

INSCRIPTIONS, PLANS, ETC., OF THE TEMPLE OF MUT PREVIOUSLY PUBLISHED OR NOTED.

Recueil, xiii., pp. 161–169, "Notes de Voyage." By Bouriant. Description of Temple; Hymn to Mut; Inscription of Rameses Meri-Tum and Nefertari Mert-en-Mut.

Karnak. By Auguste Mariette-Bey. Plan of Temple, Pl. 3; Taharqa Chamber, pl. 42, 43, 44; Description of Temple, pp. 14, 15 (text).

Monuments of Upper Egypt. A translation of the 'Itinéraire de la Haute Égypte' of Auguste Mariette-Bey. By Alphonse Mariette. Pp. 185, 186.

Mélanges d'Archéologie Égyptienne et Assyrienne. Étude sur des Monuments du règne de Tahraka. By de Rougé, T. 1ᵉʳ, fascicule 1ᵉʳ. Translation of the Inscription of the Taharqa Chamber.

Historische Inschriften. By Dümichen. Taharqa Chamber, 48. A. B.

Denkmäler. Lepsius. Plan of the Temple, I. 83. Inscription on Sekhet statue of Pi-netem, III. 249. f.

The Burton Papers (British Museum). Memorandum by James Burton on the destruction of the Temple, Add. MS. 25,639, f. 43. Plan of the Temple, 25,645, ff. 162–163.

The Hay Papers (British Museum). Plan of the Temple, Add. MS 29,825 B.

LIST OF COINS FOUND IN THE TEMPLE, 1895–1897.

FORTY-NINE POTIN COINS OF NERO STRUCK AT ALEXANDRIA.

The inscriptions and designs of type are as follows :—

Obverse.	*Reverse.*
1. Head of Nero to right. ΝΕΡΩ · ΚΛΑΥ · ΚΑΙΣ · ΣΕΒ · ΓΕΡΜ.	1. Head of Γoppaea to right. ΠΟΠΠΑΙΑ · ΣΕΒΑΣΤΗ. Date LI (A.D. 64).
2. *Idem.*	2. *Idem.* Date LIA (A.D. 65).
3. *Idem.*	3. Head of Zeus to right, wearing turreted crown. ΑΥΤΟΚΡΑ. Date LIA (?) (A.D. 65).
4. *Idem.*	4. Eagle to left. ΑΥΤΟΚΡΑ. Date LIΔ (?) (A.D. 68).
5. *Idem.*	5. *Idem,* but date LIA (A.D. 65).
6. *Idem.*	6. Head of Alexandria to right, with elephant-skin head-dress. ΑΥΤΟΚΡΑ. Date LIB (A.D. 60).
7. *Idem.*	7. *Idem,* of slightly different type of head-dress.
8. *Idem,* but head to left. Date LIΓ (A.D. 67).	8. Head of Asclepius to right. (ΑΣΚΛ)ΗΠΙΟΥ.
9. *Idem.*	9. Galley under sail. Inscription illegible.
10. *Idem.*	10. Head of Tiberius to right. ΤΙΒΕΡΙΟΣ ΚΑΙΣ.
11. *Idem,* but head to right.	11. Head of Claudius (?) to right. ΘΕΟΣ (ΚΛΑΥΔΙΟΣ).
12. *Idem,* but head to right, and no date.	12. Head to right. ΑΥΤΟΚΡΑ. Date LIΓ (A.D. 67).
13. *Idem,* but head to left.	13. Head of Hera to right, and star. ΗΡΑ.

Found 1897, Plan no. 26.

Various Coins of the Roman Emperors struck at Alexandria.

TIBERIUS.

ΤΙΒΕΡΙΟΣ · ΚΑΙΣ · ΣΕΒΑ.　　　　Eagle to right. ΑΥΤΟΚΡΑ. Date LIB (A.D. 26). (Bronze.)

NERO.

Head of Nero to right. Inscription illegible.　　　　Lotus. ΑΥΤΟΚΡΑ. (Bronze.)

HADRIAN (?).

Head of Hadrian (?). Inscription illegible.　　　　Eagle. Inscription illegible. (Potin.)

Head of Hadrian (?). Inscription illegible.　　　　Winged victory and altar (?). Inscription illegible. (Bronze.)

OTACILIA, wife of Philip (?).

Head of Otacilia (?). Inscription illegible.　　　　Eagle. Date LB (A.D. 245). (Bronze.)

Various Coins of the Ptolemies.

(In several the inscription is erased.)

Head of Cleopatra.　　　　Eagle. (Bronze.)

Head of Zeus.　　　　Eagle with thunderbolt; in one case a double-headed eagle. ΠΤΟΛΕΜΑΙΟΥ ΒΑΣΙΛΕΩΣ. (Bronze.)

INDEX AND CATALOGUE,

Including names and objects connected with the Temple of Mut, and names of contemporary Pharaohs. The names of those Pharaohs in whose reigns no monument is known or conjectured to have been added to the Temple are marked with an asterisk. Names known in connection with the Temple before the 1895–97 excavations are printed in italics.

Names of Deities will be found in alphabetical order under Deities, and not elsewhere in the catalogue.

† For fragments see under Stelae.

† Many of these were visible before the 1895–97 excavations. Many had been removed from the Temple. The numbers here given refer to those statues and fragments of statues which still remain in the Temple.

† The translations having been abbreviated, some names, offices, etc., given in the inscriptions, do not appear in the English. Official Egyptian titles being as yet imperfectly understood, the list cannot be regarded as complete.

† For pages of statues and stelae see under initial letters.

MISCELLANEOUS OBJECTS FOUND IN THE TEMPLE.
(Fragmentary.)

Bronze.
Candlestick, 10½ inches.
Lamp and tray, 5½ inches.
Tripod, 2½ inches.

CPSIA information can be obtained at www.ICGtesting.com
Printed in the USA
LVOW132243280312

275176LV00013B/142/P